W9-CND-895

DEFINING MOMENTS
THE
GILDED AGE

DEFINING MOMENTS
THE
GILDED AGE

Diane Telgen

155 W. Congress, Suite 200
Detroit, MI 48226

Omnigraphics, Inc.

Kevin Hillstrom, *Series Editor*
Cherie D. Abbey, *Managing Editor*

Peter E. Ruffner, *Publisher*
Matthew P. Barbour, *Senior Vice President*

Elizabeth Collins, *Research and Permissions Coordinator*
Kevin M. Hayes, *Operations Manager*

Allison A. Beckett and Mary Butler, *Research Staff*
Cherry Edwards, *Permissions Assistant*
Shirley Amore, Joseph Harris, Martha Johns, and Kirk Kauffmann, *Administrative Staff*

Library of Congress Cataloging-in-Publication Data

Telgen, Diane.
The Gilded Age / by Diane Telgen.
    p. cm. -- (Defining moments)
  Includes bibliographical references and index.
  Summary: "Provides a comprehensive overview of the political and economic forces that transformed the United States during the nineteenth century from a farming society to an urban, industrial one dominated by powerful industrialists and their vast corporate empires. Includes a narrative overview, biographies, primary sources, chronology, glossary, bibliography, and index"--Provided by publisher.
  ISBN 978-0-7808-1238-3 (hardcover : alk. paper) 1. United States--History--1865-1921--Juvenile literature. 2. United States--History--1865-1921--Biography--Juvenile literature. 3. United States--History--1865-1921--Sources. 4. United States--Politics and government--1865-1933--Juvenile literature. 5. United States--Politics and government--1865-1933--Sources. I. Title.
  E661.T45 2012
  973.8--dc23   2011048642

The information in this publication was compiled from sources cited and from sources considered reliable. While every possible effort has been made to ensure reliability, the publisher will not assume liability for damages caused by inaccuracies in the data, and makes no warranty, express or implied, on the accuracy of the information contained herein.

This book is printed on acid-free paper meeting the ANSI Z39.48 Standard. The infinity symbol that appears above indicates that the paper in this book meets that standard.

Printed in the United States of America

TABLE OF CONTENTS

PRIMARY SOURCES

PREFACE

Throughout the course of America's existence, its people, culture, and institutions have been periodically challenged—and in many cases transformed—by profound historical events. Some of these momentous events, such as women's suffrage, the civil rights movement, and U.S. involvement in World War II, invigorated the nation and strengthened American confidence and capabilities. Others, such as the McCarthy era, the Vietnam War, and Watergate, have prompted troubled assessments and heated debates about the country's core beliefs and character.

Some of these defining moments in American history were years or even decades in the making. The Harlem Renaissance and the New Deal, for example, unfurled over the span of several years, while the American labor movement and the Cold War evolved over the course of decades. Other defining moments, such as the Cuban missile crisis and the terrorist attacks of September 11, 2001, transpired over a matter of days or weeks.

But although significant differences exist among these events in terms of their duration and their place in the timeline of American history, all share the same basic characteristic: they transformed the United States' political, cultural, and social landscape for future generations of Americans.

Taking heed of this fundamental reality, American citizens, schools, and other institutions are increasingly emphasizing the importance of understanding our nation's history. Omnigraphics' *Defining Moments* series was created for the express purpose of meeting this growing appetite for authoritative, useful historical resources. This series will be of enduring value to anyone interested in learning more about America's past—and in understanding how those historical events continue to reverberate in the twenty-first century.

Each individual volume of *Defining Moments* provides a valuable resource for readers interested in learning about the most profound events in our nation's history. Each volume is organized into three distinct sections—Narrative Overview, Biographies, and Primary Sources.

- The **Narrative Overview** provides readers with a detailed, factual account of the origins and progression of the "defining moment" being examined. It also explores the event's lasting impact on America's political and cultural landscape.

- The **Biographies** section provides valuable biographical background on leading figures associated with the event in question. Each biography concludes with a list of sources for further information on the profiled individual.

- The **Primary Sources** section collects a wide variety of pertinent primary source materials from the era under discussion, including official documents, papers and resolutions, letters, oral histories, memoirs, editorials, and other important works.

Individually, each of these sections is a rich resource for users. Together, they comprise an authoritative, balanced, and absorbing examination of some of the most significant events in U.S. history.

Other notable features contained within each volume in the series include a glossary of important individuals, places, and terms; a detailed chronology featuring page references to relevant sections of the narrative; an annotated bibliography of sources for further study; an extensive general bibliography that reflects the wide range of historical sources consulted by the author; and a subject index.

Acknowledgements

This series was developed in consultation with a distinguished Advisory Board comprised of public librarians, school librarians, and educators. They evaluated the series as it developed, and their comments and suggestions were invaluable throughout the production process. Any errors in this and other volumes in the series are ours alone. Following is a list of board members who contributed to the *Defining Moments* series:

Gail Beaver, M.A., M.A.L.S.
Adjunct Lecturer, University of Michigan
Ann Arbor, MI

Melissa C. Bergin, L.M.S., NBCT
Library Media Specialist
Niskayuna High School
Niskayuna, NY

Rose Davenport, M.S.L.S., Ed.Specialist
Library Media Specialist
Pershing High School Library
Detroit, MI

Karen Imarisio, A.M.L.S.
Assistant Head of Adult Services
Bloomfield Twp. Public Library
Bloomfield Hills, MI

Nancy Larsen, M.L.S., M.S. Ed.
Library Media Specialist
Clarkston High School
Clarkston, MI

Marilyn Mast, M.I.L.S.
Kingswood Campus Librarian
Cranbrook Kingswood Upper School
Bloomfield Hills, MI

Rosemary Orlando, M.L.I.S.
Library Director
St. Clair Shores Public Library
St. Clair Shores, MI

Comments and Suggestions

We welcome your comments on *Defining Moments: The Gilded Age* and suggestions for other events in U.S. history that warrant treatment in the *Defining Moments* series. Correspondence should be addressed to:

Editor, *Defining Moments*
Omnigraphics, Inc.
155 West Congress, Suite 200
Detroit, MI 48226
E-mail: editorial@omnigraphics.com

HOW TO USE THIS BOOK

*D*efining Moments: The Gilded Age provides users with a detailed and authoritative overview of the formative period between the end of the Civil War and the turn of the twentieth century, as well as background on the principal figures involved in this pivotal era in U.S. history. The preparation and arrangement of this volume—and all other books in the *Defining Moments* series—reflect an emphasis on providing a thorough and objective account of events that shaped our nation, presented in an easy-to-use reference work.

Defining Moments: The Gilded Age is divided into three primary sections. The first of these sections, the **Narrative Overview**, provides a detailed, factual account of the social, political, and economic forces that transformed the United States during the second half of the nineteenth century. It traces the settling of the western frontier, the construction of the first transcontinental railroad, and the nation's shift from a rural, farming society to an urban, industrial one. This section also covers the emergence of the wealthy and powerful industrialists known as the "robber barons" and their building of vast corporate empires. It describes the atmosphere of cutthroat competition, monopolistic business practices, political corruption, and get-rich-quick attitudes that created tremendous wealth for a few fortunate Americans—and left millions of workers struggling in poverty and hardship. It traces the rise of labor unions, third-party politics, and reform movements aimed at narrowing the divide between rich and poor and restoring American democracy. Finally, it explains how the events of the Gilded Age paved the way for the reforms of the Progressive Era.

The second section, **Biographies**, provides valuable biographical background on leading figures associated with the Gilded Age, including John D. Rockefeller, who built the giant Standard Oil Company trust; J. P. Morgan, the era's leading banker and financier; American Federation of Labor president Samuel Gompers; social reformer and Populist speaker Mary Elizabeth Lease;

and President Grover Cleveland, who took a stand against the political corruption of the era. Each biography concludes with a list of sources for further information on the profiled individual.

The third section, **Primary Sources**, collects essential and illuminating documents related to the Gilded Age. This diverse collection includes excerpts from Mark Twain's recollections of greed and corruption in a western mining town; an 1883 *New York Times* article describing the ostentatious displays of wealth at a high-society costume ball; a muckraking journalist's account of the overcrowded, unsanitary conditions endured by poor residents of New York City tenement buildings; the 1892 political platform of the newly formed Populist Party; steel magnate Andrew Carnegie's influential writings about philanthropy; and point-counterpoint articles comparing twenty-first-century social and economic conditions in America to those of the Gilded Age.

Other valuable features in *Defining Moments: The Gilded Age* include the following:

- Attribution and referencing of primary sources and other quoted material to help guide users to other valuable historical research resources.
- Glossary of Important People, Places, and Terms.
- Detailed Chronology of events with a *see reference* feature. Under this arrangement, events listed in the chronology include a reference to page numbers within the Narrative Overview wherein users can find additional information on the event in question.
- Photographs of the leading figures and major events associated with the Gilded Age.
- Sources for Further Study, an annotated list of noteworthy works about the era.
- Extensive bibliography of works consulted in the creation of this book, including books, periodicals, and Internet sites.
- A Subject Index.

RESEARCH TOPICS FOR
DEFINING MOMENTS:
THE GILDED AGE

S tarting a research paper can be a challenge, as students struggle to decide what area to study. Now, each book in the *Defining Moments* series includes a list of research topics, detailing some of the important topics that recur throughout the volume and providing a valuable starting point for research. Students working on essays and reports will find this feature especially useful as they try to narrow down their research interests.

These research topics are covered throughout the different sections of the book: the narrative overview, the biographies, the primary sources, the chronology, and the important people, places, and terms section. This wide coverage allows readers to view the topic through a variety of different approaches.

Students using *Defining Moments: The Gilded Age* will find information on a wide range of topics suitable for conducting historical research and writing reports:

- How Americans spread across the western frontier during the nineteenth century, and what impact this migration had on the nation's economic and cultural growth.

- Political and economic effects of the transcontinental railroad and the extension of rail lines throughout the United States.

- Transformation of America from a rural, farming society to an urban, industrial society.

- Creation of the first great industrial corporations and factors in their growth and success.

- Rise of the industrialists known as the "robber barons" and their contributions—both positive and negative—to American business and finance.

- Contrast between glittering displays of wealth by business owners and political leaders and poverty and hardships faced by working-class Americans during the Gilded Age.
- Targets and achievements of Gilded Age political, social, and economic reforms.
- Growth and impact of the labor movement in the Gilded Age.
- History of third-party political movements in the Gilded Age.
- Factors influencing the rise of Populist movements, and how and why they succeeded or failed.
- Role of the president in the Gilded Age, especially as compared with Theodore Roosevelt's presidency in the Progressive Era.
- Contributions of "muckraking" investigative journalists to raising public awareness of corporate greed and political corruption.
- Legacy of the Gilded Age on American business, economics, politics, law, and culture.
- Whether the United States has entered into another Gilded Age of economic disparity and excess during the twenty-first century.

NARRATIVE OVERVIEW

PROLOGUE

⋙⋘

The years following the Civil War were a period of rapid change in the United States. During this period, the nation transformed itself from a rural, agricultural nation to an urbanized industrial power. Boosted by an influx of immigrants, the U.S. population more than doubled between 1865 and 1901, from 35.7 million to over 77.5 million. Some of these newcomers settled a frontier that grew increasingly connected, with 158,000 miles of new railroad track laid during the same period. City populations grew twice as fast as rural ones, as people came to work in factories that produced steel, refined oil, or processed food on a huge scale. Fueled by exponential increases in the production of wheat, corn, sugar, coal, steel, and oil, American exports more than quadrupled between 1865 and 1898. By the end of the nineteenth century the United States had become the world's leading industrial producer—and its leading businessmen had become fabulously wealthy.

America's rapid growth opened up many opportunities for citizens to achieve individual success, no matter how humble their origins. Samuel Langhorne Clemens, for instance, was born in a log cabin in rural Missouri in 1835. By 1872 he was a popular travel writer and lecturer—better known under his pseudonym, Mark Twain—who had married the daughter of a wealthy New York businessman. The couple built a house in Hartford, Connecticut, where they socialized with several notable writers and thinkers, including Charles Dudley Warner, editor of the *Hartford Courant*. At one dinner, Clemens and Warner teased their wives for reading the melodramatic books that were popular at that time. The ladies responded by challenging their husbands to write something better. The result was the 1873 novel *The Gilded Age*, a clever parody of both the sentimental fiction and the pervasive get-rich-quick attitude that characterized the era. While the novel itself has

been overshadowed by Twain's later works, historians found it an apt portray-
al of the postwar era and borrowed its title to describe the years between the
end of the Civil War in 1865 and the start of the Progressive Era in the early
twentieth century.

The Gilded Age drew from Clemens's rustic Western upbringing as well
as Warner's Eastern establishment background. It featured characters from all
walks of life trying to strike it rich by attracting government money for their
pet projects. The novel's characters become involved in a wide variety of
dubious financial schemes, including one that heroine Ruth Bolton overhears
being discussed in her father's home:

> That day Mr. Bolton brought home a stranger to dinner, Mr.
> Bigler of the great firm of Pennybacker, Bigler & Small, rail-
> road contractors. He was always bringing home somebody,
> who had a scheme to build a road, or open a mine, or plant a
> swamp with cane to grow paper-stock, or found a hospital, or
> invest in a patent shad-bone separator, or start a college some-
> where on the frontier, contiguous to a land speculation.
>
> The Bolton house was a sort of hotel for this kind of people.
> They were always coming. Ruth had known them from child-
> hood, and she used to say that her father attracted them as nat-
> urally as a sugar hogshead does flies. Ruth had an idea that a
> large portion of the world lived by getting the rest of the world
> into schemes. Mr. Bolton never could say "no" to any of them,
> not even, said Ruth again, to the society for stamping oyster
> shells with scripture texts before they were sold at retail.
>
> Mr. Bigler's plan this time, about which he talked loudly, with
> his mouth full, all dinner time, was the building of the
> Tunkhannock, Rattlesnake and Youngwomans-town railroad,
> which would not only be a great highway to the west, but
> would open to market inexhaustible coal-fields and untold
> millions of lumber. The plan of operations was very simple.
>
> "We'll buy the lands," explained he, "on long time, backed by
> the notes of good men; and then mortgage them for money
> enough to get the road well on. Then get the towns on the line
> to issue their bonds for stock, and sell their bonds for enough

to complete the road, and partly stock it, especially if we mortgage each section as we complete it. We can then sell the rest of the stock on the prospect of the business of the road through an improved country, and also sell the lands at a big advance, on the strength of the road. All we want," continued Mr. Bigler in his frank manner, "is a few thousand dollars to start the surveys, and arrange things in the legislature. There is some parties will have to be seen, who might make us trouble."

"It will take a good deal of money to start the enterprise," remarked Mr. Bolton, who knew very well what "seeing" a Pennsylvania Legislature meant, but was too polite to tell Mr. Bigler what he thought of him, while he was his guest; "what security would one have for it?"

Mr. Bigler smiled a hard kind of smile, and said, "You'd be inside, Mr. Bolton, and you'd have the first chance in the deal."

This was rather unintelligible to Ruth, who was nevertheless somewhat amused by the study of a type of character she had seen before.

At length she interrupted the conversation by asking, "You'd sell the stock, I suppose, Mr. Bigler, to anybody who was attracted by the prospectus?"

"O, certainly, serve all alike," said Mr. Bigler, now noticing Ruth for the first time, and a little puzzled by the serene, intelligent face that was turned towards him.

"Well, what would become of the poor people who had been led to put their little money into the speculation, when you got out of it and left it half way?"

It would be no more true to say of Mr. Bigler that he was or could be embarrassed, than to say that a brass counterfeit dollar-piece would change color when refused; the question annoyed him a little, in Mr. Bolton's presence.

"Why, yes, Miss, of course, in a great enterprise for the benefit of the community there will little things occur, which, which—and, of course, the poor ought to be looked to; I tell my wife, that the poor must be looked to; if you can tell who are poor—there's so many impostors. And then, there's so many poor in the legislature to be looked after," said the contractor with a sort of a chuckle, "isn't that so, Mr. Bolton?"

Eli Bolton replied that he never had much to do with the legislature.

"Yes," continued this public benefactor, "an uncommon poor lot this year, uncommon. Consequently an expensive lot. The fact is, Mr. Bolton, that the price is raised so high on a United States Senator now, that it affects the whole market; you can't get any public improvement through on reasonable terms."[1]

As this passage suggests, many Gilded Age politicians profited from their positions by receiving preferred stock sales, free railroad passes, and even outright bribes. As the novel also makes clear, for every winner in the new American economy who struck it rich speculating on railroads or stocks, there were several losers left destitute. The working poor were often among these losers. The 1890 census showed that eleven of twelve families lived on an average yearly income of $380—well below the poverty line. The same census showed that the richest 1 percent of Americans had more wealth than the other 99 percent combined. "However much movement might take place around the edges," one historian noted, "the country began the Gilded Age with a permanent lower class and a permanent upper class."[2]

During the Gilded Age, the growing gap between rich and poor led to reform movements, labor unrest, and the growth of third-party politics. Nonetheless, the nation's legislatures and courts continued to favor corporate interests, who employed all sorts of slippery practices to keep their profits rolling in. As Charles Francis Adams Jr.—the grandson and great-grandson of presidents and a railroad commissioner in Massachusetts after the Civil War—observed in 1869: "The stock exchange revealed itself as a haunt of gamblers and a den of thieves; the offices of our great corporations appeared as the secret chambers in which trustees plotted the spoliation [plunder] of their wards; the law became a ready engine for the furtherance of wrong...; the halls of legislation were transformed into a mart in which the price of votes were higgled [sic] over, and laws, made to order, were bought and sold; while under all, and through all, the voice of public opinion was silent or disregarded."[3] The new American captains of industry may have been admired for their unprecedented success and public philanthropy, but underlying the Gilded Age's glittering surface was a society in danger of being torn apart by greed, corruption, and inequality.

Notes:

[1] Twain, Mark, and Charles Dudley Warner. *The Gilded Age: A Tale of To-Day* . Hartford, CT: American Publishing Company, 1874, pp. 140-143.

[2] Summers, Mark Wahlgren. *The Gilded Age, or, the Hazard of New Functions.* Upper Saddle River, NJ: Prentice Hall, 1997, p. 122.

[3] Adams, Charles Francis, Jr., "A Chapter of Erie." *North American Review,* no. 142, July 1869. Reprinted in *Robber Barons and Radicals.* Collected and edited by T. J. Stiles. New York: Perigee, 1997, p. 133.

Chapter One

AMERICA'S POSTWAR EXPANSION

To the frontier the American intellect owes its striking characteristics. That coarseness and strength combined with acuteness and inquisitiveness; that practical, inventive turn of mind, quick to find expedients; that masterful grasp of material things, lacking in the artistic but powerful to effect great ends; that restless, nervous energy; that dominant individualism, working for good and for evil, and withal that buoyancy and exuberance which comes with freedom—these are traits of the frontier, or traits called out elsewhere because of the existence of the frontier.

—Frederick Jackson Turner, "The Significance of the Frontier in American History," 1893

From its earliest years, the United States looked west for sources of growth and opportunity. Many Americans believed that the availability of land on the western frontier was vital to the nation's prosperity. The Louisiana Purchase of 1803 doubled the size of the fledgling country and secured the important trading waterway of the Mississippi River, and the nation continued acquiring land through both treaty and war. By 1850 the United States had laid claim to the entirety of the continent between the Mississippi River and California.

The U.S. government sponsored surveys of the unsettled frontier and assessed its natural resources and potential railroad routes. Yet several limitations prevented Americans from developing the western territories. First and foremost was a lack of cheap, reliable transportation: travel from New York to

This painting, entitled "Across the Continent: Westward the Course of Empire Takes Its Way," shows the steady advance of settlements along the American frontier.

the West Coast required either a dangerous journey overland or a long sea voyage around South America. In 1857, this trip took a minimum of four weeks. There were also political obstacles to developing the West. New territories meant a congressional battle over whether to allow slavery, a contentious issue between North and South. Southerners also resisted spending federal government funds on economic development of the region because they thought it would primarily benefit northern financiers.

Following the Union's victory in the Civil War, however, northern interests dominated national politics. Federal land on the frontier was opened to railroad companies and settlers alike, and new tariff policies were crafted to support fledging industries. Development in the West proceeded rapidly. While it had taken 250 years after the first colonies were established for American settlement to reach mid-continent, it only took the 25 years from 1865 to 1890 to inhabit the rest of the frontier.

This rapid development transformed more than the U.S. map; it also changed the fundamental nature of the country's economy and government. The new railroads and mechanical inventions that made expansion possible required huge amounts of capital investment and industrial production, which led to the rise of the corporation. At the same time, federal policies had a growing impact on business. This reality led corporations to seek more political influence, both legally and illegally.

The Government Opens the Frontier

The idea that the federal government should make public lands available to individuals at low or no cost was almost as old as the country itself. If land ownership was a route to wealth, many argued, a nation founded on the idea of equality should make it accessible to all classes. In the early years of the United States, it was common for settlers to "squat" on public land, and the Preemption Acts of 1830 and 1841 gave squatters who made improvements to these lands the first chance to purchase them from the government. Others, particularly Tennessee congressman Andrew Johnson, believed that settlers willing to improve public land by farming—homesteading—should be granted land for free.

Opponents of homesteading believed offering free land would attract the wrong type of settler; many southerners saw it as a scheme to aid freed slaves. By the time Johnson became a senator in 1857, though, the idea of homesteading was gaining public support. In 1860 a homesteading bill passed Congress. Democratic president James Buchanan vetoed it, reflecting his party's belief that it might undermine land values and create labor shortages in the East. The Republican Party, however, saw the Homestead Act as a way for the working class to achieve independence, and the party of "free soil, free labor, free men" made support for homesteading a part of its 1860 platform.

The election of Abraham Lincoln brought a proponent of homesteading to the White House. As he noted in a February 1861 address: "I have to say that in so far as the government lands can be disposed of, I am in favor of cutting up the wild lands into parcels, so that every poor man may have a home."[1] A new bill allowed any family head or male over twenty-one to claim 160 acres of public land for a fee of ten dollars. If the homesteader lived on and cultivated the land for five years, the title would be theirs, free and clear. The bill easily passed Congress, and Lincoln signed it into law in 1862.

President Abraham Lincoln was a major proponent of westward expansion.

Further acts of Congress opened up more federal land to potential settlers. Not all land distributed through these acts ended up in the hands of pioneers, however. Because a homestead claimant only needed one witness to "prove" he had built on his land, many fraudulent claims fell into the hands of land speculators, especially after the Homestead Act was modified to permit settlers to buy land for $1.25 per acre after only six months of occupation. In addition, the expense of establishing a homestead— which could exceed $1,000 when considering the costs of transportation, clearing and fencing the land, purchasing tools and draft animals, and stocking up on supplies to feed the family until crops came in—was well beyond the average factory worker's yearly $250 salary. As a result, according to one historian, "The story of settlement under the Homestead Act was not one of downtrodden laborers rising to affluence through governmental beneficence, but more often a tale of fraud and monopoly which only ended with seven-eighths of the public domain in the hands of a favored few."[2]

Of the settlers who attempted to farm Homestead lands, as many as 50 percent failed to stay long enough to gain title to their claims. Still, with hundreds of thousands of families making the attempt, approximately 270 million acres of western lands were settled by some 783,000 farmers. Of those who remained, many increased their holdings or made improvements by using the property as collateral for loans. Thus while the Homestead Act may not have fulfilled all of its intended purposes, it did serve to draw people west. It would take the railroads, however, for the United States to spread settlers across the entire continent.

Building the Transcontinental Railroad

Long before California was admitted to the Union in 1850, many in the United States foresaw the need for a railroad to span the continent. Even Mississippi's Jefferson Davis, shortly before leaving the Senate to preside over the Confederacy, noted that "I have thought it an achievement worthy of our age and of our people, to couple with bonds of iron the people of the Pacific with the valley of the Mississippi, and show that even the snow-capped mountains intervening could not divide them."[3] Federal and state governments often subsidized public transportation, including roads, bridges, canals, and the 30,000 miles of railroads that had been built by 1860. A transcontinental road would require huge amounts of investment, however, and politicians argued over how much support the government should give. Further disputes arose between states when surveys showed that two northern and two southern routes were feasible, for everyone knew that such a railroad would bring new economic opportunities to its host states. The South's secession broke the political deadlock. With the onset of the Civil War in 1861, southern and border routes fell by the wayside. President Lincoln and Congress settled on a more northerly route.

"The story of settlement under the Homestead Act was not one of downtrodden laborers rising to affluence through governmental beneficence, but more often a tale of fraud and monopoly which only ended with seven-eighths of the public domain in the hands of a favored few."

The Pacific Railway Act of 1862 authorized the incorporation of the Union Pacific Railroad, issuing 100,000 shares at $1,000 each for an initial capitalization of $100 million. The Union Pacific was charged with constructing a route from Omaha, Nebraska, westward along the 42nd parallel. This same legislation authorized the Central Pacific Railroad to build eastward from Sacramento, California. The act gave both companies five alternating sections of public land per mile on each side of the track—an area of 6,400 acres per mile of track—which they could keep and develop, use as loan securities, or sell for cash. They were also granted the use of all the earth, stone, or timber from public lands they might need for construction. Finally, the government gave the companies extremely generous terms for borrowing money.

The Central Pacific broke ground first, but building was slow and expensive. Supplies had to be brought by ship from the east coast, and there was a shortage of labor until the company began importing Chinese workers.

Representatives of the Central Pacific (left) and Union Pacific celebrate the completion of the transcontinental railroad on May 10, 1869, at Promontory Point, Utah.

The company had only built 22 miles by March 1864, but with further government support the Central Pacific reached 92 miles west of Sacramento by fall 1866. Thousands of workers blasted through the Sierra Nevada range, and by spring 1868 the Central Pacific was ready to race to the finish.

The Union Pacific took longer to begin construction, as most of the materials and workers it needed were consumed by the war. By the end of 1865, the Union Pacific had only laid 40 miles of track west of Omaha. After the war ended that year, many veterans joined Union Pacific construction crews, including former general Grenville Dodge, who became chief engineer. Despite the difficulties posed by Native American raids and transportation of

The Age of Invention

For many Americans, the Gilded Age was also an age of invention. At the 1876 Centennial International Exhibition in Philadelphia, almost 10 million visitors saw Thomas Edison's multiplex telegraph, Alexander Graham Bell's telephone, and the 45-foot-tall Corliss steam engine—a 1,400-horsepower engine that could power 800 machines. The exhibits moved author William Dean Howells to write: "It is still in these things of iron and steel that the national genius most freely speaks."

Between 1860 and 1901, some 440,000 U.S. patents were issued, many of them for inventions that became regular features of American life. Edison's lab produced the phonograph in 1877 and the incandescent lamp two years later, while George Eastman introduced the Kodak camera in 1884. Electric streetcars and streetlamps came into use in the 1880s, the better to reach and illuminate the first skyscrapers, which were made possible by elevators and advances in structural steel. Refrigerator cars and air brakes revolutionized railroad transportation, while stock tickers, punch card tabulators, and the wireless telegraph revolutionized business operations. "For Americans in the Gilded Age," historian W. Bernard Carlson noted, "technology was not the cause of their troubles but rather the solution to their problems."

Sources:

Carlson, W. Bernard. "Technology and America as a Consumer Society, 1870-1900," in Calhoun, Charles W., editor. *The Gilded Age: Perspectives on the Origins of Modern America,* 2nd edition. Lanham, MD: Rowman & Littlefield, 2007, pp. 29-52.

Trachtenberg, Alan. *The Incorporation of America: Culture and Society in the Gilded Age.* New York: Hill and Wang, 1982, 25th anniversary edition, 2007, p. 47.

supplies—Dodge reported using 10,000 animals and 8,000 to 10,000 men at one point during construction—the Union Pacific built 266 miles in 1866. By spring 1868 the line had reached Wyoming's Cheyenne Pass through the Rocky Mountains.

By 1869 both companies were laying five to ten miles of track per day, hoping to claim as much land as possible for themselves before the railroad was completed. The final spike connecting the two railways was driven at

Promontory Point, Utah, on May 10, 1869. The event was covered by telegraph and newspapers nationwide and celebrated with holidays and speeches. At completion the Central Pacific had laid 689 miles of track and the Union Pacific 1,086. Although the federal government loaned the two companies over $64 million, within thirty years the loans were repaid, along with over $100 million in interest. While some believed the 21 million acres of land grants were overly generous, many thought it was a small price to pay for what historian Stephen Ambrose called "the greatest engineering achievement of the nineteenth century."[4]

Promontory Point was only the beginning of America's railroad expansion. Railroad mileage increased from 35,000 at the end of the Civil War to 190,000 miles in 1900, when most American citizens lived within earshot of a locomotive. No wonder, as one historian observed, that "railroads became the symbol for all the drive and enterprise of Gilded Age America."[5]

Native Americans Lose the Land Battle

As federal authorities and railroad companies opened up the western frontier to meet white settlers' demands for more land and more opportunity, Native Americans found themselves pushed off their traditional lands and confined to smaller and smaller reservations. Treaties were violated, especially when gold was discovered on native lands; roads and forts inevitably grew into larger settlements; and hunting destroyed the buffalo herds many tribes depended on for their livelihoods. Initially, some Native Americans were able to resist white inroads. Ultimately, though, they could not overcome the whites' overwhelming advantage in numbers and resources. As one historian noted, "What destroyed the Indian tribes far more effectively than the army was the commercial and industrial power of the East, which was able to pour settlement west in an ever-increasing flow, ever more conscious of the wealth of the West waiting to feed the mills and mints east of the Mississippi."[6]

In 1868, the Ulysses S. Grant administration decided to pursue a "peace policy" with Native Americans that would give them protected status on individual reservations and teach them to assimilate. They established a reservation in the Black Hills of Dakota Territory for 54,000 natives of the Northern Plains and set aside three million acres in Indian Territory (present-day Oklahoma) for the Kiowa and Comanche of the Southwest. In 1871, Congress decreed that Native American tribes no longer "shall be acknowledged or rec-

Native Americans who resisted the flood of white settlers into their traditional lands often met the fate of these Cheyenne Indians, killed by U.S. soldiers near Fort Robinson, Nebraska, in 1879.

ognized as an independent nation, tribe or power, with whom the United States may contract by treaty."[7] Instead, natives would be subjects and wards of the U.S. government.

Not all Native Americans would abide by these settlements, and they fought back. In the early 1870s, representatives of the Northern Pacific Railroad scouting potential routes in the Yellowstone River basin had to take both infantry and cavalry troops to protect them from Indian attacks. When gold was discovered in the Black Hills in 1874, the U.S. Army could not prevent hundreds of prospectors from entering the territory, leading to attacks by Lakota Sioux. Although the tribes united long enough to defeat the U.S. Army at the Battle of Little Big Horn, by the end of 1876 their leaders were forced to retreat to Canada or surrender. By 1883, General William T. Sherman was confident enough to declare: "I now regard the Indians as substantially eliminated from the problem of the Army."[8]

The massacre of more than 200 Sioux—including women and children—at South Dakota's Wounded Knee Creek in 1890 effectively marked the end of Native American resistance to white expansion. Afterward, the various tribes were herded onto reservations, where they were pressured to adopt white farming practices and abandon ancient traditions. Over time, even these reservation lands were pried loose from the Indians when politicians and speculators discovered that they had value for mining, ranching, or farming. The Dawes Severalty Act, which was passed by Congress in 1887, eventually resulted in nearly two-thirds of the reservation land base being made available for white settlement. "At last the restless pioneer could advance unmolested across the Great Plains where once the shaggy buffalo and free native had long held sway,"[9] one historian recounted.

> *"What destroyed the Indian tribes far more effectively than the army was the commercial and industrial power of the East, which was able to pour settlement west in an ever-increasing flow, ever more conscious of the wealth of the West waiting to feed the mills and mints east of the Mississippi."*

Waves of Migration Close the Frontier

With Civil War strife behind them, cheap frontier lands made safe from Native Americans, and railroads to take them there, Americans settled down to the business of filling the nation's interior. Except for settlements in Mormon Utah and Santa Fe, New Mexico, there were few Americans living between the Mississippi Valley and the West Coast at the close of the Civil War. Between 1870 and 1900, however, Americans would settle and cultivate more land than they had in the previous 260 years. Those seeking valuable natural resources such as animal furs or precious minerals came first. They were followed by ranchers taking advantage of free, plentiful grazing lands. Last came the farmers, lured by tales of fertile earth and independent living. While not all of these migrants found what they were looking for, enough stayed that by 1890 the head of the census bureau could say that the frontier "cannot any longer have a place in the census reports."[10] By the turn of the century, all but three continental territories—Oklahoma, Arizona, and New Mexico—had enough population to achieve statehood.

The West's natural resources brought wealth to eastern investors even before the Civil War, when John Jacob Astor monopolized the fur trade and became America's first millionaire. The rush to acquire individual riches began with the discovery of gold in California in 1848, and miners moved

A family of homesteaders stands in front of their sod house in Nebraska in 1886, shortly before mass migration closed the frontier.

east to silver strikes in Nevada and Colorado eleven years later. Of course, not all discoveries panned out (see "Mark Twain Describes the Get-Rich-Quick Mining Culture," p. 163), but enough strikes of gold, silver, copper, lead, and zinc were found in the western states to create interest in unsettled areas. While some towns lasted only as long as the mines produced, others were developed by corporations into permanent settlements.

Some of the fastest settlement after the Civil War came to the southern Plains, as cattle ranchers exploited millions of acres of federal grassland free for the grazing. Texans had discovered that wild longhorns, descended from imported Spanish cattle, thrived on the open range. A prospective rancher could purchase calves for as little as three to four dollars a head in Texas and earn up to fifty dollars apiece upon delivery to northern meatpacking companies. They hired cowboys to round up the herds twice a year and take them on the "long drive" up to railroads in Kansas, and from there the cattle headed to Chicago slaughterhouses. Between 1866 and 1885, some 5.7 million

19

head of cattle traveled this route. Other ranchers moved to open ranges in Kansas, Nebraska, and Wyoming by the early 1870s.

Prospective farmers, many of them immigrants, provided the final wave of settlement. They were encouraged by railroad companies, who stood to profit twice: first, by selling the land near their tracks; and second, by getting business from new residents. Most companies had branches overseas to encourage immigration, with some railroad land offices spending millions on attracting new settlers. As one North Dakota pioneer described in the 1880s:

> Language cannot exaggerate the rapidity with which these communities are built up. You may stand ankle deep in the short grass of the uninhabited wilderness; next month a mixed train will glide over the waste and stop at some point where the railroad has decided to locate a town. Men, women, and children will jump out of the cars and their chattels will be tumbled out after them. From that moment the building begins.[11]

Of course, the railroad companies' promotional literature failed to warn of the hot summers, frigid winters, insect plagues, prairie fires, and fuel and water shortages that immigrant pioneers frequently faced. Pioneer farmers persisted, however, overcoming hardships with the help of new agricultural inventions, new farming methods, and the assistance of the wider community.

One historian credits the Northern Pacific Railroad with doubling the population of Minnesota, the Dakotas, and the Pacific Northwest between 1880 and 1900, mostly by attracting immigrants from Germany, Scandinavia, and Great Britain. Many frontier settlers came from the eastern United States as well, including large groups of African Americans who migrated to Kansas in the 1870s. In all, over one million pioneers from Iowa, Missouri, and the Great Lakes states headed west between 1880 and 1890. The flood of settlers spread all across the continent, effectively eliminating the frontier.

In a famous 1893 speech, historian Frederick Jackson Turner suggested that the Western frontier had played a key role in building the American character. "Turner held that American democracy was not an import but a product of the American frontier," another historian explained. "The wilderness environment fostered traits of individualism, self-reliance, restless energy, and 'that buoyancy and exuberance that comes with freedom.'"[12] But the same "restless energy" that allowed Americans to conquer the frontier would also create a new breed of businessmen. These "robber barons," as they came to be called, would use any and all means at their disposal to reap financial rewards on an unthinkable scale—and in the process they would become the most prominent symbols of America's Gilded Age.

Notes:

[1] Quoted in Wexler, Sanford. *Westward Expansion: An Eyewitness History.* New York: Facts on File, 1991, p. 226.

[2] Billington, Ray Allen, and Martin Ridge. *Westward Expansion: A History of the American Frontier.* 6th edition, abridged. Albuquerque: University of New Mexico Press, 2001, p. 351.

[3] Quoted in Wexler, p. 226.

[4] Ambrose, Stephen. *Nothing Like It in the World: The Men Who Built the Transcontinental Railroad, 1863-1869.* New York: Simon & Schuster, 2000, p. 62.

[5] Summers, Mark Wahlgren. *The Gilded Age, or, the Hazard of New Functions.* Upper Saddle River, NJ: Prentice Hall, 1997, p. 75.

[6] Summers, p. 64.

[7] Quoted in Billington and Ridge, p. 318.

[8] Quoted in Davis, William C. *The American Frontier: Pioneers, Settlers, and Cowboys 1800-1899.* New York: Salamander Books, 1992, p. 235.

[9] Billington and Ridge, p. 319.

[10] Quoted in Davis, p. 227.

[11] Quoted in Wexler, p. 287.

[12] Wall, James T. *Wall Street and the Fruited Plain: Money, Expansion, and Politics in the Gilded Age.* Lanham, MD: University Press of America, 2008, p. 123.

Chapter Two

THE RISE OF
THE ROBBER BARONS

[Railroad tycoon Cornelius] Vanderbilt is but the precursor of
a class of men who will wield within the state a power created by it, but too great for its control. He is the founder of a
dynasty.

—Charles Francis Adams Jr., "A Chapter of Erie," 1869

From its earliest days, the United States was a place where individuals could take huge financial risks and reap equally huge rewards. Land speculation, get-rich-quick schemes, stock market fluctuations, and financial panics became common characteristics of the American economy. People admired businessmen who bested their competitors or government authorities to achieve the "American dream" of wealth and power. But this atmosphere of cutthroat economic competition reached new heights during the Gilded Age, which extended roughly from the end of the Civil War in 1865 to the turn of the twentieth century. Unprecedented economic development was accompanied by unbridled competition, excessive greed, manipulation of markets, and political corruption. Government officials handed out subsidies, land grants, tariffs, and other political favors in return for campaign contributions, cheap stock, free goods and services, and even outright bribes.

The Gilded Age created a new class of business owners who wielded great power and lived in great luxury. These men collectively came to be known as "robber barons." Kansas farmers originally coined the term to describe ruthless railroad owners who controlled shipping routes and charged exorbitant rates, and the term was later applied more generally to the wealthy industrialists of the era. But the era's economic competition created as many losers as winners. The robber barons built their business empires at the expense of workers who toiled long hours under difficult conditions and still struggled to make ends meet.

Railroad Expansion Spurs "Creative" Financing

Before the Civil War, the United States had few large corporations. In the 1850s, only a few factories existed that had more than $1 million invested in facilities and equipment. Railroads, however, needed huge amounts of investment. By 1859, investors had poured more than $1 billion into regional rail companies like the Erie, the Pennsylvania, the Baltimore & Ohio, and the New York Central. The transcontinental railroads were projects on another scale entirely, and they would change the nature of American finance. "They were enormous pools of capital," according to one historian, "undertakings so large that the modern institutions of the stock market and investment banking had to be created to make it possible to funnel so many millions into single enterprises."[1]

The American people demanded more railroads, and they were willing to invest in them. Like many road and canal projects before them, railroads often received government loans in the form of land grants and bonds. The ease of financing led to schemes where a corporation could create huge profits with little initial risk. First, a prospective railroad company would get a charter (a document granting rights) from the state, which was so eager to encourage new railroads that it would often bestow low-cost land grants along with the charter. The company would then use the land as collateral for a bond issue and use the bond sales to pay off the land grant (see "Stocks, Bonds, and Currency in the Gilded Age," p. 26). Sometimes the railroad would not even begin construction; chartering was enough to claim a route, and many of these "paper railroads" made a profit when sold off to a competitor. Other railroad companies were little more than investment scams, with new bonds issued to pay off old bond holders.

Railroad companies also used stock sales to make huge profits for little investment. After acquiring their charter and land, they could begin issuing stock (shares of partial ownership in the company) to investors. For instance, the "Big Four" financiers who headed the Central Pacific Railroad initially sold $8.5 million worth of stock in the company even though they had invested less than $200,000. After selling stock, companies sometimes spent

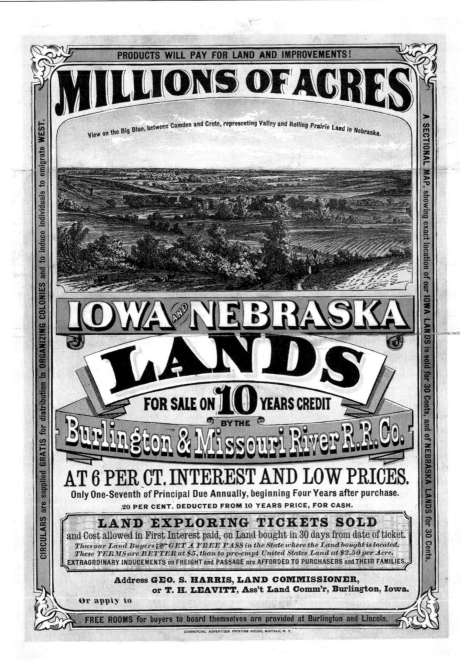

This 1872 railroad pamphlet attempted to lure settlers to newly established western towns with promises of cheap land and easy credit.

Stocks, Bonds, and Currency in the Gilded Age

During the Gilded Age, people had two main options when investing their money: stocks and bonds. Buying stock in a corporation made investors part-owners in proportion to the number of shares they held. By owning stock in a company, investors were entitled to a share of the company's profits, paid as dividends. They could buy or sell shares on a stock exchange, and stock prices rose and fell with the company's fortunes.

Investors could also purchase bonds: a guarantee by a government or corporation to repay a loan, usually with interest, at the end of a specified period of time. Bonds, especially government-issued ones, were considered less risky than stocks. The greater the risk of a borrower defaulting on repayment, the higher the interest rate bonds would promise. Like stocks, bonds fluctuated in value because they could be bought and sold.

Currency was a more complicated matter. Before the Civil War, there was no national currency in the United States. Banks chartered by individual states could issue their own paper money, and it did not have to be backed by silver or gold coins, called specie. The federal government, however, would only accept specie as payment, making the value of state bank notes unstable.

the bare minimum on actual rail line construction. After all, shoddy construction affected a railroad's future, not the current value of its stock.

Railroad owners and financiers became adept at other forms of stock manipulation as well. For example, companies needing extra money might simply issue more stock, even if it artificially inflated the company's worth. This practice was called "watering stock," a term borrowed from cattle drovers who watered their animals just before selling them so they would weigh more and bring a better price.

In addition to stock manipulations, railroad robber barons were not above using blackmail to increase their fortunes. A town without a railroad stop was at a competitive disadvantage, so some companies would threaten to move their tracks away from a town unless they received special compensation. In 1873, for example, the Denver and Rio Grande Railroad built its line

During the war, the federal government took steps to increase the money supply and create a national system of currency and banking. The Legal Tender Act of 1862 created $150 million in paper notes that were backed only by government guarantees, not specie. Because of the green ink used to print them, these notes were called greenbacks. This currency was accepted by the general public, although it was subject to inflation, meaning that its value declined over time in relation to the price of goods and services.

The Union passed two National Banking Acts during the war that created nationally chartered banks that issued a new national currency. Unlike greenbacks, these federal bank notes were redeemable in specie. The laws also taxed state-issued currencies, essentially removing them from use. By the end of the Civil War, most state banks had been converted to national charters, and the new national currency was widely accepted. The issue of how to handle the greenbacks that remained in circulation, however, remained contentious throughout the entire Gilded Age.

Source:
Office of the Comptroller of the Currency. "History." Available online at http://www.occ.treas.gov/about/history.html.

seven miles short of Cañon City, Colorado, and refused to build further until the company received $100,000 in bonds. When the town voted to pay $50,000 in bonds and $50,000 in real estate, the railroad finished the line—but it routed the track away from downtown, instead placing it on property owned by the railroad on the outskirts of town.

Land speculation was another popular moneymaking technique for railroads. The Atchison, Topeka and Santa Fe, for instance, was known for stopping a few miles short of existing towns and building its own settlements on lands that—prior to the arrival of the railroad—had been virtually worthless. Afterward, the railroad executives frequently blackmailed the existing towns into extending the tracks to their location.

To get the political influence needed to award charters, pass bond issues, and receive land grants, the robber barons often engaged in bribery of public officials. Lawmakers and officials received free railroad passes, free or heavily discounted stock, and insider information about proposed line locations. Many politicians and government agents used the latter information to snap up land at bargain rates, hold it until the railroad line increased its value, and then sell it for a tidy profit. The Union Pacific reportedly spent $400,000 on bribes between 1866 and 1872, while the Central Pacific spent as much as half a million dollars a year between 1865 and 1875. The railroad tycoons' dominance of American politics led British historian and politician Viscount James Bryce to observe in his 1888 study *The American Commonwealth:* "They have power, more power—that is, more opportunity of making their will prevail—than perhaps anyone in political life, except the President and the Speaker who, after all hold theirs only for four years and two years, while the railroad monarch may keep his for life."[2]

Cutthroat Competition: The Erie War

One of the most famous robber barons of the early Gilded Age was Cornelius Vanderbilt, who at his death in 1877 was the richest man in America. "Commodore" Vanderbilt initially made his fortune in the steamship business. In the 1860s, Vanderbilt decided to diversify into railroads and gained control of two local lines on Manhattan Island, the Harlem Railroad and the Hudson River Railroad. When the New York Central Railroad broke an agreement with Vanderbilt's Hudson River line, Vanderbilt retaliated by boycotting the New York Central, leaving its passengers two miles short of destinations in New York City. His ruthless measure ruined the New York Central, allowing Vanderbilt to take over the crippled line in 1867. He thus gained control of one of the four major trunk lines that led from the East Coast to the waterways of the heartland.

Vanderbilt soon brought the same efficiencies to the New York Central as he had to his other ventures, increasing net profits by more than 50 percent in the first year. He was concerned with how competition might affect rates, however, so he proposed to pool together with the two other trunk lines that served New York City, the Pennsylvania Railroad and the Erie Railway, and divide the city's huge shipping business between them. The Pennsylvania's directors were willing, but the Erie's board—led by influential Wall Street broker Daniel Drew—turned Vanderbilt down. Drew "regarded his fiduciary position as director of a railroad as a means of manipulating its stock for his own advantage,"[3] wrote journalist Charles Francis Adams Jr. in

Wealthy railroad owner Cornelius Vanderbilt's efforts to wrestle control of the Erie Railway away from financier Jim Fisk received sensational coverage in Gilded Age newspapers in 1870.

1869, and was little concerned with how the railroad was run as long as he could use insider information to profit. Vanderbilt, who also held shares in the Erie, was tired of Drew's stock shenanigans. In 1868 he decided to attempt to buy control of the Erie Railway.

This decision led to the infamous "Erie War," with Vanderbilt on one side and Drew and two brash young financiers, Jim Fisk and Jay Gould (see Gould biography, p. 144), on the other. Vanderbilt was well able to afford the minimum $10 million it would have cost to gain a controlling interest of Erie's outstanding 250,000 shares of stock, but Drew, Gould, and Fisk responded to his challenge by watering the stock. They secretly converted bonds into 30,000 new shares, plus they released an additional 28,000 previously unissued shares onto the market. Vanderbilt found a favorable New York judge to issue an injunction against the new Erie shares and order Drew's removal from the Erie board. Drew found an equally bribable judge to issue a counter injunction. He then released a further 50,000 new shares of

Erie stock, causing the price to drop from $95 to $50 per share. When Vanderbilt's judge ruled that Drew, Gould, and Fisk were in contempt of court, the Erie board members took their records, printing press, and $6 million in greenbacks (paper currency) and fled across the river to New Jersey.

At this point, however, Vanderbilt realized that he was losing the battle for public opinion. The newspapers accurately charged that if he added the Erie to his New York Central, Vanderbilt would have a stranglehold over New York City's rail business—which would enable him to charge inflated prices for rail service. Recognizing he was defeated, he made a deal with Drew: he would sell back 100,000 shares of Erie in return for $4.75 million in cash and bonds from a Boston branch railroad. Drew then left the Erie's board—his stock watering had scandalized the public too much for him to stay—but Gould and Fisk became Erie's president and controller, respectively. They continued abusing Erie's stock until 1872, when Fisk was murdered by a romantic rival and Gould was ousted from the board. The Erie Railway itself survived, but it paid only a single dividend until 1942.

> *"The power of the railroads gave rise to demands for a stronger government to control them," one historian explained, "yet this same power aroused fears that they would simply corrupt a strong government, and grow still more powerful."*

While the Erie War only had a short-term effect on Wall Street prices—and on Vanderbilt, who soon made up his estimated million-dollar loss on Erie—it was a source of fascination to the American public. The stock battle earned countless headlines, with one admiring editorial in the *New York Herald* noting that "however questionable these schemes may be, their skill and success exhibit Napoleonic genius on the part of him who conceived them."[4] Following the Erie War, Wall Street did adjust some of its rules regarding the registration of new stock, but the government did little to prevent such a situation from happening again. "The power of the railroads gave rise to demands for a stronger government to control them," one historian explained, "yet this same power aroused fears that they would simply corrupt a strong government, and grow still more powerful."[5]

Black Friday: Gould Manipulates Gold

Gould's experiences in the Erie War gave him an idea for an even greater speculative venture. With careful planning, he thought he might corner the gold market (buy enough gold to manipulate the price others had to pay) and earn great profits. His main obstacle was the U.S. Treasury, which was regularly redeeming U.S. war bonds with gold in an effort to reestablish government credit. A gold corner was impossible if other buyers knew the government would release millions in gold to the market every month. Despite the difficulties, Gould believed he had found a way to get around the government. "Of all financial operations, cornering gold is the most brilliant and the most dangerous," Gould's contemporary Henry Adams wrote, "and possibly the very hazard and splendor of the attempt were the reasons of its fascination to Mr. Jay Gould."[6]

Shortly after the presidential inauguration of General Ulysses S. Grant in March 1869, Grant's younger sister Virginia married a wealthy New York widower, Abel R. Corbin, who was an acquaintance of Gould. Hoping to influence the president, Gould convinced

Financier Jay Gould nearly managed to corner the market on gold in 1869, causing a financial panic.

Corbin that letting gold prices rise would be good for the American economy. To gain Corbin's support, Gould established a gold account in Corbin's name worth $1.5 million. Corbin soon introduced Gould to Grant, and although the president showed little inclination to accept their gold theory, Corbin kept lobbying him. He also recommended Daniel Butterfield for the recently opened post of assistant U.S. Treasury secretary for the New York Sub Treasury, which handled all federal gold sales. Grant appointed him. After Gould gave Butterfield a collateral-free loan of $10,000, he felt sure the assistant secretary would give him advance warning when the Treasury planned to sell gold.

Gold was selling for $135 per ounce in greenbacks when Gould and his partners, which eventually included Jim Fisk, began buying it in mid-August 1869. They used several brokers to disguise their $9 million purchase. When the price stayed bogged down, Gould planted an article in the *New York Times* suggesting that the U.S. government would hold off on further gold sales until fall harvests came in. As prices slowly rose, Gould finally got the insider information from Corbin he needed: Grant had been convinced that the government should stop selling gold to avoid appearing to take sides in the market. Once this occurred, the gold that was already on the market increased in value. By mid-September Gould's ring had $40 million in gold, and the Gold Exchange Bank was registering some $160 million in trades every day, instead of the usual $70 to $90 million. By September 22, gold had risen to $141 per ounce, leaving many bankers worried. They regularly guaranteed the price of gold to their customers, shorting the price, so the higher gold rose the greater their potential losses.

When bankers began sending messages to Treasury Secretary George Boutwell urging him to sell gold, and thus bring down gold prices, Gould's group made a misstep: they sent a letter from Corbin via special messenger to President Grant, arguing in favor of letting gold rise. Grant finally realized Corbin was involved in the speculation. The president sent a letter warning Corbin to get out, then instructed the Treasury to sell gold if necessary to prevent a panic. Gould, forewarned, sold $8.1 million of his gold on September 23. But Fisk kept buying. On September 24 Fisk bid the price of gold up to $145, then $150. Brokers panicked, believing Fisk's boast that he would see gold reach $200. Gold reached a high of $162 before news broke that the Treasury would sell $4 million in gold the next day. This announcement triggered a mad dash to sell gold. Now that it was more widely available, the value of gold plummeted with startling speed. By the end of the day, which would become known as "Black Friday," the floor of the Gold Exchange became so chaotic that police had to be called to establish order.

> *"This is a government of the people, by the people, and for the people no longer,"* declared Rutherford B. Hayes. *"It is a government of corporations, by corporations, and for corporations."*

The clerks at the Gold Exchange were overwhelmed with the $325 million in trades from Thursday, let alone the $500 million traded on Black Friday. When they tried to settle accounts, Fisk denied placing $30 million in buy orders. Having sold his $40 to $50 million stash at prices between $140 and $150, Gould might have covered his partner's losses. Instead, he used his political influence to convince a judge to put the Gold Exchange Bank into receivership. The new receiver threw out Fisk's trades, settled the bank's debts at 25 cents to the dollar, and ensured that Gould's claims were settled first. By paying off judges, Gould and Fisk easily evaded various lawsuits brought against them. Although there was no official reckoning of their profits that day, Fisk avoided a loss of $20 to $30 million, and Gould's sales before the crash netted him as much as $10 million. Since Gould and Fisk had only spent one or two million on lawyers' fees and bribes, they still raked in enormous fortunes when all was said and done.

Although Gould and Fisk emerged unscathed and even enriched by Black Friday, dozens of brokers and bankers went bankrupt. Losses on Wall Street and the Gold Exchange totaled around $100 million. Yet despite creating havoc in the markets, Gould and Fisk's bold financial maneuvering captured the public imagination. "The attempt to 'corner gold' in that terrible week was so near complete success," noted the *London Times,* "that it appeared to the imagination of Wall Street like the defeat of Hannibal or Napoleon—a victory of Fate over Genius."[7] Both men escaped prosecution, even after Congressional hearings into the scandal. From this day forward, though, Gould was tarnished with a new nickname: "The Mephistopheles [devil] of Wall Street."

Railroad Money and the Crédit Mobilier Scandal

In 1873 the United States was rocked once again by a scandal involving railway men, many of whom had infiltrated the highest levels of government. Of the 73 men who served as cabinet officers between 1868 and 1896, 48 had either served railroad clients, lobbied for railroads, sat on railroad boards, or had relatives connected to railroads. Central Pacific president Leland Stanford even served in the U.S. Senate from 1885 to 1893. "Shall the railroads govern the country, or shall the people govern the railroads?" future president Rutherford B. Hayes wrote in his diary. "This is a government of the people, by the people, and for the people no longer. It is a government of corporations, by corporations, and for corporations."[8]

Another politician with close ties to the railroad industry was Massachusetts congressman Oakes Ames, a tool manufacturer and early investor in both the Central Pacific and the Union Pacific Railroads. When the Union Pacific was having difficulty raising funds in 1865, President Lincoln reportedly summoned the lawmaker and told him, "Ames, you take hold of this. If the subsidies provided are not enough to build the [transcontinental railroad] ask double and you shall have it. The road must be built, and you are the man to do it. Take hold of it yourself. By building the Union Pacific, you will be the remembered man of your generation."[9]

During the Crédit Mobilier railroad financing scandal, Massachusetts congressman Oakes Ames sold deeply discounted shares of stock to dozens of high-ranking federal government officials.

Ames and his brother Oliver subsequently became major shareholders in Crédit Mobilier of America, the company that had been set up to perform construction for the Union Pacific. Crédit Mobilier was established as a separate entity so that the brothers could overcharge for construction, then pass along the excess profits to shareholders in the form of stocks and bonds. Because the same men ran both companies, no one detected the fraud. By marking up construction costs, Crédit Mobilier passed along some $50 million to its stockholders, while spending only $44 million on actual railroad construction. In 1868, when the Union Pacific itself was $10 million in debt, a Crédit Mobilier investor with 100 shares received $28,200 in stocks, bonds, and dividends—a 280 percent return on a $10,000 investment.

This creative financing was scandalous enough, although some suggested that outrageous profits were a just reward for taking on the risky business of building the transcontinental railroad. But beginning in 1867, Oakes Ames had sold deeply discounted shares of Crédit Mobilier stock to more than twenty members of Congress—stock they could quickly sell for big profits. Ames held most of the stock "in trust" to keep the recipients' names off the books, but the scandal broke in the *New York Sun* in late 1872. The public was shocked to see some of the names on the list: current vice president Schuyler Colfax, vice president-elect Henry Wilson, Ohio representative (and future president) James Garfield, and House minority leader James Brooks.

Ames claimed he was not trying to influence his colleagues: "I did not know that they required it, because they were all friends of the [railroad] and my friends; if you want to bribe a man you want to bribe one who is opposed to you, not to bribe one who is your friend."[10] Nevertheless, Congress immediately began an investigation that sparked newspaper headlines throughout 1873. Accusations and denials were exchanged until Ames, tired of being called a liar, produced a book with the names of the men who had taken

Crédit Mobilier stock. The investigating committee, however, ruled that while most of the congressmen had been imprudent in accepting stock, they had not intended to be dishonest. Only Brooks was found guilty of accepting bribes from Ames, and the two men were censured (formally condemned for their behavior) rather than expelled from Congress.

Soon after the Crédit Mobilier scandal broke, the financing and business operations of the Central Pacific—the railroad responsible for the western-most sections of the transcontinental railroad—came under investigation as well. The Big Four had been more careful in setting up their construction company, the Contract and Finance Company. While they had indulged in the same fraud—inflating construction costs and pocketing the difference—they dissolved the company after the line was completed, then burned their accounting records to "save space" in their offices.

The revelations disappointed many people who had supported the transcontinental railroad project. "When the greatest railroad of the world, binding together the continent and uniting the two great seas which wash our shores, was finished," Massachusetts senator George Hoar recalled, "I have seen our national triumph and exaltation turned to bitterness and shame by the unanimous reports of three committees of Congress that every step of that mighty enterprise had been taken in fraud."[11] In the end, however, the financial consequences of the Crédit Mobilier scandal were worse than the political ones. A sharp drop in the value of Union Pacific stock contributed to the nation's slide into an economic depression in the final months of 1873.

Bad Railway Financing and the Panic of 1873

The first major financial crisis of the Gilded Age was precipitated by the failure of Jay Cooke. Prior to 1873, according to one biographer, "no American financier enjoyed greater prestige, esteem and public confidence than he."[12] Cooke had gained prominence during the Civil War by using patriotic adver-tising to sell war bonds to hundreds of thousands of ordinary citizens. He sold over $1.6 billion in bonds—accounting for more than a quarter of the Union's war chest—and became a millionaire in the process. Cooke saw his success as fated: "I have been—I firmly believe—God's chosen instrument, especially in the financial work of saving the Union."[13]

Once the war ended, Cooke grew determined to bring a transcontinental railroad to the Northwest. In 1869 Cooke agreed to sell bonds and serve as

SUPPLEMENT TO NO. 940 OF "FRANK LESLIE'S ILLUSTRATED NEWSPAPER."

THE GREAT FINANCIAL PANIC.—CLOSING THE DOORS OF THE STOCK EXCHANGE ON ITS MEMBERS, SATURDAY, SEPT. 20TH.

This newspaper illustrates the desperation in the financial industry during the Panic of 1873, when the stock market shut down for the first time in history.

banker for the Northern Pacific Railroad, which had been chartered to run from Duluth, Minnesota, to Puget Sound on the West Coast. Unfortunately for Cooke, the Northern Pacific's management spanned "a rainbow of inexcusably poor planning, weak personnel, cronyism, kickbacks, lack of financial controls, questionable purchases, 'creative' bookkeeping, absentee decision-making, woeful ethics, and a bureaucratic chain of command characterized by evasion and buck-passing,"[14] according to one historian. Cooke's bank held almost $7 million in Northern Pacific debt by August 1873. On September 18, when Cooke's partners could not raise the $1 million needed to keep the bank running, they suspended operations at the firm's New York City branch.

The failure of one of the nation's most trusted financiers set off a run on banks, as panicked account holders tried to withdraw their savings before funds disappeared. Cooke was forced to close branches in Philadelphia and Washington, D.C., and the panic spread down the eastern seaboard and into the Midwest. On Wall Street, stocks dropped sharply and more than thirty brokerages became insolvent. The stock market was forced to close for the first time in history, for ten days, beginning on September 20. Overall, almost 5,000 banks, brokers, and commercial houses went bankrupt, and the country fell into a depression that would last five years. As people hoarded money, more businesses became starved for revenue. An estimated 6,000 businesses carrying 500,000 employees failed in 1874 alone. By 1877, national unemployment reached 20 percent, with another 40 percent only working half the year.

Railroads were hit hard by the depression, and many former robber barons went bankrupt. Cooke lost control of the Northern Pacific and had to sell his mansion and live with his daughter. The Northern Pacific itself went bankrupt in 1875 and would not complete its transcontinental path until 1883. At the same time, though, shrewd businessmen like Jay Gould took advantage of the depression to buy failing companies on the cheap, turn them around, and expand them when good economic times returned. A handful of these men would create companies of unprecedented size and scale. After a while, the newspapers stopped referring to them as robber barons. Instead, they became known by a much more admiring term: captains of industry.

Notes:

[1] Porter, Glenn. "Industrialization and the Rise of Big Business." In Calhoun, Charles W., editor. *The Gilded Age: Perspectives on the Origins of Modern America.* 2nd edition. Lanham, MD: Rowman & Littlefield Publishers, 2007, pp. 11-27.

[2] Bryce, James. *The American Commonwealth,* Vol. 2. New York: Macmillan, 1888. Quoted in Josephson, Matthew. *The Robber Barons.* New York: Harcourt, 1934, p. 244.

[3] Adams, Charles Francis, Jr. "A Chapter of Erie." *North American Review,* no. 142, July 1869. Excerpted in Stiles, T. J., editor. *Robber Barons and Radicals.* New York: Perigee, 1997, p. 110.

[4] *New York Herald,* November 19, 1868. Quoted in Gordon, John Steele. *The Scarlet Woman of Wall Street: Jay Gould, Jim Fisk, Cornelius Vanderbilt, the Erie Railway Wars, and the Birth of Wall Street.* New York: Weidenfeld & Nicolson, 1988, p. 206.

[5] Stiles, T. J. *The First Tycoon: The Epic Life of Cornelius Vanderbilt.* New York: Knopf, 2009, p. 470.

[6] Adams, Henry. *Chapters of Erie, and Other Essays,* Boston: James R. Osgood, 1871, p. 114.

[7] *London Times,* January 9, 1872. Quoted in Gordon, p. 277.

[8] Quoted in Summers, Mark Wahlgren. *The Gilded Age, or, the Hazard of New Functions.* Upper Saddle River, NJ: Prentice Hall, 1997, p. 89.

[9] Quoted in Bain, David Haward. *Empire Express: Building the First Transcontinental Railroad.* New York: Viking, 1999, pp. 211-12.

[10] Quoted in Bain, p. 689.

[11] Quoted in Josephson, p. 165.

[12] Pollard, James E. *The Journal of Jay Cooke: Or, The Gibraltar Records, 1865-1905.* Columbus: Ohio State University Press, 1935, p. 96.

[13] Quoted in Lubetkin, M. John. *Jay Cooke's Gamble: The Northern Pacific Railroad, the Sioux, and the Panic of 1873.* Norman: University of Oklahoma Press, 2006, p. 13.

[14] Lubetkin, p. 288.

Chapter Three
CAPTAINS OF INDUSTRY

I believe the true road to preeminent success in any line is to make yourself master in that line. I have no faith in the policy of scattering one's resources, and in my experience I have rarely if ever met a man who achieved preeminence in money-making—certainly never one in manufacturing—who was interested in many concerns. The men who have succeeded are men who have chosen one line and stuck to it.

—Steel magnate Andrew Carnegie,
The Autobiography of Andrew Carnegie

In the unregulated financial environment of the Gilded Age, many individuals manipulated the system to their advantage. While some industrialists deserved the "robber baron" label, historian H. Wayne Morgan cautioned that the stereotype of greedy, power-hungry manipulator "must be balanced with a fuller picture, showing the new technology he often brought to his industry, the wealth and resources he developed for the economy in general, the social good he sometimes did with his money, offsetting the bitter fact that he paid little in taxes."[1]

The most successful businessmen of the Gilded Age squeezed every drop of extra cash from their enterprises through superior equipment, careful management, and large volumes of business. James J. Hill, for instance, built his Great Northern Railway without federal subsidies by carefully surveying the best routes, thus lowering building costs; using quality materials, thus ensuring lower maintenance costs; and waiting to build until his route was sufficiently populated to support the line, thus bringing quick profits. As a result, one historian noted, "Hill's [rail]road was the best built, the least corrupt, the most popular, and the only transcontinental never to go bankrupt."[2]

Railroads revolutionized business management along with transportation. By nature, railroads were sprawling enterprises that had to coordinate carefully to prevent tracks and trains from lying idle and wasting money. Many railroads adopted a military structure, with autonomous regional divisions reporting to a central staff. Through careful record-keeping and use of the telegraph's instant communications capacity, companies could integrate their efforts over huge distances. This pyramidal structure was also central to the new corporations, as a single board of directors took responsibility for directing the capital of thousands of investors.

Corporations grew larger and more powerful as they found new ways to expand operations, generate profits, and take advantage of the public's growing taste for material comforts. The most successful of these Gilded Age enterprises were commanded by three men: John D. Rockefeller, Andrew Carnegie, and J. P. Morgan. These powerful industrialists were "walking whirlwinds," according to one historian. "Over some twenty-five years they forced the pace in all the critical underpinnings of the modern industrial state—steel, oil, railroads, coal, telegraphs—constantly driving to larger scales and lower costs, constantly attacking the comfortable settling points where normal businessmen paused to enjoy their success."[3] Their success was often portrayed as a Darwinian struggle, a survival of the fittest, and many believed these titans came out on top because of superior talent. Others criticized them as ruthless monopolists who crushed anyone who got in their way. While the truth lay in between these extremes, there is no doubt that these men captured the imagination of their era.

Rockefeller and Standard Oil

When John D. Rockefeller was born (see Rockefeller biography, p. 156), few would have predicted a future as one of America's wealthiest tycoons. The son of a shady traveling salesman, Rockefeller nonetheless grew up with a dedicated work ethic, and by the early 1860s he had gained a foothold in the relatively young industry of oil refining. Rockefeller soon discovered that his Cleveland-based refinery held the potential for great profit. While crude oil prices fluctuated wildly, the market for refined products like kerosene was only growing. It was so cheap to build and staff a refinery that the initial

John D. Rockefeller built the Standard Oil Company into a business empire by taking over competitors and making deals with railroad lines.

investment could be recouped after the first production run. In addition, Cleveland's location—close to oil fields yet serviced by two major railroads—made it an ideal distribution center. Rockefeller built on these advantages by adopting new technology early, hiring the best talent, developing new petroleum by-products, making his own barrels, and acquiring his own storage and loading facilities. By cutting waste and underselling his competitors to gain market share, Rockefeller soon had the city's largest refinery.

In 1870 Rockefeller incorporated his business with five other small refineries as Standard Oil. By then his company was refining some 600 barrels of oil every day, about 5 percent of the national total. Rockefeller continued to improve his product and increase his refining capacity, expanding to the west and south and setting up an export business in New York. He reduced transport costs through shrewd negotiation: in exchange for a price rebate, he would guarantee a railroad a specific volume of shipping and allow it to use his loading facilities and tanks. When other refiners could not match his terms—or his profits—he bought them out. By 1872, Standard Oil's refining capacity had jumped to 12 million barrels a year.

> *"All seem to have bought into [Rockefeller's] quiet insistence that consolidation was the path to salvation; that the Standard would be the entity that survived the mergers; and that he was the man to lead them."*

In 1871 Thomas A. Scott of the Pennsylvania Railroad approached Rockefeller with a proposal to collaborate on a new business venture. The South Improvement Company (SIC) would be jointly owned by railroads and refiners and would set production and shipping quotas for member companies. The plan was to sharply raise shipping rates for non-members. Besides receiving a 50 percent rebate for shipping his oil over SIC rail lines, Rockefeller would also receive a "drawback": a 40 percent rebate on competitors' shipments. In addition, the member railroads would pass along information to Standard Oil on its competitors' shipping schedules and customers. The arrangement appealed to Rockefeller, who was looking for ways to control the oil industry's boom-and-bust cycle of overproduction, lower prices, and business failures. If he could not convince other refiners to enter his alliance, he was happy to drive them out of business instead.

The SIC operated in secret until its planned rate increases were accidentally published in early 1872. Rockefeller's competitors threatened legal action, the press vilified Standard Oil and Rockefeller, and crude oil producers threatened to boycott SIC railroads and build pipelines to ship their product to market. The railroad owners blinked first, dropping rates. Pennsylvania's legislature also revoked the SIC's charter. Even though crude oil producers refused to sell to Standard Oil refineries, Rockefeller rode out the controversy. By the end of 1872 another bout of overproduction allowed him to buy 22 of Cleveland's 26 refineries. He sold many for scrap and consolidated the rest into six newly designed facilities.

Rockefeller Builds an Empire

Although the SIC failed, it convinced Rockefeller that pooling and rebate schemes could produce windfall profits. He thus created a new secret rebate agreement with railroads while simultaneously gobbling up an ever larger share of the nation's refining business. In 1874 and 1875 he brought major refineries from New York, Pittsburgh, and Philadelphia into Standard Oil with little struggle. "All seem to have bought into his quiet insistence that consolidation was the path to salvation; that the Standard would be the entity that survived the mergers; and that he was the man to lead them,"[4] as one historian recounted. Standard Oil took over an additional 24 companies in 1876 and 35 more in 1877. In many cases Rockefeller kept the acquisitions secret, leaving the new partner with its old name while allowing it to share Standard's freight rebates. If potential targets were reluctant to merge—and few were, after seeing the profits on Standard's books—Rockefeller used price wars, railroad drawbacks, industrial espionage, and even political bribery to force them to their knees. By 1878, Standard Oil controlled 80 percent of the U.S. refining trade, a number that increased to 90 percent in the 1880s. Economists call Rockefeller's method of gaining dominance of an industry—through mergers with competing companies in the same line of business—"horizontal integration."

At the same time that Rockefeller tightened his stranglehold over American oil refining, he also looked to further expand his business empire through what economists refer to as "vertical integration"—merging with companies in related lines of business, such as oil transport and retail oil sales. In 1872 Standard Oil absorbed United Pipelines, and by 1876 the company controlled almost half of the existing pipelines that delivered refined oil to terminals and shipping points. The company also moved into distribution, cutting out wholesalers and middlemen by opening its own stores. If railroads or pipelines tried their own vertical expansion into refining, Rockefeller was quick to shut them out.

Gilded Age Philanthropy

Although greed and excess defined much of the Gilded Age, unprecedented fortunes also led to unprecedented charity. As Andrew Carnegie explained (see "Andrew Carnegie's 'Gospel of Wealth,'" p. 177), philanthropy was "the true antidote for the temporary unequal distribution of wealth, the reconciliation of the rich and the poor." Led by Carnegie's example, captains of industry donated millions of dollars to museums, libraries, universities, concert halls, and other cultural institutions.

Gilded Age business leaders used their wealth to support such institutions as the Metropolitan Opera.

Carnegie began by building libraries, spending $38 million to fund 2,811 libraries in the United States and Europe. Over the years he gave his adopted hometown of Pittsburgh $28 million to build schools, museums, assembly rooms, and the Carnegie Institute, a technical training school. He set up educational trusts, public parks, and libraries in his native Scotland and established commissions for peace and international cooperation in Europe. After selling his company in 1901, Carnegie donated $4 million in bonds to a pension fund for his workmen, along with $1 million to fund the libraries and halls he had built for them.

A tithing Christian, John D. Rockefeller gave away $550 million during his lifetime, including $35 million to the University of Chicago. His most notable cause was the Rockefeller Foundation (founded in 1913), which became a steadfast supporter of education, public health, scientific research, and the arts. J. P. Morgan's notable donations included $500,000 to build a church and $1 million for a hospital serving poor pregnant women. Morgan was also a major patron of New York City's Metropolitan Museum of Art.

Many Gilded Age philanthropists are remembered today for their educational bequests. Some financed professorships or specialty training schools, while others founded entire universities. Western Union founder Ezra Cornell, Baltimore & Ohio Railroad financier Johns Hopkins, Central Pacific Railroad president Leland Stanford, and New York Central Railroad owner Cornelius Vanderbilt all endowed private universities. These Gilded Age names live on, connected with some of the finest educational institutions in the country.

Sources:

Carnegie Institute of Science. "Andrew Carnegie's Organizations." Available online at http://carnegiescience.edu/andrew_carnegies_organizations.

Rockefeller Foundation. "Our History—A Powerful Legacy." Available online at http://www.rockefellerfoundation.org/who-we-are/our-history.

By the early 1880s Rockefeller had business interests scattered throughout the East Coast and Midwest. Since Ohio laws prohibited individuals from owning companies in multiple states, Rockefeller decided that a reorganization was in order. In 1882 his lawyers devised a new form of business organization called a trust, which created a holding company for the various state Standard Oil companies. The board of trustees of the holding company took control of the stock of more than 40 companies, whose shareholders received "trust shares" in return. Although the individual companies were run somewhat independently, the trust decided who sold in what region, which plants should open or close, and coordinated the buying of crude oil. Over the next few years, the trust closed 30 underperforming refineries and built three massive new facilities. Its refining costs dropped to 1.5 cents per gallon, then to only half a cent. By 1886 Standard Oil posted net earnings of $15 million per year. Some states enacted monopoly laws in an effort to limit the trust's operations or outlaw it altogether. But Standard Oil fended off these threats, either by using high-priced lawyers to win its court cases or by reincorporating in states with looser financial laws.

During this same period, Rockefeller and Standard Oil became the targets of "muckraking" investigative journalists and Congressional inquiries (see "Exposing the Price-Fixing Schemes of the 'Lords of Industry,'" p. 170). An 1886 Senate committee concluded that the company represented the "perfection of corporate greed in its fullest development."[5] Although Standard Oil did earn huge profits—from 15 to 80 percent return on investment during the 1890s—it also brought down wholesale oil prices over twenty years, from 58 cents per gallon to only 8 cents. As Rockefeller wrote to a colleague in 1885, "We must ever remember we are refining oil for the poor man and he must have it cheap and good."[6] Rockefeller was an innovator—the trust format was increasingly adopted by various industries—who for the most part worked within the laws of the time. Because he built "a modern organization that was both highly decentralized and highly unified," one historian noted, Rockefeller "has a claim to be not only the first great corporate executive but one of the greatest ever."[7]

Andrew Carnegie and Steel

The rags-to-riches story of Andrew Carnegie (see Carnegie biography, p. 129) was another tale that captured the American imagination during the

Gilded Age. A self-taught Scottish immigrant, Carnegie was mentored by Thomas A. Scott of the great Pennsylvania Railroad and quickly rose through the ranks. His early investments in shipping and construction soon exceeded his railroad salary, and in 1865 Carnegie left the Pennsylvania Railroad to focus on his own businesses.

Carnegie became a major player in iron and bridge-building through tough negotiating, superior products, and on-time construction. He knew, however, that the future of railroad construction was in steel. This material made stronger and longer-lasting rails than iron. After careful research, he decided to build a plant that would use the Bessemer method of producing steel, a technique new to America. He raised $700,000 to begin construction and hired engineer Alexander Holley, Bessemer's foremost champion, to design the plant. He named his new plant the J. Edgar Thomson Works, after the president of the

Andrew Carnegie acquired interests in every aspect of steel production, from iron ore to finished products.

Pennsylvania Railroad. The plant opened in 1875, and by its second full year of operation was returning 20 percent on its original investment.

Carnegie's success also came from finding the best technical experts and implementing revolutionary methods of management. Upon Holley's recommendation, he hired "Captain" William R. "Bill" Jones, a self-taught mechanic who would patent more major improvements to the Bessemer process than any of his contemporaries. Under his guidance, the Thomson works implemented several time-saving mechanisms, increasing efficiency. Carnegie also hired a chemist to analyze steel output and iron ore. Most importantly, he brought "railroad-style accounting" to manufacturing. When Carnegie first entered the iron industry, he was appalled at the shoddy recordkeeping of his competitors. "I heard of men who thought their business at the end of the year would show a loss and had found a profit, and vice-versa," he recalled in his autobiography. "I felt as if we were moles burrowing in the dark, and this to me was intolerable."[8] Instead, he tracked costs at every stage of production, found new ways to use scrap materials, and discovered the most efficient methods of running his equipment. Being able to calculate the lowest profitable price for his steel meant Carnegie could undersell—and outclass—his competition.

Carnegie Dominates through Vertical Integration

Unlike Rockefeller, who first dominated his industry through horizontal integration—pooling with or taking over his competition—Carnegie succeeded through vertical integration. He established a presence in all aspects of steel production, from iron ore to finished product. He rarely bought out rival steel makers, although he did purchase the Homestead and Duquesne plants from other companies when he was looking to expand production. By 1880, the Thomson steel works were producing profits of 130 percent per year. Although Carnegie Steel earned higher profits than its competitors— and Carnegie himself held almost 60 percent of the company's stock— Carnegie Steel rarely paid dividends of more than 1 percent. Instead, Carnegie poured his profits back into his operations, retiring debt and investing in new technologies and plants.

One resource crucial to steel-making was coke, a type of coal that has been heated to eliminate waste elements and increase its carbon content, which is needed to help turn iron into steel. One of Carnegie's biggest coke suppliers was Henry Clay Frick, who controlled 80 percent of Pennsylvania's huge coal fields and coke ovens. His near-monopoly also made him a potential threat to Carnegie, so the steel magnate bought half of Frick Coke in 1883 and made Frick a partner. Six years later Carnegie named the shrewd young manager chairman of their joint coke and steel company.

Carnegie also grew the company by expanding the number of products Carnegie Steel offered for sale. Besides steel rails—a market subject to fluctuations in the railroad business—Carnegie Steel came to produce structural beams for buildings and plated armor for ships. Carnegie won contracts to provide steel for the Brooklyn Bridge, the Washington Monument, and Chicago's Home Insurance Building, the first skyscraper in the United States.

Since he controlled almost every aspect of the steel-making process, Carnegie was able to cut costs at every step and maximize profits. Meanwhile,

Carnegie Steel, including the state-of-the-art Thomson Works in Pennsylvania, produced one-quarter of the world's steel by 1900.

Carnegie Steel's enormous financial resources enabled it to slash prices whenever it pleased. Many smaller competitors were driven out of business by this strategy, for they could not match Carnegie's prices without falling deeply into debt. Once the competitor had been vanquished, Carnegie would put its prices back up again.

Within four years of the opening of Thomson Steel Works, the plant was rolling 10,000 tons of steel every month. Carnegie's companies expanded production from 322,000 tons in 1890 to four million tons in 1900—accounting for almost half of all steel produced in the United States and a quarter of world production. Profits likewise jumped, from $1 million in 1883 to $40 million in 1900. By the time Carnegie was ready to retire from the steel business, only one financier had the clout to arrange the deal: J. P. Morgan.

J. P. Morgan and Finance

Unlike Rockefeller and Carnegie, John Pierpont Morgan (see Morgan biography, p. 150) was born into wealth and privilege. His banker father found experienced partners to support his early banking efforts, but Morgan quickly found success on his own. By 1873 Morgan's banking firm was the nation's leading seller of government securities abroad.

Besides selling securities, Morgan became known for lending to American industries, especially railroads. Unlike Rockefeller's oil empire and Carnegie's steel business, railroads relied on stocks and bonds to raise capital—and on bankers to sell those stocks and bonds. Morgan protected his railroad interests by placing his trusted finance men on their managing boards. "In practice, their guardianship came to mean everything from giving financial advice and bailing out bankrupt roads to firing and hiring managers, appointing new directors, fighting off hostile takeover attempts, and trying to control duplicate building and 'ruinous' competition,"[9] one biographer noted. Morgan's reputation for judicious management brought him a huge client: William H. Vanderbilt, who had inherited majority control of the New York Central from his late father, Cornelius. In 1879, when the New York legislature considered making single-family control of railroads illegal, Vanderbilt asked Morgan to arrange the sale of the line.

Morgan earned a seat on New York Central's board after the sale and set about reducing the unbridled building and competition that kept the railroad industry in a state of perpetual chaos. He negotiated a swap of lines between the Pennsylvania and the New York Central to reduce competition, and he invited other railroads to participate in a pool to split business and set rates. After the federal government made such arrangements illegal, Morgan held a summit of owners in early 1889. The result was a "gentlemen's agreement" between railroads—representing some two-thirds of U.S. railroad mileage—to regulate rates, settle disputes, and impose fines on railroads that did not behave themselves. Bankers like Morgan would enforce the agreement by holding positions on railroad boards and refusing to fund duplicate routes. The Panic of 1893 brought several failing companies under Morgan's control. By 1898, one-sixth of total U.S. mileage had been "morganized," including the Erie, the Southern, the Northern Pacific, the Baltimore & Ohio, and the former Vanderbilt lines.

The Nation's Banker

Morgan's reputation as the country's leading banker was cemented in 1895, when federal gold reserves tightened following the Panic of 1893. As

J. P. Morgan, known as "The Nation's Banker," worked out of this stately office building in New York City.

foreign investors worried about American markets, they cashed in millions of securities and took gold out of the country. Because the dollar was backed by gold, the U.S. Treasury was supposed to hold $100 million in gold reserves, but by early 1895 the reserve had dropped to $45 million. When Congress would not approve the sale of public bonds, Morgan stepped in to arrange a private loan to the Treasury. Not only did his banking consortium subscribe to $65 million in bonds, Morgan made sure that most of the gold stayed in the United States. Although critics complained that his 3.75 percent interest rate was much too high, Morgan's actions restored European confidence in U.S. markets. In 1907, the semi-retired Morgan stepped in again, halting a banking panic by coordinating contributions from banks and brokerages to shore up businesses at risk. This kind of work would later be done by the Federal Reserve, a centralized government banking system created in 1913, the year Morgan died.

By 1898, one-sixth of total U.S. railroad mileage had been "morganized," or brought under the control of leading Gilded Age financier J. P. Morgan.

Morgan's biggest banking deal created the world's first billion-dollar corporation. Alarmed by potentially ruinous competition in the steel industry, Morgan attended a dinner where Carnegie Steel president Charles M. Schwab spoke of the benefits of a possible steel supermerger. After Morgan and Schwab discussed the possibility of a merger between Carnegie Steel and fellow industry giant Federal Steel, Schwab brought the merger proposition to his boss, who was pondering retirement. Carnegie demanded $480 million for his company, including $160 million in gold bonds and $240 million in the new company's stock. Morgan agreed to his terms, and in March 1901 he announced the formation of U.S. Steel, which would be capitalized at $1.4 billion dollars.

With Carnegie on board, Morgan pursued other steel interests Schwab had indicated were crucial to the new company. He bought out John W. Gates of American Steel & Wire Co., and he negotiated with Rockefeller for his Lake Superior Consolidated Iron Mines, which controlled much of the Mesabi iron ore range. By the time Morgan was done, U.S. Steel controlled 37 percent of American pig-iron production, 74 percent of Bessemer steel production, 55 percent of open-hearth steel production, and around 50 percent of various steel products. Investors were eager to buy into U.S. Steel's initial public stock offering. Even as the price of common stock rose 45 percent, Morgan sold over 3 million shares in a single day and over 10 million in one week. For his efforts, Morgan earned $10 million in fees for his company.

Morgan's creation of U.S. Steel marked the pinnacle of a new movement towards consolidation and control of the wild American economic landscape. For some critics, however, this movement was not seen as consolidation but as monopoly, which had long been reviled by Americans as an unfair restraint of trade. To them, one historian noted, the U.S. Steel deal was "the culmination of a quarter-century of financial intrigue and political chicanery by leading industrialists, the so-called robber barons of the Gilded Age, to achieve oligopoly, dominance by plutocrats of a particular industry."[10] Those critics argued that reform and regulation were desperately needed to counter the dangers of monopoly.

Notes:

[1] Morgan, H. Wayne. *The Gilded Age.* Syracuse, NY: Syracuse University Press, 1963, pp. 1-2.

[2] Folsom, Burton W., Jr. *The Myth of the Robber Barons,* 3rd edition. Herndon, VA: Young America's Foundation, 1996, p. 17.

[3] Morris, Charles R. *The Tycoons: How Andrew Carnegie, John D. Rockefeller, Jay Gould, and J. P. Morgan Invented the American Supereconomy.* New York: Times Books, 2005, p. 389.

[4] Morris, p. 151.

[5] Quoted in Cashman, Sean Dennis. *America in the Gilded Age: From the Death of Lincoln to the Rise of Theodore Roosevelt,* 3rd edition. New York: New York University Press, 1993, p. 53.

[6] Quoted in Folsom, p. 83.

[7] Morris, p. 158.

[8] Carnegie, Andrew. *The Autobiography of Andrew Carnegie.* London: Constable & Co., 1920, p. 135. Available online at http://www.gutenberg.org/files/17976/17976-h/17976-h.htm.

[9] Strouse, Jean. *Morgan: American Financier.* New York: Random House, 1998, p. 197.

[10] Cashman, p. 38.

Chapter Four

GILDED AGE POLITICS, REFORMERS, AND REGULATORS

I have heretofore been treating of the fundamental principles of government and here I am considering all day whether A or B shall be appointed to this or that office. My God! What is there in this place that a man should ever want to get into it.

—President James A. Garfield,
writing to Secretary of State James G. Blaine, 1881

During the Gilded Age, national elections were closely contested, and neither the Democratic nor the Republican party was able to gain a significant edge. There were only four years between 1875 and 1897 when one political party controlled the presidency and both houses of Congress at the same time. Political stalemates often occurred at the local level as well. In some places, majority control was rigged by the allocation of districts. Some states assigned representatives and senators by town or county, instead of on the basis of population; as a result, a small minority of voters could elect a majority of a state's legislators. Because U.S. senators were elected by state legislatures at the time, these minority blocs also influenced national politics. Many western states admitted to the union during the Gilded Age had small populations compared to their eastern counterparts. Since every state had two senators regardless of its size, this imbalance meant that by 1900, a majority of Americans lived in states represented by only 21 percent of the Senate.

Some Americans sought political reform, but effective grassroots activism was difficult within the two existing political parties. In many areas, candidates were determined by the party "machine," which consisted of party leaders, local officials, and perhaps the local newspaper editor, who was paid to serve as a party mouthpiece. Party bosses were governors or senators—or those responsible for nominating them—and derived their power from financial or industrial interests. Party machines discouraged voters from participating in primaries, and during general elections they presented a slate of candidates on pre-printed ballots for "straight ticket" voting. Party loyalty was strong among Gilded Age voters, as supporters were often rewarded with government jobs or contracts. The number of federal government positions grew from 53,000 at the start of the Gilded Age to over 130,000 by 1885.

This patronage or "spoils" system was a tradition in American politics. Whenever control of city, state, or federal government passed from one political party to the other, the incoming party purged the old party's officeholders and replaced them with supporters. Party loyalists especially sought jobs where they could demand bribes in return for their cooperation. In New York City, the port's federally appointed collector of customs employed 1,000 agents who were notorious for "misplacing" the shipments of importers who refused to make extra payments to them.

Since political power in the federal government was usually split between Democrats and Republicans, it was very difficult for either party to transform its agenda into legislation. If one party did pass sweeping changes, voters frequently threw them out at the next election. Nonetheless, a gradual expansion of government size and power became evident over time. Some Gilded Age government expansions included the elevation of the Department of Agriculture to cabinet-level status, the creation of the Justice Department, and the formation of new bureaus and commissions tracking labor statistics, weather, education, immigration, and fisheries. Major political reforms and business regulations, however, rarely originated within the federal government during the Gilded Age. Instead, such changes were often inspired by state laws, third-party platforms, or corruption scandals.

Political Scandals Outrage the Public

Government corruption existed before the Gilded Age, of course, but a continuous parade of scandals characterized its early years. Many were due to the weak leadership of Ulysses S. Grant, the first president elected after the Civil War. While Grant had been a superb general, after the war he had befriended robber barons like Jay Gould and Jim Fisk without regard for appearances. And when he won the White House, he filled his cabinet with friends and patrons, regardless of their qualifications. "In his personal and professional values Grant was a typical representative of the age," one historian noted. "He had little understanding of the new industrial and economic forces."[1] Valuing personal loyalty over competency, Grant had high turnover in his cabinet, with five attorneys general, five secretaries of war, and four treasury secretaries during his two terms.

A number of political scandals erupted during the presidency of Ulysses S. Grant (1869-1877).

Grant was barely into his first term when the Black Friday scandal implicated his brother-in-law in an attempt to corner the gold market. The president was also criticized for many of his patronage appointments. In addition to bestowing federal jobs on many of his Army buddies, Grant gave forty-two of his relatives federal posts through nepotism. In the worst instance, his wife's brother-in-law siphoned off a fortune in customs fees as collector of customs in New Orleans. The Crédit Mobilier scandal also broke during Grant's presidency. Although the bribes occurred during the previous administration, both of Grant's vice-presidents were involved in the scandal. Shortly after members of Congress chose to censure rather than expel the two worst Crédit Mobilier offenders, they approved a bill retroactively increasing their salaries by 50 percent. Grant was heavily criticized for signing the bill, which critics called the "Salary Grab Act."

Other scandals were uncovered during Grant's second term. In 1874 the public learned that contractor John D. Sanborn, hired to collect outstanding debts for the Internal Revenue Service, had kicked back revenues into Republican campaign funds. The following year, Secretary of the Interior Columbus Delano was forced to resign for taking bribes and paying his son for surveying work that was never done. Most outrageous was the 1875 Whiskey Ring scandal, a conspiracy between tax officials and distillery owners to defraud the government of $1.2 million in taxes—much of which was funneled into Grant's 1872 re-election campaign. Among the 230 men indicted were several of Grant's appointees, as well as his personal secretary, Orville Babcock. While most were convicted, Grant used his influence to secure Babcock's acquittal. Not long after the Whiskey Ring trials ended in 1876, Grant's secretary of war, William Belknap, was forced to resign after it was revealed that he had taken thousands of dollars in bribes in exchange for prime trading posts in Indian Territory.

Gilded Age corruption was not limited to the Republicans in Grant's administration. Democrats were also implicated in the Crédit Mobilier scandal, and the party was even more notorious for its brazenly corrupt local political machines. These machines thrived in the nation's crowded cities, where millions of European immigrants were settling in search of better lives. They provided needed services like sewage, water, street maintenance, poverty relief, and medical treatment. Under the machines' grassroots structure, neighborhood representatives would help the needy, resolve business conflicts, and bribe residents for their support in the voting booth. The most infamous of the machines was New York City's Tammany Hall, run by William M. "Boss" Tweed. Tweed rose from city alderman to the board of supervisors to state senator through judicious awarding of contracts and patronage jobs. By the 1870s, his ring controlled New York City Hall, the New York Hall of Justice, and the state capital in Albany, in addition to the Democratic Party headquarters at Tammany Hall.

> *"I made up my mind not long ago to put some of those fellows behind bars, and I'm going to put them there,"* Harper's Weekly *cartoonist Thomas Nast said of corrupt New York City official William "Boss" Tweed and his ring.*

Tweed's ring regularly cheated the government by collecting extra payments on patronage jobs and building contracts. Tweed collected a 65 percent "commission" on a $13 million project to build a new courthouse in New York City, for instance; it remained unfinished for over a decade. The press, particularly *Harper's Weekly* cartoonist Thomas Nast, was relentless in unearthing and publicizing Tweed's crimes. When the Tweed Ring tried to get Nast out of the way by offering him $500,000 to study art in Europe, he responded, "Well, I don't think I'll do it. I made up my mind not long ago to put some of those fellows behind bars, and I'm going to put them there."[2] Still, Tweed's Tammany Hall cheated the government out of an estimated $30 million to $200 million before he was finally prosecuted in 1873. Tweed was convicted on more than 200 misdemeanor counts and eventually died in jail, but the Tammany machine continued under new bosses into the next century.

Early Third-Party Movements

Public outrage over the excesses of these Gilded Age politicians led to calls for reform and the creation of splinter groups and third-party movements. After Grant's scandal-filled first term, for example, a group of reform-minded Liberal Republicans broke away and nominated Horace Greeley, influential editor of the *New York Tribune,* for president. Although the Democratic Party also supported Greeley's candidacy, he lost the 1872 election to Grant in a landslide. The Liberal Republican Party soon dissolved, but the Republicans remained wracked by internal divisions. The "Half-Breed" faction, led by Speaker of the House (and later Senator) James G. Blaine of Maine, held to the Liberal Republican reformist beliefs. The "Stalwarts," led by New York senator Roscoe Conkling, wanted the party to maintain the status quo and the patronage system.

Despite such internal conflicts, the mainstream political parties remained reluctant to debate controversial issues or address major problems facing the nation. These matters were left to emerging nonpartisan organizations and third parties. One such organization was the Grange (also known as the Order of the Patrons of Husbandry), which was founded in 1867 by a Department of Agriculture official to promote cooperation between farmers. The Grange began as a fraternal order focused on social events, but as farming became more dependent on credit, the group grew to include cooperative businesses like grain elevators and mills, mutual insurance companies, and even banks. After the Panic of 1873, agricultural prices fell, putting even more pressure on the farmers who lived in debt until they could sell their crops. As the costs of tariff-protected machinery, barbed wire, and fertilizer rose, many farmers struggled to stay afloat.

The Grange stepped in to promote the interests of its members. By 1874 Grange chapters boasted 1.5 million members and had organized political parties in 11 states. Granger political action focused on the "middlemen"—commodity brokers, grain elevators, and especially railroads—who claimed a large portion of farmers' profits. They sought relief by creating state or local commissions to inspect and regulate warehouses and railroads. While railroads successfully defeated many of these "Granger laws," the farmers did have success in Illinois, where the state set up a commission to establish maximum freight and storage rates. One warehouse prosecuted for violating the law appealed all the way to the Supreme Court. In the 1877 case *Munn v. Illinois,* the Court ruled that states had the right to regulate businesses that affected the public interest. Not long afterward, however, the Grange ceased to have much political influence.

The Grange was a third-party movement that sprung up to protect the interests of farmers against railroads and other corporate middlemen.

Another third party that emerged during this time was the Greenback Party—at times called the Greenback-Labor or National Party. As their name suggests, Greenbackers were primarily concerned with federal monetary policies ("greenbacks" were the non-specie-backed currency the government began issuing during the Civil War). During the Gilded Age, the federal government's official policy was to move away from greenbacks and issue a national currency backed by gold. Those dependent on credit liked the idea of keeping greenbacks in circulation, however, as its depreciated value (compared to gold) made it easier to repay debts. Greenbackers also wanted the currency expanded to include silver coins, which had been removed from circulation under the Coinage Act of 1873. The Greenbackers never attracted widespread support, however. In the mid-1880s the party broke apart and its members dispersed to various labor-related groups.

The early Gilded Age also saw the rise of several other issue-related parties and movements, but only two would have a lasting impact. The Prohibition Party worked to ban the sale and distribution of alcohol. The party fielded its first presidential ticket in 1880 and had its best presidential showing in 1888, when Clinton B. Fisk polled almost 2.2 percent of the popular vote. Kansas wrote a prohibition clause into its state constitution in 1880, and by 1889 five other states were dry. Third-party movements also arose promoting women's right to vote. The Equal Rights Party held two conventions and nominated lawyer Belva A. Lockwood for president in 1884 and 1888. Although Lockwood polled fewer than 5,000 votes in her first election, the issue was kept alive by various suffrage movements. Again, state successes came first: Wyoming maintained voting rights for women upon becoming a state in 1890, and Colorado voters passed a suffrage referendum in 1893. Prohibition and women's suffrage would eventually gain national acceptance in 1919 and 1920 with the passage of the 17th and 18th Amendments, respectively.

Early Government Reforms

In 1877 Grant was succeeded in the White House by Republican Rutherford B. Hayes, who had a reputation for personal integrity. He took steps towards civil service reform by bypassing several traditional patronage appointments. Hayes gave the prime patronage position of postmaster general—responsible for appointing local postmasters—to a Democrat. Hayes also issued executive orders that forbade government officeholders from managing political organizations, outlawed the practice of forcing government

Notable Third-Party Successes

Candidates from large and small third parties had varying success at different levels of government. During its decade or so in existence, the Greenback Party (also known as the National Party) had 19 congressmen in the U.S. House, representing states from Maine to Texas. The short-lived Silver Party, formed in Nevada in the 1890s, sent two former Republicans to the U.S. Senate. Five other western senators switched to the Silver Republican splinter party after the 1896 election. The People's or Populist Party had the greatest success during the Gilded Age, tallying six U.S. senators, forty U.S. representatives, and control of the governorship and legislature in four states.

Short-lived parties could have big impacts. In New York City's 1886 mayoral race, the United Labor Party sprung up in support of Henry George, author of the 1879 economic treatise *Progress and Poverty*. George explored the reasons why poverty persisted in the industrial age and argued for a single tax on land values. A coalition of labor groups backed him for mayor. In response, Tammany Hall nominated a reformer for the Democratic slate, industrialist and former congressman Abram Hewitt. The Republican candidate, a young Theodore Roosevelt, was virtu-

employees to make political contributions, and banned state party bosses from political intimidation of civil servants. Hayes was unable to get a divided Congress to enact civil service reform legislation, however, during his single term in office (he kept a promise not to run for a second term).

Republicans were still divided between traditional Stalwarts and reform-minded Half-Breeds at the 1880 party convention. The party compromised to nominate nine-term Ohio representative James A. Garfield for president and Stalwart choice Chester A. Arthur as vice-president. Despite polling only 8,355 more popular votes than Democratic nominee Winfield S. Hancock, Garfield easily won the presidency with 214 of 369 electoral votes.

Like his predecessor, Garfield pledged to reform the civil service by hiring trained, competent professionals to fill increasingly complex government jobs. His plan faced stiff opposition from party members who expected gov-

ally ignored during the campaign. Although Hewitt won the election with 41 percent of the vote, George's strong showing at 31 percent resulted in several new state and local regulations to appease labor.

In Argonia, Kansas, Prohibitionist involvement in the town's 1887 election produced a historic result. Argonia women had just been granted voting rights by the Kansas legislature, and a group from the Women's Christian Temperance Union decided to nominate a slate of male candidates for the village government. Offended by the women's presumption, several men decided to play a joke by printing up the same slate, only with WCTU member Susanna Salter's name at the head of the ticket. Local Republicans, angered by the prank, asked Salter if she would serve. When she agreed, they threw their support behind her. Salter won the election with a two-thirds majority, becoming the first woman to be elected mayor in the United States.

Sources:

Billington, Monroe. "Susanna Madora Salter—First Woman Mayor." In *Kansas Historical Quarterly*, Autumn 1954, pp. 173-183. Available online at *The Kansas Collection*, http://www.kancoll.org/khq/1954/54_3_billington.htm.

Biographical Directory of the United States Congress, 1774 to Present. Available online at http://bioguide.congress.gov.

ernment posts as a reward for political loyalty. Garfield stood by his promise, however, and openly challenged the established spoils system. When he refused Senator Roscoe Conkling's choice for New York City's collector of customs, both Conkling and fellow New York senator Thomas C. Platt resigned in protest. The senators expected to be reappointed to their seats by the New York state legislature, but both lost in a special election. Garfield's political victory was a landmark in establishing presidential control over federal appointments. Tragically, he had little opportunity to take advantage of his triumph over Conkling. In July 1881 Garfield was shot and seriously wounded by a rejected applicant for a government job. The president died from complications of the wound two months later, leaving Arthur—Conkling's former protégé—to lead the country.

Arthur proved to be a more independent president than critics predicted. He kept many of Garfield's appointees and distanced himself from Con-

This 1881 political cartoon, which depicts members of the U.S. Senate demanding favors from President Chester A. Arthur (left), satirizes the patronage or spoils system of government.

kling and the Stalwarts. He also vetoed a major spending bill and supported an ongoing investigation of corruption in the awarding of postal route contracts. Arthur's greatest achievement was signing the Pendleton Civil Service Reform Act in 1883, which one historian called "the most significant reform in the civil service enacted in the nineteenth century."[3] The act required federal applicants to pass a merit-based exam, forbade campaign solicitations of public employees, and established a bipartisan Civil Service Commission to supervise the new system. Although the act initially applied to fewer than 15 percent of federal jobs, the number of positions included on the Pendleton list grew throughout the Gilded Age, reaching almost 40 percent by 1900.

Hampered by a debilitating kidney disease, Arthur did not fight for his party's nomination in 1884. The Republicans, who had become displeased with the president's nonpartisan appointments and vetoes of questionable spending bills, supported former Secretary of State Blaine instead. Democrats nominated New York Governor Grover Cleveland (see Cleveland biography, p. 133), a blunt-speaking reformer who had been a thorn in the side of Tammany Hall. Cleveland won the election with an electoral margin of 219 to 182, making him the nation's first Democratic president since before the Civil War. Cleveland did not rejoice in his victory, however. "I look upon the four years next to come as a dreadful self-inflicted penance for the good of my country," he wrote prior to his inauguration. "I can see no pleasure in it and no satisfaction, only a hope that I may be of service to my people."[4]

Early Federal Regulation Efforts

Cleveland entered the White House in 1885 with no federal or legislative experience and no particular agenda, except for the traditional Democratic belief in smaller, more frugal government. As the first Democratic president in almost twenty-five years, he was inundated with patronage requests—or what he termed a "damned everlasting clatter for offices."[5] Cleveland initially left many Republican officials in place, as long as they were not overly partisan. Democratic candidates for government jobs, meanwhile, had to demonstrate ability as well as loyalty. Seeing the president's role as a restraint on congressional excess, Cleveland vetoed a record 413 bills, more than twice as many as all of his predecessors combined. More than half were veteran pensions granted through "private bill," a law passed to apply to one person. Many of these bills were based on fraudulent disability claims, one reason that veterans' pensions made up one-quarter of federal expenditures by 1886. Cleveland also directed the Justice Department to challenge railroads about unused land grants. This directive resulted in the return of 81 million acres to the government.

As the first Democratic president in almost twenty-five years, Grover Cleveland was inundated with requests for government jobs—or what he termed a "damned everlasting clatter for offices."

The signature achievement of Cleveland's first term was federal legislation to regulate the nation's railroads. Previous congressional efforts to regulate railroads had met with little success, because many politicians were beholden to railroad interests or viewed regulation as a state matter. Various state railroad commissions had been created after the Supreme Court's 1877 *Munn v. Illinois* decision affirmed states' right to regulate. In 1886, however, the Court decided in *Wabash v. Illinois* that states had no direct right to regulate interstate commerce, as the Constitution reserved that power for

President Grover Cleveland defied the patron-age system and passed several significant reform bills during his time in office.

Congress. This ruling meant that Illinois and other states would no longer be able to set maximum rates for shipments crossing state lines. Public concerns about the decision—from farmers, independent merchants, and even smaller railroads hoping for market stability—led to bipartisan support for the Interstate Commerce Act, which Cleveland signed in 1887.

The Interstate Commerce Act prohibited a wide range of anti-competitive practices by railroad companies and required them to publish rate schedules and charge "reasonable and just" fees. The law also created the country's first federal regulatory agency, the Interstate Commerce Commission (ICC), which had authority to review rates and investigate abuses. The ICC also collected statistics on railroad accidents and enforced new safety regulations requiring air brakes and automatic couplers. While the latter provision helped cut the number of railroad employees killed or injured while coupling cars in half within six years, the ICC was less effective in managing railroad rates. They could not set maximum rates or levy penalties—only judges had that power—and companies found sympathetic judges to help them evade the law. As former railroad attorney and future attorney general Richard Olney would say of the ICC: "It satisfies the popular clamor for government supervision of the railroads at the same time that that supervision is almost entirely nominal."[6]

One historian called Cleveland "the sole reasonable facsimile of a major president between Lincoln and Theodore Roosevelt,"[7] yet he faced a difficult 1888 re-election campaign. His Republican opponent was former Indiana senator Benjamin Harrison, grandson of President William Henry Harrison.

The Republicans used more than $3 million in campaign contributions from businesses to distribute thousands of pamphlets, but Cleveland considered active campaigning beneath his dignity as president. Cleveland paid a heavy price for this stance. Although the president won the popular vote by more than 100,000, Harrison carried the swing states of New York and Indiana for a 233-to-168 electoral victory. In his outgoing message to Congress, Cleveland warned of "wealth and capital,… which insidiously undermines the justice and integrity of free institutions."[8]

When Harrison began his term as president, Republicans controlled both the House and Senate. Although Harrison increased the number of federal offices covered by the Pendleton Act and showed some independence in his appointments, he did little to check a spending-happy Congress. The federal surplus accrued under the Cleveland administration quickly turned into a deficit. The most significant reform legislation enacted during Harrison's term was the Sherman Antitrust Act, which passed with little opposition in 1890. Reinforcing earlier state efforts to curb monopolistic business practices, the act banned contracts and combinations made "in restraint of trade" and gave U.S. circuit courts the authority to investigate and punish violations. It took direct aim at the giant trusts, or groups of related businesses, that had come to dominate major industries by crushing smaller competitors. Because the bill did not clearly define business offenses or create an independent authority for enforcement, the legislation had only a limited immediate impact. Eventually, though, the Sherman Antitrust Act would become an important weapon for reformers seeking to curb the powerful monopolies created by the robber barons (see "The Sherman Antitrust Act," p. 186).

The Rise of the Populists

After the Grange's political influence died off, a new farmers' movement arose. The first Farmers' Alliance began in Texas in the mid-1870s, and it spread north and east over the next decade. Like the Grange, the Farmers' Alliance began with education programs, then moved into cooperative exchanges. Key to the movement's growth was its charismatic and colorful traveling lecturers, which included firebrand Mary Elizabeth Lease (see Lease biography, p. 147) and several other women speakers. By 1889 the Alliance had three million members across the country. Women made up a quarter of the membership in many chapters. In the segregated South, the Colored Farmers' National Alliance grew to include almost 250,000 members.

In this political cartoon, a farmer armed with government authority fights the monstrous reach and power of the railroads.

This growth was fed by difficult economic struggles for farmers. Wheat prices continued to fall, while corn sold so cheaply that some farmers chose to use it for fuel instead. Small farmers had to rely on credit—often at 100 to 200 percent annual interest—to purchase equipment, fertilizer, and other supplies. Many farmers went so deeply into debt that they were forced to sell their land or lost it to banks in foreclosure. Although some state Alliances, especially in Texas, made progress in establishing cooperative exchanges, they could not secure enough cash to keep the concerns going. Other Alliance cooperatives were met with political opposition or even violence.

The head of the National Farmers' Alliance, Charles W. Macune, proposed a radical solution for the farmers' continuing economic woes in late 1889. He called for the federal government to establish government warehouses—called subtreasuries—to sell crops when demand was high. Farmers would deposit their crops in the subtreasuries in return for government-backed certificates or greenbacks worth up to 80 percent of the crop, at 2 percent interest. This plan would return profits to the producer instead of the middlemen who profited from price speculation.

Macune and other Alliance leaders met in St. Louis and agreed that the group should move into politics. In some areas, this action came through partnerships with the existing two parties. In southern states, for example, farmers applied an "Alliance yardstick" to Democratic candidates. As a result, Democrats with Alliance ties won four governorships and control of eight state legislatures in 1890. In Kansas and Nebraska, Alliance men elected officials from the newly formed People's Party, also known as the Populist Party, including seven U.S. congressmen and two U.S. senators. Their initial success led one Alliance speaker to note that "the time grows near when the great highways of commerce will be the property of the people; and our Alliance business agency shall bring the producers and consumers together to the exclusion of useless middlemen."[9] To continue growing the party, however, the Populists would have to consider an alliance with labor unions, another group of "producers" struggling against the wealthy business interests that ruled the country.

Notes:

[1] Cashman, Sean Dennis. *America in the Gilded Age: From the Death of Lincoln to the Rise of Theodore Roosevelt.* 3rd edition. New York: New York University Press, 1993, p. 215.
[2] Quoted in Clark, Judith Freeman. *The Gilded Age.* Revised edition. New York: Facts on File, 2006, p. 47.

[3] Calhoun, Charles W. *From Bloody Shirt to Full Dinner Pail: The Transformation of Politics and Governance in the Gilded Age.* New York: Hill and Wang, 2010, p. 79.

[4] Quoted in Clark, p. 104.

[5] Quoted in Wall, James T. *Wall Street and the Fruited Plain: Money, Expansion, and Politics in the Gilded Age.* Lanham, MD: University Press of America, 2008, p. 90.

[6] Quoted in Zinn, Howard. *A People's History of the United States: 1492-Present.* New edition. New York: HarperCollins, 2003, p. 259.

[7] Hofstadter, Richard. *The American Political Tradition and the Men Who Made It.* New York: Knopf, 1948. Vintage edition, 1989, p. 232.

[8] Quoted in Calhoun, p. 123.

[9] Quoted in McGrath, Robert C. *American Populism: A Social History, 1877-1898.* New York: Farrar, Straus, & Giroux, 1992, p. 119.

Chapter Five

THE RISE OF LABOR

—⦻—

If workingmen and capitalists are equal co-partners, why do they not share equally in the profits? Why does capital take to itself the whole loaf, while labor is left to gather up the crumbs? Why does capital roll in luxury and wealth, while labor is left to eke out a miserable existence in poverty and want?

—William Sylvis, founder of the National Labor Union

"Free labor," or the right to rise in wealth and status through hard work, had long been a tradition of American culture. During the Gilded Age, however, free labor increasingly became a myth, as independent artisans and entrepreneurs of the pre-industrial era were replaced by factory laborers working for daily wages. "The trade has been subdivided and those subdivisions have been again subdivided, so that man never learns the machinist's trade now," a mechanic testified before the Senate in 1883. "You simply go in and learn whatever branch you are put at, and you stay at that unless you are changed to another."[1] Between 1865 and 1900 the number of manufacturing workers tripled to 4.5 million and factory output multiplied by eleven times as the United States became the world's leading industrial power. But as unskilled laborers became interchangeable cogs in the industrial machine, their wages fell accordingly. In addition, they had little control over their working conditions. If a man refused to work twelve-hour shifts, six or even seven days per week, he could easily be replaced by one of the millions of immigrants arriving on U.S. shores every year.

As more manufacturers became corporate concerns rather than family enterprises, factory owners became distanced from their employees. The wealthy moved to newly built suburbs and segregated themselves from the poorer classes by attending different churches, schools, and civic organizations. In 1892, one New York City newspaper counted over 4,000 millionaires in the United States, many of whom indulged in ostentatious displays of wealth. Financier Jay Cooke owned a fifty-two-room mansion outside of Philadelphia, while William K. Vanderbilt, grandson of Cornelius, built an opulent "Petit Chateau" on Manhattan's Fifth Avenue—one of seventeen large houses costing more than $1 million that various Vanderbilt heirs built before World War I. These lavishly appointed mansions hosted glittering society parties populated with guests who thought nothing of spending thousands of dollars on jewelry, clothing, or costumes (see "The Glitter of Gilded Age High Society," p. 166). Because corporations cut wages or jobs before dividends, even an economic depression did not halt the free-spending ways of their owners and top executives.

Life in the New Urban Slums

Although the industrialization of America created tremendous wealth for a few, it also turned life into a daily struggle for many others. One out of every three industrial workers was an immigrant. Many new arrivals to the United States formed ethnic enclaves in squalid city slums where population densities reached more than 300 people per acre. Relegated to difficult but poor-paying jobs in the nation's foundries and factories, immigrants and uneducated, native-born Americans often lived in dim, unventilated tenement buildings with inadequate sanitation and fire protection. Child mortality in the slums was two to three times higher than in middle-class areas, with diseases caused by unsanitary conditions causing one out of every three deaths (see "'The Problem of the Children' in New York City," p. 183).

While yearly wages rose between 1860 and 1890, few unskilled laborers got a full year's work, and wages remained the first things cut during economic downturns. Some workers were only paid in "scrip," a form of substitute currency that could only be used at company-owned stores, where prices were marked up. Others had little left once the company deducted rent for tools, machines, or company housing. In addition, working conditions in many late-nineteenth-century industries were uncomfortable and even dangerous, and employers provided no compensation for worker injuries or deaths. "The general trend of the Gilded Age was unmistakable," one historian noted. "The search for profit left workers without protection. The law of

New York socialite Mrs. W. K. Vanderbilt (right) and friends show off the latest fashions at a polo match.

supply and demand assured more goods and cheaper. It did not guarantee safer and better conditions in the workplace."[2]

Most Gilded Age millionaires felt little responsibility for the poverty and hardships experienced by workers, however. As one popular minister to the wealthy noted: "While we should sympathize with God's poor—that is, those who cannot help themselves—let us remember there is not a poor person in the United States who was not made poor by his own shortcomings, or by the shortcomings of some one else. It is all wrong to be poor, anyhow."[3] Not surprisingly, the growing economic divide between rich and poor became a source of great resentment in Gilded Age America. In his 1886 study *Progress and Poverty*, economist Henry George wrote: "There is a vague but general feeling of disappointment; an increased bitterness among the working classes; a widespread feeling of unrest and brooding revolution."[4]

Some frustrated Americans began exploring new political belief systems that held out the hope of a better life. These political philosophies included anarchism (a belief that society should have no government), communism (a belief that private ownership should be abolished and all wealth shared equally within the community), and socialism (a belief that society should be organized for the benefit of all members, with state ownership of industry). Other struggling workers hoping to improve their pay and working conditions turned to a growing national movement: labor unions.

Early Labor Movements and Conflicts

Before the Civil War, unions were mostly localized groups of skilled or craft workers, and they often acted as benevolent societies rather than negotiating groups. During the Gilded Age, however, more unions grew into national organizations, including the National Typographical Union, the Iron Molders' Union, the Machinists and Blacksmiths, the Brotherhood of Locomotive Engineers, and the iron and steel workers of the Sons of Vulcan. Molder William Sylvis saw a need for all workers to band together to fight for their rights against powerful corporations. He joined with representatives from twenty trades to found the National Labor Union (NLU) in 1866.

"There is a vague but general feeling of disappointment; an increased bitterness among the working classes; a widespread feeling of unrest and brooding revolution," economist Henry George wrote in 1886.

The NLU advocated creating a federal Department of Labor to oversee workers' rights, equal pay for equal work by women, and the eight-hour work day, which they felt could give workers time to educate themselves and become informed citizens. Responding to pressure from the NLU and other labor organizations, several states and cities passed eight-hour laws, and Congress passed one applying to workmen in federal arsenals and navy yards. The NLU even successfully lobbied for a proclamation from President Ulysses S. Grant in 1869 stating that any federal workers who had their hours reduced under the eight-hour law would not have their wages reduced. Nevertheless, employers found ways around these provisions, especially after courts ruled that employment contracts for ten- or even fourteen-hour days were legal. Many workers reluctantly signed these contracts, for they knew they would be replaced if they refused.

Sylvis had an inclusive vision for the NLU. He opened it to all workers, regardless of skill level or industry. Sylvis even wanted to include women and African Americans in the union, which was a radical idea in the nineteenth century. Although female and black representatives attended various NLU

This image by documentary photographer Lewis W. Hine shows a group of steel industry workers waiting to enter a factory.

conventions, the membership at large voted to exclude them from the union. African Americans subsequently organized separately as the Colored National Labor Union (see "African Americans in Early Labor Movements," p. 76). Sylvis died in 1869, and factionalism split the NLU when the organization made an unsuccessful move into presidential politics under the banner of the National Labor Reform Party in 1872. After drawing a negligible number of votes, both the party and the union died off. Nevertheless, the trend towards national unions continued. By 1873, 170,000 workers had joined twenty-five national unions.

One of these early unions was the Miners Benevolent Association (MBA), which Pennsylvania coal miners founded in 1868 during an unsuccessful strike for an eight-hour day. Membership jumped the next year following a fire and tunnel collapse that killed 110 miners at the Avondale Colliery. The tragedy, coupled with MBA pressure, convinced state politicians to pass a law that guaranteed safety exits and regular inspections in the coal mines. In 1870

African Americans in Early Labor Movements

During the Gilded Age, mainstream labor unions viewed African Americans as a threat, as it was common for businesses to import Southern blacks to replace striking workers. Nevertheless, African Americans had been involved in labor movements even before the Civil War. Black workers in the caulking trade—a job necessary to make ocean vessels seaworthy—went on strike as early as 1835. One skilled caulker from Baltimore, Isaac Myers, would become one of the most prominent African American labor activists during the Gilded Age. Myers addressed the National Labor Union (NLU) in 1869 as one of nine black representatives at the convention. "The white men of the country have nothing to fear from the colored laboring man. We desire to see labor elevated and made respectable; we desire to have the highest rate of wages that our labor is worth," he stated. "American citizenship with the black man is a complete failure, if he is proscribed from the workshops of this country."

When the NLU convention rejected the admission of African American unions, Myers led them to form a parallel organization, the Colored National Labor Union (CLNU), and served as its first president. The group

MBA representatives signed the first written contract between miners and coal operators. Franklin B. Gowen of the Philadelphia & Reading Railroad was determined to smash the MBA, however. He tried to connect the union with the Molly Maguires, a secret society of Irish immigrants known for arson, sabotage, and even murder. When the MBA organized a strike in early 1875 in response to a 20 percent wage cut, Gowen hired his own police force and brought in the state militia to break picket lines. He had the MBA's president and twenty-five other union leaders arrested on trumped-up charges of conspiracy, arson, and murder, and prosecuted them himself. Ten of the MBA's leaders were executed. Six months later the MBA gave in, crushed by rising hunger among the mining families and a cascade of negative press from Gowen-controlled newspapers. One historian described Gowen's breaking of the MBA as "an early example of capital energizing the courts and the press to paint labor with the broad brush of treason and criminality."[5]

was open to women and even Chinese immigrants, and it soon petitioned Congress to create forty-acre plots and provide low-interest loans to black farmers. Although noted abolitionist speaker and editor Frederick Douglass took over as CNLU president in 1872, the group declined along with the National Labor Union.

Many African Americans joined the Knights of Labor, including activist and educator Booker T. Washington. When it was replaced by the American Federation of Labor (AFL) as the country's leading labor organization, however, black workers found themselves shut out. The AFL came to accept segregated chapters, and African American chapters had no delegates on the national labor council. Some multiracial labor efforts did succeed—an 1892 walkout by black and white streetcar drivers in New Orleans, for example—but on the whole Africans Americans were driven out of skilled labor positions by white unions in the North and by violence and intimidation in the South. Not until the civil rights movement of the mid-twentieth century would African Americans begin to make real progress in labor unions.

Source:

Hill, Herbert. "The Problem of Race in American Labor History." In *Reviews in American History*, Vol. 24, No. 2, 1996, pp. 189-208.

It became easier for management to break unions during the depression of the mid-1870s. With as many as three million unemployed and desperate for work, unions had trouble keeping members united. The number of national unions dropped from thirty to nine by 1876, with total membership falling to fewer than 50,000. Nevertheless, the growing number of jobless workers demonstrated to make themselves heard, especially in larger cities. In Chicago, 20,000 people marched to demand that the city distribute excess monies from a fund intended for victims of the Great Fire of 1871. One New York City rally ended in disaster in January 1874, when police withdrew permission for a labor group to meet at Tompkins Square. Few heard of the last-minute cancellation and 7,000 men, women, and children showed up anyway, only to be met by mounted police with clubs. "The horsemen beat the air with their batons, and many persons were laid low," wrote journalist John Swinton. "There seemed to be a determination on the part of the mounted police to ride over somebody, and they showed no mercy."[6]

The Great Strike of 1877

As the depression dragged on, railroads cut wages by up to 35 percent while maintaining 8 to 10 percent dividends for shareholders. When leaders of several major railroads met in 1877 to pool shipping and set rates, they also agreed to take turns cutting wages by another 10 percent. The Baltimore & Ohio (B&O) also announced it would "doublehead"—double the size of—its trains, effectively putting half of the company's employees out of work. Railroad executives, according to one historian, "felt morally bound to put maintenance of dividends ahead of their own humanity or sense of social justice. By 1877 the phrase 'soulless corporation' had become a cliché, and it almost always referred to a railroad."[7] Owners were confident workers would not strike, because too many jobless men were waiting to take their places. But railroad workers had become fed up. "It's a question of bread or blood, and we're going to resist," one worker remarked. "If I go to the penitentiary I can get bread and water, and that's about all I can get now."[8]

The Great Labor Strike of 1877 began on July 16, when workers at the key B&O junction of Martinsburg, West Virginia, took over the railroad yard and stopped all freight trains. Police and local militia tried unsuccessfully to clear the yard, and within two days the line was blocked two miles in each direction. Although the governor called out the National Guard to unblock the rail lines, a crowd of locals sympathetic to the strikers prevented the soldiers from leaving their train. The spontaneous protest spread to B&O yards in Maryland, where firemen began deserting freight trains. Maryland's governor called out the National Guard and requested federal troops. In Baltimore, the soldiers found themselves outnumbered by strikers, supportive townspeople, and teenagers looking for trouble. Although troops were eventually able to disperse the mob and send a few freight trains out, overall the strike held.

Within a week the strike had spread to all major railroad lines east of the Mississippi. Labor unrest then moved west to Kansas, Iowa, Nebraska, and eventually California. In many cities the protest spread from railroad workers to other laborers, and general strikes erupted in Buffalo, Baltimore, St. Louis, Louisville, Cleveland, and Columbus. Some strikes were relatively peaceful and short, with management giving in to worker demands, but in other cities

During the Great Strike of 1877, violent clashes centered in the Pittsburgh railroad depot resulted in at least 20 deaths and $5 million in property damage.

strikers were supplemented by mobs of dissatisfied youths and unemployed workers. In Chicago, 30 protesters were killed in clashes with the National Guard and another 200 were wounded.

News of the nationwide Great Strike alarmed many Americans. "It seemed to the upper and middle class like a slave uprising," one historian noted. "Miners in Martinsburg and Scranton, mill-hands in Pittsburgh, sewermen in Louisville, and stevedores in Cairo, Illinois, as well as small businessmen and farmers across the country had actively assisted the strike."[9] Within two weeks of the first action, the strike had stopped freight traffic on two-thirds of the country's 75,000 miles of railroad track.

The results of the strike were especially alarming in heavily industrialized Pittsburgh, Pennsylvania, a major railway crossroads with dozens of glass factories, iron and steel mills, oil refineries, and coal mines. The strike in Pittsburgh began spontaneously on July 19, when workers refused to take trains out after the Pennsylvania Railroad announced pay cuts and the use of doubleheaders. Strikers occupied the line's Pittsburgh depot and were joined by non-railroad workers and freight crews. Local police were ineffective in their efforts to end the strike, and the Pittsburgh militia was sympathetic to the strikers. Some members even joined in the blockade.

Trouble began when the governor sent 600 militiamen from hated rival Philadelphia. They arrived to find 2,000 cars and locomotives idled by a crowd of 5,000 to 7,000. Members of the crowd threw stones and firecrackers at the Philadelphians, and shots were exchanged. At least 20 people were killed and dozens more wounded, including a woman and a four-year-old girl who were merely spectators. The outraged crowd went on a rampage, burning and looting railroad property along a three-mile stretch of the city. Only when the flames threatened local houses and shops did the crowd allow firemen to fight the blaze. By the time order was restored by a volunteer citizen force, 40 buildings, 104 locomotives, and more than 2,000 freight cars had been destroyed. An estimated $5 million in property was lost in the violence.

The Great Strike posed a problem for newly elected president Rutherford B. Hayes. Railroad executives prodded their governors to request federal troops to put down the strike, but the U.S. Army only had 25,000 soldiers, many of whom were fighting Native Americans in the West. Hayes was hesitant to involve the federal government, especially as it had been forty-two years since federal troops had responded to a labor action. Many politicians had ties to the railroads, however. They asserted that railroads were public "highways" necessary for trade or that the strikers posed a threat to public order. Hayes reluctantly acceded to their demands, sending federal troops to many of the most troubled cities. The troops managed to get the rail lines moving again, but the knowledge that labor had temporarily paralyzed the nation was retained by worker and owner alike.

The Growth of the Knights of Labor

The next few years after the Great Strike of 1877 saw the growth of several national labor unions. One such organization was the Noble and Holy Order of the Knights of Labor, which had been formed in 1869 by a group of Philadelphia garment cutters. The Knights of Labor was originally structured as a secret lodge along the lines of the Freemasons. It grew locally at first, establishing eighty craft unions around Philadelphia. Unlike other trade unions, however, it was open to all members of the "producing class," and many chapters permitted unskilled workers, African Americans, and women as members. The Knights not only focused on member education and "uplift," it advocated working within the system by passing labor-friendly laws and using arbitration rather than strikes to settle labor disputes. "It was a bold project bringing the conventional goals of a political party, a fraternal lodge, and a trade union under a single umbrella,"[10] one historian noted. By 1878 the Knights had 10,000 members nationally.

Terence V. Powderly assumed leadership of the Knights of Labor in 1879.

The Knights of Labor held its first national assembly that year, formally stating goals that included an eight-hour day, a federal bureau to track labor statistics, cooperatives for production, equal pay for equal work, and bans on child, prison, and contract labor. In 1879 Terence V. Powderly (see Powderly biography, p. 153) became the group's Grand Master Workman. Under his leadership the Knights gave up secrecy in favor of expanding further and making the union available to settle disputes between workers and management. By 1880 the group boasted 30,000 members belonging to 1,600 assemblies. Although Powderly's speeches were often fiery—in 1884 he told the Knights' general assembly that "the attitude of our order to the existing industrial system is necessarily one of war"[11]—his actions were conservative, emphasizing political action and arbitration over strikes. "Powderly grasped something essential in the discontent over the new industrial order," one historian observed. "Workers were not objecting to the rich having grown rich. They did resent how monopoly and large-scale capitalism had narrowed the right to rise to a privileged few, and robbed the rest of their control over their fate."[12]

The Knights of Labor won several political and strike victories in the early 1880s. Its lobbying helped pass the Chinese Exclusion Act of 1882, which suspended Chinese immigration for ten years and thus eliminated one source of cheap replacement labor for western railroad and mining interests. The Knights' legislative achievements also included the establishment of the Bureau of Labor in 1884. Several of the union's early strike victories came against the railroad lines of Jay Gould, who by the 1880s held a controlling interest in almost 10 percent of U.S. railway mileage. Although Powderly originally opposed the walkout, an 1884 Knights strike against Gould's Union Pacific line won the repeal of a 10 percent pay cut. The following year three more Gould lines announced a 10 percent pay cut. After arbitration failed, the union called a strike against all of Gould's lines. Gould was forced to meet with Powderly—the first time a major capitalist met with a labor leader—and the railway baron agreed to allow the Knights to organize his workers. In return, Powderly promised that the Knights would not strike against any of Gould's roads without talking to management first. The Knights' victory over Gould—who once said that labor unions "create evils which do not exist"[13]—brought a flood of new members. Membership jumped from 100,000 in 1885 to over 700,000 in 1886, including an estimated 65,000 women and 60,000 African Americans. As many as 20 percent of all U.S. industrial workers belonged to the Knights of Labor, making it the largest, most inclusive labor organization in American history.

With a growing membership, the Knights attempted to broaden its reach even further. The union sponsored libraries, lectures, newspapers, cooperatives, and even parades and sporting clubs. Such quick expansion brought troubles to the Knights, however, because its diverse membership had differing expectations for the union. Many rank-and-file members were more militant than the union's leaders, and some local chapters declared strikes without support from Knights leadership. One local action against Gould's Union Pacific and Missouri Pacific Railroads in 1886 led to disaster. When the workers struck for higher wages, Gould decided that his agreement with Powderly had been broken. He subsequently used Pinkerton detectives, state militia, and Texas Rangers to protect "scabs," break up union meetings, and intimidate journalists. When violence broke out between the strikers and Gould's forces, the public blamed the union for the bloodshed. The failed strike harmed the Knights' reputation, as did Powderly's often inconsistent support of other actions. It was a tragic event in Chicago, however, that played the greatest role in bringing about the union's downfall.

The Haymarket Riot and the Fall of the Knights

As the American economy rebounded from the long depression of the 1870s and a smaller one in 1883, many workers thought it was time to press for a universal eight-hour work day. The Federation of Organized Trades and

Labor Unions (FOTLU), a group of trade unions that arose as an alternative to the Knights of Labor, called for a general strike to take place on May 1, 1886. Although Powderly opposed the strike, fearing it would create class conflict, many local Knights assemblies joined in. As many as 350,000 workers nationwide participated. The largest demonstration took place in Chicago, where an estimated 40,000 to 100,000 workers marched without incident.

The strike continued peacefully on May 3, with some shops and stockyards agreeing to workers' demands. At the nearby McCormick Reaper Works, however, Chicago police shot and killed two striking workers who were demonstrating outside the factory. Local anarchist and labor journalist August Spies witnessed the conflict and published an editorial calling on workers to "rise in your might ... and destroy the hideous monster that seeks to destroy you. To arms, we call you."[14] Nevertheless, he insisted that the words "arm yourself and appear in full force" be removed from a flyer announcing a protest rally against police brutality to be held the next day in Chicago's Haymarket Square.

"Workers were not objecting to the rich having grown rich," noted one historian. "They did resent how monopoly and large-scale capitalism had narrowed the right to rise to a privileged few, and robbed the rest of their control over their fate."

When the rally took place on May 4, city police assembled 176 officers a block away in case of trouble. The 3,000 protesters that showed up were a smaller crowd than expected, however, and they were peaceful. Late in the evening the weather turned rainy, and by the time the last speaker appeared on stage there were fewer than 500 spectators left. Just as the last speaker was concluding his remarks, someone in the crowd threw a bomb into the police ranks. One policeman was killed almost instantly, and the others opened fire into the crowd of mostly unarmed men and women. A full-blown riot erupted, and by the time it was over seven policemen and eight civilians were dead.

The Haymarket Riot became the biggest news story since Lincoln's assassination. Panic gripped Chicago. As future labor activist Mary "Mother" Jones recalled, "The city went insane and the newspapers did everything to keep it like a madhouse."[15] Appalled at the violence, the public and press assumed that anarchist rebels were responsible for the bombing and demanded swift vengeance. Authorities quickly arrested eight anarchist leaders, including Spies, and their murder trial began in late June. None of the eight defendants had thrown the bomb—only three had even been pre-

The labor movement lost a great deal of popular support following a violent clash between activists and police in Chicago's Haymarket Square in 1886.

sent at the rally—nor was there any evidence demonstrating a conspiracy. Nevertheless, all eight were found guilty by a jury that included a relative of one of the slain police officers, and seven were sentenced to death. As defendant Adolph Fischer summarized: "I was tried here in this room for murder, and I was convicted of Anarchy"[16] (see "An Anarchist Protests His Haymarket Death Sentence," p. 174). Labor forces were not the only ones appalled at the unfairness of the trial, and several notable figures called for clemency, including a former senator and congressman. Two of the convicted men disavowed their actions and had their death sentences commuted, but four others—including Spies and Fischer—were executed in 1887, while a fifth committed suicide in his cell.

Although Powderly and the Knights of Labor leadership had little to do with the May Day protests, the Haymarket Affair gave corporations an opening to link them and other labor groups with anarchy and violence. With the press and public increasingly suspicious of strikes, employers had little incentive to negotiate with the Knights. A final blow occurred in 1887 when a Knights strike of 10,000 Louisiana sugar workers was put down violently, with dozens of members killed. Membership in the union dropped by half that year, and by the time Powderly was ousted as the Knights' Master Workman in 1893, the organization had declined to only 75,000 members, most of whom were farm workers from rural areas. Despite the Knights' eventual fall, the organization made important gains in unionizing unskilled and semi-skilled workers. Its success inspired some workers to create new industrial unions, including the United Mine Workers Union (founded 1890) and the American Railway Union (founded 1893). Many skilled workers, however, would return to the trade union model favored by a new organization: the American Federation of Labor.

The American Federation of Labor

Although the Haymarket incident shocked the nation, it did not mark the end of labor strife or union actions. Still, the failure of the Knights of Labor led many union leaders to adopt a more conservative approach to activism. One such leader was Samuel Gompers (see Gompers biography, p. 141), who in the fall of 1886 reorganized various FOTLU unions to form the American Federation of Labor (AFL). Determined to avoid the mistakes the Knights had made, Gompers based the AFL on traditional craft unions. It was open only to skilled workers who could bargain from a position of strength. It excluded unskilled workers, many of whom were immigrants. Gompers wanted to include African Americans in the AFL, because he recognized that excluding black craftsmen from the union gave them little choice but to become strikebreakers if they wished to work in their field. Individual local chapters, however, were less open to diverse membership, so the AFL leadership was forced to accept some measure of segregation. Women were also marginalized (see "Women in Early Labor Movements," p. 86). Although the union hired Mary Kenney as an organizer in 1892, she was let go after only five months.

The AFL was a true federation. Member unions retained their autonomy while national and state leadership resolved jurisdictional disputes and promoted federal labor legislation. Gompers believed the forces of industrialism were too powerful to overcome, so the AFL limited itself to working within the system on specific, achievable goals. The union also resisted affiliation with radical socialist groups who were calling for federal ownership of railroads or factories. "Gompers's group harbored no illusions about shaping a new world more

Women in Early Labor Movements

Although some early labor leaders—including those of the National Labor Union and the Knights of Labor—believed unions should be open to women, most rank-and-file members were not so progressive. They viewed women as competition for jobs and as potential strikebreakers, so they moved to exclude or segregate them from their unions.

Nevertheless, women did participate in early labor movements. In the textile industry, where many factories had predominantly female workforces, women had been active since before the Civil War. In 1860, Clara Brown led a modestly successful strike by "factory girls" at a shoemaking factory in Lynn, Massachusetts. Irish immigrant Kate Mullany organized the all-female Collar Laundry Union in 1864, and it remained active even after a successful strike for a wage increase. Mullany went on to become an assistant secretary of the National Labor Union in 1868, making her the first woman appointed to a labor union's national management.

Leonora Barry was another textile worker to gain national recognition. As master workman of her local chapter of the Knights of Labor, she was one of sixteen female delegates to attend the 1886 national convention in Richmond, Virginia. There she was elected a general investigator in charge of the new department of women's work. As a paid organizer, she

favorable to the proletariat [working class]," one historian noted. "It focused instead on wages, hours, and working conditions, and the effective power of trade unions fighting for these goals within the industrial status quo."[17]

Knowing that it was easier to negotiate from a position of economic strength, the AFL levied higher dues on its members so that it could offer them benefits in case of a strike. Strikes and boycotts were only used as a tactic of last resort, however, in the union's quest for recognition, collective bargaining rights, and higher wages. Gompers wanted to avoid the problems that faced the fast-growing Knights, so the AFL grew slowly, from 150,000 members at its founding in 1886 to only 250,000 by 1892. Several major trade unions chose not to join the AFL, but those that did join tended to remain with the group. The AFL's ability to retain members would help it become the

traveled across the country for the next four years. Although she retired from the Knights in 1890 to get married, she remained active in suffrage and other social reform movements.

Perhaps the most famous woman in the early labor movement was Mary Harris "Mother" Jones, best known for her efforts on behalf of textile workers and miners. A widowed dressmaker who witnessed violent labor conflicts in Chicago in 1877 and 1886, Jones only became active in the movement in her fifties. She led a "children's crusade" march to protest child labor, and she organized workers during miners' strikes despite threats to her life. She stressed solidarity of all workers, male and female. "You will never solve the problem until you let in the women," she declared in a speech. "No nation is greater than its women."

Despite the efforts of these early pioneers, women made little progress in the mainstream labor movement. Although by 1910 one in five wage workers was a woman, organizations like the American Federation of Labor shut them out, leaving them to form their own associations and mutual-aid societies. Female workers were limited to specific fields under male authority until well into the twentieth century.

Sources:

Jones, Mary Harris. *Mother Jones Speaks: Speeches and Writings of a Working-Class Fighter.* Edited by Philip S. Foner. New York: Pathfinder, 1983, p. 92.

most influential union in the country. Despite its influence, however, the AFL represented very few of America's workers. Unskilled laborers who were not eligible for the AFL made up some 70 percent of America's total workforce in the late nineteenth century.

Notes:

[1] Quoted in Meltzer, Milton. *Bread—and Roses: The Struggle of American Labor, 1865-1915.* New York: Facts on File, 1991, p. 4.

[2] Summers, Mark Wahlgren. *The Gilded Age, or, the Hazard of New Functions.* Upper Saddle River, NJ: Prentice Hall, 1997, p. 138.

[3] Quoted in Meltzer, p. 42.

[4] George, Henry. *Progress and Poverty.* New York: D. Appleton & Co., 1886, p. 487.

[5] Dray, Philip. *There Is Power in a Union: The Epic Story of Labor in America.* New York: Doubleday, 2010, p. 98.

[6] Quoted in Meltzer, p. 48.

[7] Bruce, Robert V. *1877: Year of Violence.* New York: Bobbs-Merrill, 1959. Elephant Paperback edition, Chicago: Ivan R. Dee, 1989, p. 56.

[8] Quoted in Dray, p. 111.

[9] Cashman, Sean Dennis. *America in the Gilded Age: From the Death of Lincoln to the Rise of Theodore Roosevelt,* 3rd edition. New York: New York University Press, 1993, p. 111.

[10] Kaufman, Jason. "Rise and Fall of a Nation of Joiners: The Knights of Labor Revisited." In *Journal of Interdisciplinary History,* Spring 2001, p. 557.

[11] Quoted in Clark, Judith Freeman. *The Gilded Age.* Revised edition. New York: Facts on File, 2006, p. 102.

[12] Summers, p. 139.

[13] Quoted in Clark, pp. 98-99.

[14] Quoted in Dray, p. 143.

[15] Quoted in Green, James. *Death in the Haymarket: A Story of Chicago, the First Labor Movement, and the Bombing That Divided Gilded Age America.* New York: Anchor Books, 2007, p. 9.

[16] Fisher, Adolph. "Speech of Adolph Fischer," from *The Accused, the Accusers.* Chicago: Socialistic Publishing Society, 1886, pp. 36-38. Available online at Chicago Historical Society, Haymarket Affair Digital Collection, http://www.chicagohistory.org/hadc/books/b01/B01S004.htm.

[17] Dray, p. 161.

Chapter Six

THE 1890s:
A DECADE OF UPHEAVAL

───◦◦◦◦◦───

Either capital will be master, and the people slaves, or the
people of the country will be involved in anarchy, and capital
destroyed.

—Senator John M. Palmer of Illinois, July 7, 1892

During the 1890s, Gilded Age social and economic trends further
intensified. Many businesses expanded from single corporations into
huge trusts that monopolized their industries. Labor conflicts also
increased in response to the ever-widening income gap between rich and
poor. The 1880 census showed that 25,000 U.S. families controlled half the
nation's wealth. A mere decade later, that same percentage of wealth was held
by only 4,047 families.

The decade also featured startling changes in the political landscape.
The Republicans had won the presidency and both houses of Congress in
1888, but their unchecked spending earned public disapproval, as did their
protectionist trade policies. The McKinley tariff had raised duties on imported products such as textiles and metal goods to an unprecedented 49.5 percent. Although this measure protected various U.S. manufacturers from foreign competition, it also kept equipment prices high for farmers. Frustrated
voters became even more convinced that the U.S. Senate was a "Millionaire's
Club," filled with wealthy industry heads and corporate lawyers prone to represent railroad, mining, or oil interests over their constituents. The GOP paid
for its activism in the 1890 mid-term elections, losing control of the House as
well as three state legislatures in the Midwest.

The Homestead Conflict

As the 1892 presidential election approached, a huge labor conflict involving Carnegie Steel arrested the country's attention. The Pittsburgh Bessemer Steel Works of Homestead, which was perched on the banks of the Monongahela River six miles outside of Pittsburgh, had a long tradition of labor strength. The Amalgamated Association of Iron and Steel Workers (AAISW) won a strike at Homestead in 1882 and another in 1889. The latter defeat was especially difficult for Carnegie to stomach, for it gave the AAISW a strong voice in the factory's operations. Although Carnegie publicly supported unions and criticized the use of replacement workers, in practice he was firmly anti-union. By 1892 Homestead was the only AAISW plant in the Pittsburgh area, and its workers made up to 50 percent more than their non-union counterparts. But the union's Homestead contract expired that year, and Carnegie was determined to roust the AAISW from his facility.

Although the newly incorporated Carnegie Steel earned $4.3 million in profits in 1891, the company demanded that Homestead's workers accept a new sliding wage scale that would result in a 25 percent pay cut, as well as an increase in the length of shifts from eight to twelve hours. Chairman Henry Clay Frick announced these changes in May 1892 and threatened to dismiss workers if the AAISW did not approve the new contract. Union leaders refused to accept Frick's terms, which would have spelled the end of the AAISW at Homestead. In response, Frick surrounded the works with a ten-foot barbed-wire fence, searchlights, and platforms with water cannons. On June 29, Frick locked out more than 3,400 union workers and made plans to bring in 300 Pinkerton detectives to protect his replacement workers.

The union responded by taking control of the plants, setting up patrols to repel scabs, and closing saloons in the town (AAISW leaders worried that drunk members might become violent). The company, however, sent the Pinkertons down the Monongahela River to Homestead on two barges outfitted with pistols and rifles. The union men, supported by many of Homestead's 10,000 citizens, gathered on July 6 to repel them. Shots were exchanged, killing men on both sides, and the Pinkertons were eventually forced to surrender. As they were taken to the local jail, they were assaulted by a mob that included many women, a development that appalled outside observers. Frick ignored the union's attempts to restart negotiations, knowing that as conditions deteriorated local authorities would be forced to call for federal help. When workers

Escalating labor conflicts, such as the 1892 strike at the Carnegie Steel plant in Homestead, Pennsylvania, shocked the American people and led to calls for reform.

from neighboring plants joined in the action, Pennsylvania's governor finally called in the National Guard. Union leaders planned to welcome them peacefully with a parade, but the 8,500 troops arrived in secret and took control of several factory buildings. By July 17 Homestead was under martial law.

Several union leaders were prosecuted for incitement to riot, murder, and even treason. Although no one was convicted, the cost of defending its leadership against the charges hurt the union financially. Even more damaging were the actions of immigrant anarchist Alexander Berkman, who attempted to murder Frick on July 23. Although Frick survived the attack, and the union condemned Berkman's actions, the assassination attempt turned public opinion in the company's favor. By November the AAISW—the nation's largest trade union—was forced to accept Frick's terms. The steel industry would not be effectively unionized for another forty years.

The union was not the only one whose public image suffered from the Homestead incident, however. Carnegie, who spent the summer in Scotland, was roundly criticized in the press for his hypocrisy and neglect. The *St. Louis Post-Dispatch* charged that a "single word from him might have saved the battle—but the word was never spoken.... Say what you will of Carnegie, he is a coward."[1] His company also suffered financial losses associated with the Homestead conflict, although it still earned $4 million in profits in 1892. Finally, the Homestead conflict shocked the American people into a pro-reform frame of mind. As one historian noted, "Even in an era marked by decidedly tempestuous industrial relations, the fierceness of the lockout at Andrew Carnegie's prized steel mill alarmed the public in the United States and abroad."[2]

The Populists and the 1892 Election

Many reform-minded voters found little difference between the Democratic and Republican parties. In 1892 many of these people turned to the People's (or Populist) Party. Populism was based on the belief that the two major political parties failed to represent the interests of common people because they were largely controlled by wealthy bankers and business owners. The Populist message found a ready audience among farmers, miners, small ranchers, and railroad workers. It also attracted former members of the Greenback and labor parties. In fact, many of their ideas influenced the political platform written at the group's first presidential convention in Omaha in July 1892 (see "The Populists Articulate Their Principles," p. 189).

From the Greenbackers, the Populists adopted free coinage of silver and an expanded greenback supply. Another plank came from the Farmers' Alliance subtreasury plan. To reduce the political power of capital, the Populists called for a graduated income tax, the direct election of U.S. senators, and government ownership of railroads and telegraph lines. To appeal to labor, they advocated the eight-hour day, immigration restrictions, and a ban on the use of injunctions and private armies (like the Pinkertons) in labor disputes. The party's selection of a presidential candidate was complicated by the unexpected death of National Farmers' Alliance president Leonidas L. Polk, a popular lecturer and former Confederate soldier who could have appealed to Southern Alliance voters. In his place the Populists chose James B. Weaver of Iowa, a former Union general who had been the Greenback candidate for president in 1880.

During the campaign Weaver toured the country, often speaking with firebrand Mary E. Lease. Weaver argued that, unlike his opponents—Republican president Benjamin Harrison and Democratic former president Grover Cleveland—he and the Populists would battle corporate interests. "There is no power on earth that can defeat us," he said. "It is a fight between labor and capital, and labor is in the vast majority."[3]

The turnout for the 1892 election was the lowest in twenty years, but Weaver made the best showing for a third-party presidential candidate since the two-party era began. He became the first third-party candidate to poll more than one million votes. He carried four states—all in the West—and finished second in eight others. The Populists also picked up three governorships and sent three more con-

Populist Party candidate James B. Weaver made an impressive showing in the 1892 presidential election.

gressmen and another senator to Congress. Nevertheless, the party received little support in the South and the Northeast. Weaver's 22 electoral votes were not enough to affect the outcome of the election, and Cleveland reclaimed the presidency with 277 electoral votes to Harrison's 145. The Democrats also kept their advantage in the House and gained ten Senate seats, giving them control of the presidency and both houses of Congress for the first time since 1859.

Depression Creates More Political Reversals

Cleveland's second term got off to a promising start in 1893. The World's Columbian Exposition was held in Chicago that year in honor of the 400th anniversary of Christopher Columbus's voyage to North America. A fabulous showcase of art, architecture, technology, and culture, it attracted more than 25 million visitors and became a symbol of America's industrial power and optimism. Soon after the president officially opened the event on May 1, however, Wall Street was hit with one of its severest panics to date. The panic began when the National Cordage Company, a hemp rope trust that began the year by paying out a 100 percent dividend, was found to be insolvent. Its bankruptcy set off a frenzy of selling on Wall Street as the stocks of other

As the 1893 World's Columbian Exposition in Chicago showcased America's industrial strength and technological achievements, the U.S. economy entered into a severe depression.

financially troubled companies—including many railroads—plummeted. Banks failed when they could not cover withdrawals, and as the cash supply contracted many companies could not meet their payroll obligations. By the end of the year, 500 banks around the country had declared bankruptcy and 15,000 businesses and factories had closed.

The panic set off a severe depression that would last for the next four years. Unemployment in the winter of 1893-94 was almost 20 percent nationwide. Millions of people were without jobs, while many others held only part-time or seasonal jobs or endured pay cuts. As agricultural prices dropped below production costs, many growers lost their farms to foreclosure. Concerned

European investors exchanged U.S. government bonds for payment in gold, further reducing the Treasury's gold supply. The drain on the gold supply continued until financier J. P. Morgan arranged a bailout of the Treasury in 1895.

People argued over the causes of the depression. Many Democrats blamed the McKinley tariff, while AFL head Samuel Gompers blamed "greed of the capitalist class."[4] The Cleveland administration came under heavy criticism for not doing more to help struggling Americans. An Ohio quarry owner named Jacob Coxey called for the government to mint $500 million in greenbacks to pay for a road-building program that would provide work for thousands. When Congress failed to respond, "General" Coxey led the first protest march on Washington, D.C. "Coxey's Army" of 500 demonstrators was intercepted by D.C. authorities. They arrested Coxey and his followers for trespassing, clubbing many of them in the process. Although Coxey and other protest leaders failed to affect political change, they showed many Americans the uncomfortable reality that "poverty and unemployment did not stem from laziness or even bad luck, but rather from larger, systemic problems in the economy, in society—factors that were beyond any one person's control,"[5] as one historian explained. This rising sentiment was a direct challenge to the upper-class embrace of Social Darwinism—the belief that the "fittest" survived and prospered, while poor people were innately inferior (see "Social Darwinism and Attitudes toward the Poor," p. 100).

The Pullman Strike

The ongoing troubles of the depression also triggered one of the most widespread labor actions since the Great Strike of 1877. The Pullman Palace Car Company, which made luxury railroad sleeping cars, kept dividends steady during economic hard times by laying off more than half of its workers and cutting wages by as much as 70 percent. But the company made no corresponding reduction in prices in the company town of Pullman, Illinois, which provided housing, shops, and entertainment for Pullman workers. When an employee delegation seeking higher wages or reduced fees was laid off, Pullman workers went on strike in May 1894. A month later they were joined by the 150,000-member American Railway Union (ARU), which had been founded in 1893 by Eugene V. Debs (see Debs biography, p. 137) as the first nationwide labor organization for railway workers. The ARU voted to boycott any train carrying a Pullman car, and within a month railroad traffic was disrupted nationwide. Harvested crops rotted at depots and factories shut down for lack of coal. The strike also hit railroads hard. The Southern Pacific, for example, lost $200,000 a day due to the Pullman strike.

Debs insisted on peaceful, passive resistance, but some militants ignored his instructions by overturning Pullman cars, blocking tracks, and physically removing workers who would not comply with the boycott. Railroad owners countered with the usual tactics: strike-breakers, court injunctions, and calls for military invention. They also deliberately attached U.S. Mail cars to trains. This scheme was designed to maneuver the union into interfering with mail delivery, which was a federal offense. President Cleveland eventually sent in 14,000 U.S. Army troops, which gained control over Chicago following clashes that killed thirteen people and wounded many others.

> *The depression of the mid-1890s convinced many Americans that "poverty and unemployment did not stem from laziness or even bad luck, but rather from larger, systemic problems in the economy, in society—factors that were beyond any one person's control."*

The strike was broken after Cleveland's attorney general initiated conspiracy and contempt of court proceedings against Debs and other union leaders. Debs was found guilty of "restraint of trade" under the Sherman Antitrust Act, and the ruling was later confirmed by the Supreme Court. With its leadership jailed and no support from the AFL or railroad craft unions, the ARU dissolved. From this point forward, many former ARU members found it impossible to obtain work in the railroad industry.

The 1896 Election and the Decline of Populism

Continuing economic troubles and labor unrest caused many Americans to lose faith in Democratic leadership. State elections in late 1893 went heavily in the Republicans' favor, and the 1894 elections continued the trend. In the biggest mid-term election swing in history, the Democrats lost over 120 House seats, giving the Republicans a two-thirds majority in that chamber as well as a slight majority in the Senate. The Populists were disappointed that voters had not turned to them instead. They gained one senator but lost two congressmen in the 1894 elections and also lost ground in state offices in the West. As one historian observed: "The People's Party needed to broaden its base or see the cause of reform die completely."[6]

Eager to take on the weakened Democrats in the 1896 presidential race, the Republicans nominated former Ohio governor and congressman William McKinley on the first ballot and chose New Jersey legislator Garret A. Hobart as his running mate. Events at the Democratic National Convention took an unexpected turn, however. With President Cleveland deeply unpopular, there was no clear frontrunner for the nomination. As members worked out the party's platform, silver advocates gained the upper hand. Silver advocates believed that the gold standard limited the amount of currency in circulation, which hurt farmers and industrial workers who had to pay off debts and benefited wealthy bankers and business owners who extended credit.

William Jennings Bryan was the presidential nominee of both the Democratic and Populist parties in 1896.

Former Nebraska congressman William Jennings Bryan (see Bryan biography, p. 125), who had traveled the nation speaking on the silver issue, viewed the convention as an opportunity. Bryan closed the platform debate on the silver issue with a rousing speech that held his audience spellbound. "We shall answer their demands for a gold standard by saying to them, you shall not press down upon the brow of labor this crown of thorns," he declared. "You shall not crucify mankind upon a cross of gold"[7] (see "William Jennings Bryan's 'Cross of Gold' Speech," p. 192). The following day, the thirty-six-year-old Bryan clinched the Democratic presidential nomination on the fifth ballot. "He set them on their heads and stole away their hearts,"[8] Missouri congressman Champ Clark said of Bryan's effect on his fellow delegates.

The Populists who had hoped to draw Democrats to their party now found themselves facing a dilemma. They could choose their own ticket and risk dividing silver supporters, or nominate Bryan and undermine the party's independence. They eventually decided to support Bryan's candidacy, although they nominated their own vice-presidential candidate, former Georgia representative Thomas E. Watson, over the Democratic choice, Maine shipbuilder and banker Arthur Sewall. Bryan refused to replace Sewall on the ticket, however, and Watson ended up campaigning around the country by himself.

Many historians consider the Bryan-McKinley race of 1896 to be the first modern presidential campaign. Bryan set off on an unprecedented campaign tour, logging 18,000 miles over 29 states and making more than 600 speeches to upwards of two million people. McKinley knew he could not compete with Bryan's eloquence, so he took the opposite tactic instead. He stayed home and let reporters and prospective voters come to him. McKinley's "front porch" campaign drew almost 750,000 people to his home in Canton, Ohio. The GOP also employed a revolutionary new strategy of distributing campaign literature. With a war chest of $3.5 million—more than ten times the Democrats'—the Republicans produced over 200 million pamphlets in a dozen languages, or 14 per eligible voter. They also sent out 1,400 speakers to stump for the party during the last two weeks alone.

The result was a resounding victory for McKinley and the Republicans. Many voters were put off by Bryan's confrontational rhetoric and use of biblical imagery in his speeches. Others worried that his support among Populists would provoke class warfare. McKinley won the popular vote by over half a million—the largest margin in twenty-four years—and earned a 271 to 176 electoral college victory. The GOP also regained control of both the House and Senate. It was the beginning of a new period of Republican dominance in Washington.

The 1896 election also marked the beginning of the end for the People's Party. Two main difficulties doomed the long-term prospects of the Populists: a failure to appeal to labor in the North and racial conflict in the South. While the Populists were trying to change the existing capitalist system, Gompers and the AFL were trying to work within it. As a result, the labor leader noted, cooperation between the two groups was "impossible, because it is unnatural."[9] The Southern issue was equally problematic. African Americans could not be coaxed to leave the Republican Party, which had once championed their rights, and the Populist message held little appeal to white Democrats in the South. Nevertheless, as one writer observed, the Populist movement "had awakened American politics from slumber and transformed the election of 1896 into a high tide of radical dissent and a final flow of the controversy over the currency. Thus were the forces arrayed for the election of 1896, the political climax of the Gilded Age."[10]

The Trusts Flex Their Muscles

The victory of the Republicans was also a victory for business leaders, many of whom had made major contributions to McKinley's campaign. The GOP raised $250,000 each, for example, from Standard Oil and J. P. Morgan's company. Corporate interests recognized that a McKinley administration was unlikely to change the federal government's feeble enforcement of the Sherman Antitrust Act. In fact, the depression of the 1890s had further accelerated the movement toward consolidation that Standard Oil had pioneered in the late 1880s with its holding company structure. Weak companies went under in economic hard times, to be absorbed by stronger ones. In the decade after the Panic of 1893, more than 1,800 previously independent companies entered into some form of combination or trust. Even after the economy rebounded in 1898, the trend toward consolidation continued, with more than 300 major consolidations between 1898 and 1902 alone.

Although there were approximately 100 industrial pools at the beginning of the 1890s, most of them were loose or secret combinations. As the decade progressed, however, these arrangements were formalized using the lenient holding company laws of states like New Jersey and Delaware. Most of these new trusts were set up by financiers like J. P. Morgan and Charles R. Flint, who became known as the "father of trusts." The promoter would first set up a new corporation as a holding company to buy the companies to be combined, then find other bankers to provide cash or credit for the purchases. Once the properties had been bought and combined, the new holding company could sell stock, thus multiplying the value of the trust. The most successful trusts of the decade included Standard Oil, American Tobacco, Quaker Oats, Singer Manufacturing, Otis Elevator, and National Lead. The biggest merger was a 1901 transaction that combined Carnegie Steel and Federal Steel to form U.S. Steel, the first billion-dollar corporation. After a decade of mergers and consolidations, fifty industries were dominated by a single company that controlled at least 60 percent of production, and trusts controlled about 40 percent of all capital invested in manufacturing.

In the decade after the Panic of 1893, more than 1,800 previously independent companies entered into some form of combination or trust. As a result of these mergers and consolidations, fifty American industries were dominated by a single company that controlled at least 60 percent of production.

Although most Americans were distrustful of huge corporations and hoped the Sherman Antitrust Act would prevent the unfair business practices of monopolies, the federal government brought only eighteen antitrust lawsuits during the 1890s—and only three after McKinley's election. Few trusts were successfully prosecuted, especially after the Supreme Court's 1895 decision in *United States v. E. C. Knight and Co.* weakened Congress's power to regulate business operations

Social Darwinism and Attitudes toward the Poor

In his 1859 work *On the Origin of Species,* English naturalist Charles Darwin first introduced the concept of natural selection. According to this theory, species evolve over time in ways that allow them to better adapt to their environment. In the late nineteenth century many people reduced Darwin's argument to the idea of "survival of the fittest," meaning that if certain species were not as successful as others, it was because they were not as advanced. Before long, this same concept was being applied to different socioeconomic and ethnic groups. Known as "Social Darwinism," it was used by wealthy whites to justify white domination over African, Asian, South American, and Southern European peoples. It was also employed by middle- and upper-class Americans to explain the growing divide between rich and poor in the United States.

Social Darwinism dovetailed with American ideas about self-improvement and upward mobility. In a democratic country with vast resources, according to popular wisdom, anyone willing to work hard should be able to succeed. This idea was so ingrained that even the Great Emancipator,

under the Sherman Antitrust Act. Two years later, the Supreme Court also ruled that the Interstate Commerce Commission had no explicit authority to set railroad rates, further undermining government attempts at regulation.

The Supreme Court did issue several rulings against obvious monopolies or pools. The most notable such ruling came in the 1897 case *U.S. v. Trans-Missouri Freight Association,* which involved a group of eighteen railroads that pooled together to set rates. More often, however, U.S. courts weakened the ability of states to regulate railroad rates or pools. In the 1898 case *Smyth v. Ames,* also known as the *Maximum Freight Case,* the Supreme Court overturned a Nebraska law setting maximum freight rates for railroads in the state, arguing that excessive regulation deprived the railroads of property without due process.

Court rulings also favored business when dealing with labor disputes or labor regulations. Often judges took their reasoning from laws that had been designed to prevent business overreach, such as the Interstate Commerce Act and the Sherman Antitrust Act. The latter's provision outlawing "restraint of

Abraham Lincoln, noted that if people remained wage laborers, "it is not the fault of the system, but because of either a dependent nature which prefers it, or improvidence, folly, or singular misfortune." This attitude was also reflected in the Gilded Age novels of Horatio Alger, a popular children's writer. In many of Alger's works, a plucky young man lifts himself from poverty to success with just a little luck or friendly help. (Ironically, Alger himself died in poverty before his works were rediscovered in the early twentieth century.)

With their belief in Social Darwinism, many Americans were wary of laws that seemed to hamper natural competition. Laws that benefited one particular group, such as loans to homesteaders or the eight-hour day for industrial workers, were frowned upon by business owners as "class legislation." Yet these same business owners were quick to praise laws that helped fill their own pocketbooks, such as protective tariffs or railroad subsidies.

Source

Beatty, Jack. *Age of Betrayal: The Triumph of Money in America, 1865-1900*. New York: Alfred A. Knopf, 2007, p. 48.

trade" was used to outlaw union meetings and justify the imprisonment of the ARU's Debs during the Pullman strike. As states passed more laws to expand the rights of workers and rein in corporate excess, an increasingly conservative court system kept overturning them. Courts often found state laws restricting working hours to be unconstitutional, calling them restrictions on workers' right to contract their labor as they saw fit. The Supreme Court did uphold a Utah law restricting hours for miners in 1898. Even then, however, the justices were careful to note that the dangerous nature of the work made it a special case, and that other state statutes limiting work hours remained unconstitutional. Another ruling overturned a congressional ban on "yellow-dog" contracts, which made workers promise not to join a union.

The End of the Gilded Age

Not long after McKinley's inauguration in 1897, the American economy began bouncing back from depression. As the country regained its economic strength, the government increased its involvement in international affairs.

The 1901 assassination of President William McKinley brought reformer Theodore Roosevelt to office and marked the beginning of the Progressive Era.

Some Americans, known as imperialists, believed that the United States should seek to acquire new territory and expand its influence overseas. But others criticized America's growing role in world affairs. Some argued that the country had no business getting involved in disputes between other nations. Others claimed that exerting control over smaller, weaker countries betrayed the principles of freedom and equality on which the United States was founded. Economist William Graham Sumner, for instance, described imperialism as "a grand onslaught on democracy."[11]

The debate intensified when the Spanish colony of Cuba, a Caribbean island located only ninety miles from Florida, fought for independence.

102

Imperialists pressured McKinley to approve U.S. military involvement in the conflict in order to protect U.S. sugar interests in Cuba and push Spain out of the western hemisphere. After the American battleship *Maine* exploded in Havana harbor under mysterious circumstances on February 15, 1898, the United States declared war against Spain. The Spanish-American War lasted only 100 days and ended in a decisive victory for the United States, which gained possession of the former Spanish colonies of Puerto Rico, Guam, and the Philippines, as well as temporary control of Cuba. During McKinley's tenure the United States also annexed the Republic of Hawaii and explored options for building a shipping canal across Central America.

In 1900 the Democrats once again selected William Jennings Bryan to be their candidate in that year's presidential election. For Republicans, the only issue was who would replace Vice President Hobart, who had died in office, as McKinley's running mate. New York governor and Spanish-American War hero Theodore Roosevelt was the popular choice among delegates, and Roosevelt accepted the slot when it was offered to him. The McKinley-Roosevelt ticket proved to be a formidable one. Mounting a campaign emphasizing the nation's prosperity under his leadership—which he described as a "full dinner pail"—McKinley easily won a second term with the largest popular vote margin to date.

Only a few months after his second inauguration, however, McKinley was shot by anarchist Leon Czolgosz while visiting the Pan-American Exposition in Buffalo, New York. Eight days later, McKinley died of an infection and Roosevelt was sworn in as president. Although one historian noted that "McKinley proved so effective as an administrator and legislative leader that recent scholars consider him the first modern president,"[12] Roosevelt introduced a whole new level of activism to the office. A supremely confident and tough-minded reformer, the new president led the nation out of the Gilded Age and into the Progressive Era. Many of the reforms that Roosevelt muscled into existence, however, had first been suggested during the Gilded Age. As Roosevelt began his tenure in 1901, another writer remarked, "America was just on the cusp of the modern era, but the extraordinary Gilded Age had brought it thus far."[13]

Notes:

[1] Quoted in Morris, Charles R. *The Tycoons: How Andrew Carnegie, John D. Rockefeller, Jay Gould, and J. P. Morgan Invented the American Supereconomy.* New York: Times Books, 2005, p. 206.
[2] Krause, Paul. *The Battle for Homestead, 1880-1892: Politics, Culture, and Steel.* Pittsburgh, PA: University of Pittsburgh Press, 1992, p. 13.

[3] Quoted in Clark, Judith Freeman. *The Gilded Age.* Revised edition. New York: Facts on File, 2006, p. 156.

[4] Quoted in Cherny, Robert W. *American Politics in the Gilded Age, 1868-1900.* Wheeling, IL: Harlan Davidson, 1997, pp. 110-118.

[5] Dray, Philip. *There Is Power in a Union: The Epic Story of Labor in America.* New York: Doubleday, 2010, pp. 195-96.

[6] Goodwyn, Lawrence. *The Populist Moment: A Short History of the Agrarian Revolt in America.* New York: Oxford University Press, 1978, p. 84.

[7] Bryan, William Jennings. "Cross of Gold." Speech made at the Democratic National Convention, Chicago, IL, July 9, 1896. Available online at http://historymatters.gmu.edu/d/5354/.

[8] Quoted in Williams, R. Hal. *Realigning America: McKinley, Bryan, and the Remarkable Election of 1896.* Lawrence: University Press of Kansas, 2010, p. 76.

[9] Quoted in Trachtenberg, Alan. *The Incorporation of America: Culture and Society in the Gilded Age.* New York: Hill and Wang, 1982, 25th anniversary edition, 2007, p. 176.

[10] Cashman, Sean Dennis. *America in the Gilded Age: From the Death of Lincoln to the Rise of Theodore Roosevelt.* 3rd edition. New York: New York University Press, 1993, p. 335.

[11] Quoted in Clark, p. 196.

[12] Calhoun, Charles W. "The Political Culture: Public Life and the Conduct of Politics." In *The Gilded Age: Perspectives on the Origins of Modern America,* 2nd edition. Edited by Calhoun. Lanham, MD: Rowman & Littlefield, 2007, pp. 239-264.

[13] Wall, James T. *Wall Street and the Fruited Plain: Money, Expansion, and Politics in the Gilded Age.* Lanham, MD: University Press of America, 2008, p. 370.

Chapter Seven

LEGACY OF
THE GILDED AGE

⊷⊶

The man who wrongly holds that every human right is secondary to his profit, must now give way to the advocate of human welfare, who rightly maintains that every man holds his property subject to the general right of the community to regulate its use to whatever degree the public welfare may require it.

—Theodore Roosevelt

When Theodore Roosevelt ascended to the presidency in 1901, he found a nation thirsty for a new era in government. This situation delighted Roosevelt, who fervently believed in the need for change and felt no reluctance to expand the role of the president in pursuing it. "No hard-and-fast rule can be laid down as to the way in which such work [reform] must be done; but most certainly every man, whatever his position, should strive to do it in some way and to some degree,"[1] he asserted. With a solid Republican majority in Congress to push through legislation, Roosevelt led the country into a period of rapid and far-reaching reform known as the Progressive Era.

One reason the general public supported many of Roosevelt's reforms was the growing trend toward muckraking journalism. The writers known as the muckrakers investigated and exposed the worst excesses of the age, from the tragic poverty of American slums to the corruption that characterized many city governments. Although a few muckraking books and articles were written in the 1890s—most notably Jacob Riis's *How the Other Half Lives*, which examined urban poverty—it was not until the early 1900s that they became a regular feature in American newspapers and magazines. Articles by

Ray Stannard Baker uncovered appalling working conditions for miners, railroad workers, and laborers in the garment and meatpacking industries, while Ida Tarbell's *The History of the Standard Oil Company* (1904) portrayed John D. Rockefeller's oil trust as a merciless monopoly. Upton Sinclair's *The Jungle* (1906) horrified readers with its account of unsanitary conditions in Chicago's meatpacking industry, while Lincoln Steffens reported on political corruption in several major U.S. cities, including New York, Chicago, and Philadelphia. Americans were outraged by what they read and increasingly looked to the federal government for meaningful reform.

Middle-class support for the Progressive platform arose from more than indignation and charity, however. Many Americans worried that the vast divide between rich and poor that arose during the Gilded Age was tearing the country apart. While giant corporate trusts were booming, anger and frustration were on the rise among struggling immigrants and native-born laborers. Worried about potential financial instability from either a plutocracy (government by the rich) or a worker revolution, the middle class joined long-suffering mine workers, factory employees, and other laborers in calling for reform. Educated professionals, small businessmen, and settlement houses and churches all came together to demand new laws revolutionizing labor conditions, voting rights, and finance and trade. As one historian noted, "What Progressives of all kinds shared was American confidence that, given goodwill and intelligent analysis, the United States' political, social, and economic problems could be solved by reform of the existing system."[2]

Changing political trends also helped the state-level reforms of the Gilded Age become the national laws of the Progressive Era. McKinley was the last Civil War veteran to occupy the White House, and with his death a new generation rose to the forefront of American politics. This generation was less attached to the sectional loyalties of their forebears, and Americans became less inclined to form ties to an individual party. Voters were more willing to split their tickets, especially as states adopted the secret ballot. Newspapers also became less tied to parties. In the new age of advertising, publishers became less dependent on financial support from political machines.

Roosevelt's Progressive Presidency

Roosevelt's reform agenda was focused on regulating business and finance and improving the social welfare of the American people. The new president demonstrated his willingness to stand up to business interests early in his first term. In May 1902, over 140,000 anthracite coal miners went on strike for higher wages and an eight-hour day. The mine owners responded by closing their mines and refusing to deal with the United Mine Workers union. The owners' spokesman, George F. Baer of the Philadelphia & Reading Railroad, claimed that "the rights and interest of the laboring man will be protected and cared for by the Christian men to whom God has given control of the property rights of the country."[3] By October, with coal reserves decreasing (and owner profits increasing as looming shortages drove up coal prices), Americans became worried about heating their homes during the coming winter.

"What Progressives of all kinds shared was American confidence that, given goodwill and intelligent analysis, the United States' political, social, and economic problems could be solved by reform of the existing system."

Roosevelt offered federal arbitration, but the owners refused to negotiate. Unlike past presidents, however, Roosevelt did not accept the mine owners' stance. To the contrary, their arrogant refusal to consider any compromise angered Roosevelt so much that he threatened to take over the mines and run them with federal troops. The president's shocking threat convinced the mine owners to accept arbitration. The settlement that was subsequently brokered by an independent commission doled out benefits to both sides. It gave workers a 10 percent wage increase and a nine-hour day, but it gave owners a price increase and no union recognition. Roosevelt called his actions in considering the needs of both sides a "square deal" and adopted the phrase to describe his political agenda.

Roosevelt was also quick to ramp up federal antitrust efforts in his administration. Although not opposed to trusts on principle, he was determined to rein in unfair practices like rebates (deep discounts to preferred customers), watering stock, and corruption of public officials. After pushing through legislation to create a Bureau of Corporations to investigate large interstate trusts, Roosevelt gained his first major victory in an antitrust case against the Northern Securities Company, a monopoly of northwestern railways put together by J. P. Morgan, John D. Rockefeller, Edward Harriman, and James J. Hill. The Roosevelt administration accused Northern Securities of illegally restraining trade and manipulating its stock to generate unreasonable profits. After Morgan protested to the president personally, Roosevelt noted that "Mr. Morgan could not help regarding me as a big rival operator,

Theodore Roosevelt's presidency marked the end of the Gilded Age and the beginning of the Progressive Era.

who either intended to ruin all his interests or else could be induced to come to an agreement to ruin none."[4] In 1904 the Supreme Court ordered the dissolution of Northern Securities in a 5-4 decision. In total, Roosevelt's administration would prosecute forty-four antitrust cases—including ones against American Tobacco, DuPont, American Sugar Refining, and Standard Oil—with results including multi-million dollar fines and the conviction of company officials for bribery.

Several other initiatives to regulate business were enacted during Roosevelt's two terms. In 1903 he convinced Congress to establish the Department of Commerce and Labor as a cabinet-level agency, giving it power to investigate interstate business. He also supported several laws designed to increase the effectiveness of the Interstate Commerce Commission (ICC). A 1903 law made rebates illegal and gave the ICC the ability to fine violations and issue injunctions. Three years later Congress gave the ICC the ability to set railroad rates.

Roosevelt's administration also oversaw the creation of important new policies in the realms of food safety and conservation of natural resources. After the abuses uncovered in Sinclair's *The Jungle*, the public demanded regulation of food production. The president responded by working with Congress to pass the Pure Food and Drug Act in 1906. Roosevelt was also a pioneer in conservation programs. He ended longstanding federal policies of unlimited exploitation and created a far-reaching program to regulate the use of public lands. He added almost 125 million acres to the National Forest system, established the national monument and bird reserve systems, and increased federal supervision of inland waterways, irrigation projects, and water power sites. By the time Roosevelt left office in 1909, the Progressive Era was in full swing, with important reforms in politics, labor policy, and economics on the horizon. Many of these reforms were implemented by his hand-picked successor, President William Howard Taft.

New Reforms in Politics

The Progressives sought to bring more fairness to government by reducing the political influence of corporations, stamping out corruption, and increasing the power of the people. They backed several reforms that would create a more direct democracy. One of the most important was the secret ballot. Prior to its adoption, individual political parties printed up ballots listing only their own candidates, often on distinctly colored paper. Because this made it almost impossible for voters to split their vote or keep it secret, it made voter intimidation—and vote buying—very easy. Under the new system, however, the state printed an official ballot listing all candidates, and voters marked it in secret. Massachusetts became the first state to adopt the secret ballot in 1888, and by 1910 all but four southern states were using the system.

Progressive reformers also succeeded in passing legislation that mandated the direct election of U.S. senators by popular vote—an idea that the Populists had long advocated. For many years senators had been elected by state legislatures, but this system was riddled with corruption and political machinations. Twenty-nine states enacted some form of direct election of U.S. senators by 1912, and this trend convinced Congress to pass national legislation.

Securing voting rights for women was one of the major achievements of the Progressive Era. In this photo, a group of suffrage activists look on as Edwin P. Morrow, the governor of Kentucky, ratifies the 19th Amendment.

The 17th Amendment to the Constitution, providing for the direct election of senators, was ratified in 1913.

Other democratic reforms included recall elections, referendums, and voter initiatives. The recall—a special election that gave voters a way to remove elected officials and appointed judges from office—was seen as a check on corruption. The first recalls were used in cities in 1903. Oregon became the first state to adopt the recall in 1908, and by 1914 ten other states had recall policies in place. Referendums were designed to give the public a chance to inspect proposed laws and ordinances and petition that they be subject to a vote at the next election. Voter initiatives allowed the public to petition directly to enact a law, which would be submitted for approval at the next election. In 1898 South Dakota became the first state to adopt the initiative and referendum, and by 1912 seventeen states offered one or both of these options to their citizenry.

The most far-reaching political reform of the Progressive Era was granting women the right to vote. The first women's suffrage organizations had been founded in 1848, but women struggled for the next seventy years to gain the same political rights as men. Many women found their political voice through Gilded Age organizations like the Farmers' Alliance. In 1890 Wyoming became the first state to grant women the right to vote, and several other western states followed suit. To secure women's voting rights nationwide, however, suffragist leaders believed that a Constitutional amendment was needed. The 19th Amendment was finally passed by Congress in 1919 and ratified a year later. According to one historian, "the 'new woman' associated with the Progressive Era—educated, informed, and more free of the separate sphere—was clearly the legacy of Gilded Age activists on all fronts."[5]

Labor Reforms Come to Fruition

Many states had passed laws regulating labor conditions before the Progressive Era, but in the absence of strong federal laws, conditions remained difficult and dangerous for many workers. In 1914 the average U.S. laborer worked 55.2 hours per week, the equivalent of six nine-hour workdays per week. The United States also had one of the world's highest industrial accident rates. A 1913 national survey showed 25,000 workers had been killed and 750,000 seriously injured on the job. A particularly horrifying example occurred in 1911 at the Triangle Shirtwaist Company, which occupied the upper floors of a New York City building. Factory owners had padlocked stairwell and exit doors to prevent theft by garment workers. When a fire broke out in the factory, 146 workers—mostly young women—burned to death or died jumping from windows. The tragedy inspired a wave of new state laws regulating workplace safety. Many of these measures later became models for national laws.

Before the twentieth century, few workers injured on the job were able to get compensation from their employers. Courts generally assumed that workers accepted the risks of employment when they took a job, and judges rarely

Gilded Age Glamour in Literature

For many people, the term "Gilded Age" conjures visions of a glamorous society where millionaires competed to find new ways to flaunt their riches. New York City was the social center of the Gilded Age, with prominent families like the Astors and Vanderbilts leading the way. Society events received extensive coverage in the city's newspapers, giving everyday readers a chance to marvel at the ostentatious displays of wealth.

Many American novelists portrayed the glitter of the Gilded Age in their works, as well, including William Dean Howells (1837-1920) and Henry James (1843-1916). Edith Wharton (1862-1937) was perhaps the most insightful writer to portray the Gilded Age. Growing up in an "old money" New York family, Wharton was acquainted with the Vanderbilts and Tafts. She became intimately familiar with high society's strengths and weaknesses, and she often used them to create dramatic tension in her works. In *The House of Mirth* (1905), for example, a spirited young socialite faced with a choice between wealth and self-respect ends up committing suicide.

Wharton's 1920 novel *The Age of Innocence*—a best-seller and Pulitzer Prize winner—examines the emotional sacrifices that Newland Archer makes in choosing his wealthy fiancée over her unconventional cousin. In the following passage from the novel, Wharton reveals New York society's pretensions in her description of a garden party at a wealthy family's summer home:

> The small bright lawn stretched away smoothly to the big bright sea.

awarded damages unless employers had been clearly negligent. The first federal workers' compensation law was passed in 1882, but it only applied to a few employees in "life-saving" agencies such as the Coast Guard. Speaking in favor of a broader law, Roosevelt noted that it was "a matter of humiliation" that there was no law to aid employees injured in public service, and he argued that "this same broad principle which should apply to the Government should

The turf was hemmed with an edge of scarlet geranium and coleus, and cast-iron vases painted in chocolate colour, standing at intervals along the winding path that led to the sea, looped their garlands of petunia and ivy geranium above the neatly raked gravel.

Half way between the edge of the cliff and the square wooden house (which was also chocolate-coloured, but with the tin roof of the verandah striped in yellow and brown to represent an awning) two large targets had been placed against a background of shrubbery. On the other side of the lawn, facing the targets, was pitched a real tent, with benches and garden-seats about it. A number of ladies in summer dresses and gentlemen in grey frock-coats and tall hats stood on the lawn or sat upon the benches; and every now and then a slender girl in starched muslin would step from the tent, bow in hand, and speed her shaft at one of the targets, while the spectators interrupted their talk to watch the result....

The Newport Archery Club always held its August meeting at the Beauforts'. The sport, which had hitherto known no rival but croquet, was beginning to be discarded in favour of lawn-tennis; but the latter game was still considered too rough and inelegant for social occasions, and as an opportunity to show off pretty dresses and graceful attitudes the bow and arrow held their own.

Source

Wharton, Edith. *The Age of Innocence.* New York: Appleton, 1920, Book II, Chapter XXI. Available online at Project Gutenberg, http://www.gutenberg.org/files/541/541-h/541-h.htm.

ultimately be made applicable to all private employers."[6] In response, Congress passed the first Federal Employers Liability Act in 1906 to protect railroad workers, who had a high rate of injury on the job. Two years later Congress passed a law that covered workers at federal manufacturing sites, arsenals, and Navy yards, as well as employees engaged in hazardous jobs on construction sites. In 1916 Congress passed the Federal Employees' Compensation Act, which extended workers' compensation to all federal employees injured or killed on the job and created a commission to administer claims.

Federal regulation of working hours also began with the railroad system. In 1916 four railway brotherhoods demanded an eight-hour day with no reduction in wages. When federal mediation failed, the unions' 400,000 members voted overwhelmingly to strike. As the nation's commerce was increasingly conducted by rail, potential stoppages meant widespread economic disruption. To avert the stoppage, Congress quickly passed the Adamson Act, which established an eight-hour day for railroad workers. Although railroad companies challenged the law, the Supreme Court ruled 5-4 in *Wilson v. New* that it was within Congress's powers to regulate working hours to prevent interruption of interstate commerce. Justice James Clark McReynolds accurately predicted the sweeping impact of the law in his dissent: "It follows as of course that Congress has power to fix a maximum as well as a minimum wage for trainmen; to require compulsory arbitration of labor disputes which may seriously and directly jeopardize the movement of interstate traffic; and to take measures effectively to protect the free flow of such commerce against any combination."[7]

The Court did not approve all federal labor legislation, however. In 1916 Congress passed the Keating-Owen Child Labor Act, which banned the sale of goods made by children in the United States. The law was aimed at states in the South that had failed to follow the industrial North's lead in outlawing child labor. But the Supreme Court overturned the law in its 1918 ruling in *Hammer v. Dagenhart*. The Court asserted that the issue was not one of interstate commerce but one of labor, and thus a responsibility left to the states. Although the demand for child labor was largely eliminated by the Great Depression of the 1930s, it would not be banned nationwide until the Fair Labor Standards Act (FLSA) of 1938. The FLSA also established a minimum wage, a maximum work week of forty-four hours, and overtime pay at one-and-a-half times the normal rate for employees in most manufacturing businesses. In 1941 the Supreme Court upheld the new labor regulations, expressly overturning *Hammer* in its unanimous *United States v. Darby* decision.

Reforms in Finance

Legislators also turned their attention to matters of finance and business during the Progressive Era. Before this time the federal government had traditionally collected most of its revenue through tariffs, which are taxes on goods imported into the country. Although legislators had made a few attempts at taxing personal and corporate income to raise revenue, the Supreme Court had held that certain income taxes—including those levied on interest, dividends, and rent income—were unconstitutional. Because wealthy Americans and corporations earned more money from such sources than poor and middle-class workers, Progressives believed a direct income tax could make the tax base broader and more fair. In 1909 they secured passage of the 16th Amendment to the Constitution, which gave Congress the ability to "lay and collect taxes on incomes, from whatever source derived," and it was ratified in 1913.

The Federal Trade Commission, which operates out of this building in Washington, D.C., emerged from antitrust efforts during the Progressive Era.

After J. P. Morgan had to step in to help the country's banks avoid financial disaster during the Panic of 1907, politicians and financiers alike recognized the need for banking and currency reform. Democratic president Woodrow Wilson (who had been elected in 1912, when Roosevelt ran as a Progressive and split the Republican vote between himself and Taft) brokered a compromise between banking interests and those who wanted a government-controlled central bank. The Federal Reserve Act of 1913 set up twelve regional Federal Reserve banks that would hold reserves to meet commercial bank demand. The system would be supervised by a presidentially appointed Federal Reserve Board, which would set interest rates for reserve bank loans. Congress set up a similar banking system to aid small farmers with the Federal Farm Loan Act of 1916. The act created twelve district Farm Loan Banks that could give long-term, low-interest loans to farmers. Combined with the Bonded Warehouse Act of 1916, which allowed farmers to exchange crops for receipts that could be used as collateral for bank loans, the law fulfilled many of the provisions of the Populists' old subtreasury plan.

Wilson also took a more cooperative approach to antitrust conflicts than his predecessor. The Taft administration had concluded a high-profile antitrust case against Standard Oil the year before Wilson took office. Standard Oil had long been viewed by the public as an unfair monopoly, thanks to an 1886 congressional investigation and Tarbell's muckraking book *The History of the Standard Oil Company*. In its 1911 decision *Standard Oil Co. of New Jersey v. United States*, a unanimous Supreme Court ordered the breakup of Standard Oil. The Court based its decision on its belief that the company had "the intent to drive others from the field and to exclude them from their right to trade, and thus accomplish the mastery which was the end in view."[8] The company was forced to split into various subsidiaries as a result of this ruling. Ironically, the sell-off resulted in huge profits for Standard Oil founder Rockefeller and his shareholders. While the decision seemed a victory for antitrust forces, the Court's decision also restricted future cases by declaring that monopolies were not inherently illegal unless they "unreasonably" restricted trade.

In response, Congress passed a new bill intended to strengthen the government's antitrust powers. Wilson was not an ardent supporter of the new law, however, so by the time the Clayton Antitrust Act became law in 1914 it had been watered down considerably. Although the act banned price discrimination, exclusive selling agreements, holding companies, and common directors among competing firms, the legislation deemed these acts illegal only if the government could prove the companies involved had unreasonably restricted trade. Although the act failed to exempt labor unions from its application, it did note that farmers' groups or unions engaged in lawful protests could not be ruled in restraint of trade. Nevertheless, the Supreme Court continued ruling against labor unions throughout the 1920s. It was not until the Norris-LaGuardia Act of 1932 that strict limits were placed on injunctions against union activities.

Wilson was more of a leader in establishing the Federal Trade Commission (FTC) in 1914. He presented Congress with his initiative for an agency that could not only investigate unfair trusts, but could also advise businesses on whether a proposed merger might violate the law. The FTC Act outlawed unfair practices in general terms and gave the new commission the power to investigate corporations and issue injunctions. The first commissioners Wilson named were sympathetic to business, and the new FTC tended to negotiate with companies rather than prosecute them, using consent decrees to bring them in line with the new rules. Wilson's cooperation with business interests reflected a similar attitude adjustment among average Americans. "As the new century unfolded and the consumer carnival spilled forth its treasures, the corporation's values, methods, and influence spread into many other walks of life," according to one historian. "Americans would never manage to love the corporation, but they certainly came to accommodate it and to learn from it."[9]

A New Gilded Age?

The Progressive Era came to an end after the United States entered World War I. A war-weary public gave Republicans control of Congress in 1918 and the White House in 1920. When Democrat Franklin D. Roosevelt became president in 1933 during the depths of the Great Depression, however, his New Deal programs to aid the working class and poor incorporated many of the progressive ideals of the earlier era. The country was emerging from depression by the time it entered World War II in 1941, and wartime increases in industrial production helped launch a new economic boom in the late 1940s and 1950s. Programs like the GI Bill, which helped veterans obtain college educations and buy homes and businesses, helped more people move into the middle class. By the 1960s, the disparity between the highest-earning and lowest-earning Americans was smaller than ever before.

"The chances of a poor citizen, or even a middle-class citizen, making it to the top in America are smaller than in many countries of Europe."

Economic troubles in the 1970s led to a new political movement that favored deregulation and tax cuts as a way to aid the economy. Over the next thirty years, more people began investing in the stock market through mutual funds and retirement plans. Financiers created new investment instruments to garner unprecedented profits, and tax rates on those capital gains dropped drastically. These changes enabled some Americans to accumulate tremendous wealth. The incomes of the top 1 percent of Americans grew from 8.9 percent of the country's pre-tax income in 1976, to 22.9 percent in 2006, to almost 25 percent in 2011. In 2004 the top 1 percent of Americans accounted for 34.4 percent of the nation's wealth—a total of nearly $16.8 trillion, $2 trillion more than the wealth of the bottom 90 percent of Americans combined—and by 2011 this figure increased to 40 percent of American wealth. As the rich grew richer, however, the incomes of average workers remained flat or even declined. By the late 1990s and early 2000s, many observers of this widening divide

Deregulation of the financial industry created opportunities for some American investors to accumulate tremendous wealth in the late 20th and early 21st centuries.

between America's wealthy elite and the rest of the country were comparing the situation to the United States of the late nineteenth century (see "A Second Gilded Age? The Income Gap Says Yes," p. 197). "We are in fact in the second Gilded Age," Nobel Prize-winning economist Paul Krugman wrote. "A lot of behavior is the same: the giant private philanthropies, which is one of the giant mitigating factors, the exhibitionist display of wealth and, of course, the malefactors [criminals] of great wealth all insisting that they're doing great things for us all."[10]

Although the gap between the highest-earning and lowest-earning Americans increased to Gilded Age levels in the early twenty-first century, other observers noted that several factors distinguished the two eras. In the early 2000s, for instance, over three-quarters of American families within the top 20 percent of incomes had two wage earners, meaning many of these "new rich" had earned their wealth through long hours and hard work. In addition, much of the overall disparity in income levels resulted from an explosion in incomes for the top 1 percent. When modern fortunes were ranked in proportion to national income, only software pioneer Bill Gates and investor Warren Buffett had accumulated wealth comparable to that of the top thirty tycoons of the Gilded Age. Finally, living standards and opportunities were vastly better for modern-day low-income Americans than for their counterparts in the Gilded Age, who had little education, worked up to six days a week with no vacations, and often lived in overcrowded, unsanitary slums with no plumbing or running water (see "A New Gilded Age? Living Standards Say No," p. 203).

The economic downturn that began in the fall of 2008 led some to conclude that the new Gilded Age was at an end. A sudden decline in housing values endangered financial companies that traded in mortgages and mortgage-backed securities, tightening credit for consumers and businesses and leading to a $700 billion federal government bailout of the financial industry. The result, one economic historian noted, was that the "kind of economy that supported a certain kind of gildedness is ending."[11] The political fallout of the post-2008 recession, however, had several aspects that recalled the Gilded Age. Republicans and Democrats argued over how to regulate the financial sector, while massive budget deficits on the state level created new conflicts with labor unions. In Wisconsin, for instance, a 2011 budget bill that eliminated collective bargaining for state unions led thousands of public employees to demonstrate in the state capital. Meanwhile, grassroots demonstrations by self-described "tea-party" anti-tax protesters reminded some of old populist movements.

As in the Gilded Age, modern protests were generated by economic uncertainty. "The anger fueling the populism of both the Left and the Right is not so much jealousy and envy that a tiny minority is making pots of money; it is anxiety and disappointment about the darkening prospects of everyone else,"[12] one observer noted in 2011. Nobel Prize-winning economist Joseph Stiglitz also noted a growing concern about the opportunities available for average people to achieve the American dream: "America has long prided itself on being a fair society, where everyone has an equal chance of getting ahead, but the statistics suggest otherwise: the chances of a poor citizen, or even a middle-class citizen, making it to the top in America are smaller than in many countries of Europe."[13]

Whether or not the United States entered a new Gilded Age in the early twenty-first century, such comparisons show beyond doubt that the Gilded

The income gap between rich and poor Americans has led some historians to observe that the United States may have entered a new Gilded Age.

Age of the late 1800s was a formative period in American history. The era was characterized by stark contrasts. It saw rapid advances in transportation, communication, and other technologies; the development of booming industrial corporations and advanced business strategies; and the glittering display of tremendous wealth. Yet it also saw government corruption and political scandals; greedy "robber barons" making shady business deals to crush competitors; laborers forced to work long hours in hazardous conditions; and families living in extreme poverty and squalor. These Gilded Age contrasts led to the Progressive Era, when a broad coalition of Americans came together to support reforms that made the nation more fair and democratic. "Progressivism built on the precedents that the Gilded Age had set," one historian remarked. "It improved on them, and over time, deflected further from the principles that guided them. But to the end, it owed a debt to the society passing away."[14] Many of the ideas considered radical during the Gilded Age—labor protections, government regulation of corporations, social welfare programs, a more direct democracy—would become an integral part of American life over the next hundred years. Writing of the leaders of the Gilded Age, another historian concluded: "In important ways they helped lay the groundwork for the twentieth-century American polity."[15]

Notes:

[1] Quoted in "People & Events: The Progressive Era, 1900-1918." In *American Experience: Eleanor Roosevelt.* Available online at http://www.pbs.org/wgbh/amex/eleanor/peopleevents/pande08.html.
[2] Cashman, Sean Dennis. *America in the Gilded Age: From the Death of Lincoln to the Rise of Theodore Roosevelt.* 3rd edition. New York: New York University Press, 1993, p. 371.
[3] Quoted in Josephson, Matthew. *The Robber Barons.* New York: Harcourt, 1934, p. 374.
[4] Quoted in Josephson, p. 449.
[5] Cordery, Stacy A. "Women in Industrializing America." In *The Gilded Age: Perspectives on the Origins of Modern America.* 2nd edition, p. 137.
[6] Quoted in Nordlund, Willis J. "The Federal Employees' Compensation Act." In *Monthly Labor Review.* September 1991, p. 5. Available online from the Bureau of Labor Statistics, http://www.bls.gov/opub/mlr/1991/09/art1full.pdf.
[7] *Wilson v. New,* 243 U.S. 332. Available online at http://laws.findlaw.com/us/243/332.html.
[8] *Standard Oil Company of New Jersey v. United States,* 221 U.S. 1. Available online at http://laws.findlaw.com/us/221/1.html.
[9] Porter, Glenn. "Industrialization and the Rise of Big Business." In *The Gilded Age: Perspectives on the Origins of Modern America.* 2nd edition, p. 25.
[10] Krugman, Paul. "Making Banking Boring." *New York Times,* April 10, 2009, p. A23.
[11] Quoted in McGeehan, Patrick. "Body Blow to Wall Street Will Test Resilience of New York's Economy." *New York Times,* September 21, 2008, p. A37.
[12] Mead, Walter Russell. "American Dreams, American Resentments." *The American Interest,* January-February, 2011.
[13] Stiglitz, Joseph E. "Of the 1%, by the 1%, for the 1%." *Vanity Fair.* May, 2011, p. 126.
[14] Summers, Mark Wahlgren. *The Gilded Age, or, the Hazard of New Functions.* Upper Saddle River, NJ: Prentice Hall, 1997, pp. 291-292.
[15] Calhoun, Charles W. "The Political Culture: Public Life and the Conduct of Politics." In *The Gilded Age : Perspectives on the Origins of Modern America.* 2nd edition. Edited by Calhoun. Lanham, MD: Rowman & Littlefield Publishers, 2007, p. 260.

BIOGRAPHIES

William Jennings Bryan (1860-1925)
Populist Leader and Three-time Democratic
Candidate for President

William Jennings Bryan was born in Salem, Illinois, on March 19, 1860. He was the second child and eldest son of five surviving children in his family. His father, Silas Lillard Bryan, served as a lawyer, circuit court judge, and Democratic state senator. Bryan's mother, the former Mariah Elizabeth Jennings, helped run the family farm and homeschooled her children. She also instilled a strong Christian faith in William and his siblings.

At age fifteen Bryan moved to Jacksonville, Illinois, where he attended Whipple Academy and Illinois College. He graduated as valedictorian from the latter, earning a bachelor's degree in 1881 and a master's in 1884. He then studied at Chicago's Union Law School while simultaneously working for former U.S. senator Lyman Trumbull. He received his law degree in 1883, passed the bar in 1885, and began practicing law in Jacksonville. On October 1, 1884, Bryan married Mary Elizabeth Baird. She became an indispensible partner, helping develop her husband's essays and speeches and passing the bar herself in 1888. They had two daughters and a son.

"Boy Orator" Takes National Stage

The family moved to Lincoln, Nebraska, in 1887, where Bryan continued practicing law and also became involved in Democratic politics. He ran for the U.S. House of Representatives in 1890, winning as a Democrat in a previously Republican district. When he first addressed the House in 1892, listeners responded so positively to his eloquent words and strong speaking style that even New York papers took note. His remarks launched a speaking career for the "Boy Orator of the Platte," who won a second term in 1892. While in Congress, Bryan worked for lower tariffs, the establishment of an income tax, and the free coinage of silver. Bryan and other silver advocates argued that using gold as the standard value for U.S. currency favored

125

wealthy bankers and industrialists. They believed that replacing gold with silver would help working-class farmers and laborers. In 1894 he ran for the Senate, but Nebraska's Republican state legislature elected one of its own to the position.

Bryan spent the next two years lecturing on the silver issue and serving as editor-in-chief for the *Omaha World-Herald*. At the 1896 Democratic convention, Bryan was considered a dark-horse candidate for president. During debate on the silver issue, however, Bryan gave his famous "Cross of Gold" speech (see p. 192). The speech not only earned him a half-hour ovation, it also convinced the delegates to give him the Democratic presidential nomination. The People's (Populist) Party likewise selected Bryan as its candidate. During the ensuing campaign he broke with tradition by traveling and making speeches all around the country. Despite cementing his reputation as "the most remarkable orator of the century,"[1] in the words of one Republican admirer, Bryan could not overcome Republican William McKinley's well-funded campaign. Unable to attract voters in urban centers and the Northeast, Bryan lost both the popular and electoral vote.

Bryan and his wife wrote a book about the 1896 presidential campaign called *The First Battle*. It sold 200,000 copies in eight months and demonstrated his devotion to progressive issues. Although Bryan rejected imperialism (the idea that the United States should expand its territory and influence overseas), he volunteered as a colonel in the Nebraska National Guard during the Spanish-American War. He contracted typhoid at a Florida training camp, however, and resigned at war's end without seeing action. When the Democrats unanimously nominated him for president in 1900, he made anti-imperialism and free silver his main campaign issues. McKinley rode his wartime popularity to easy reelection, however. Bryan won fewer votes and fewer states than he had in 1896.

Wins Third Democratic Nomination

At this point Bryan turned from politics to writing and lecturing. He launched the weekly newspaper *The Commoner* (a play on his nickname, "The Great Commoner") in 1901, and circulation grew to 145,000 within five years. Bryan also became the most popular speaker on the Chautauqua circuit, an adult education and culture series that traveled the country in the late 1800s and early 1900s. Although Bryan wrote that "both writing and speaking furnish such agreeable occupation that one does not notice the loss of a little thing like the presidency,"[2] he remained a force in Democratic politics. Bryan did not run for the 1904 nomination—gold-standard advocate Alton Parker was chosen instead—but he wrote most of the party's platform and gave another well-received speech. Parker ended up losing to Republican president Theodore Roosevelt in a landslide.

Bryan toured Asia, the Middle East, and Europe in 1905 and 1906, giving speeches and writing *The Old World and Its Ways* about his travels. In 1908 he secured a third Democratic presidential nomination. Armed with the campaign slogan "Shall the People Rule?," Bryan spoke against the power of big business and earned the American Federation of Labor's endorsement. Nonetheless, Bryan only won three states outside the solidly Democratic South and lost to Republican nominee William Howard Taft.

After his third defeat, Bryan continued speaking around the country, adding prohibition of alcohol and women's voting rights to the issues he supported. In 1912 he wrote most of the Democratic platform—for the fifth consecutive time—and led Nebraska's delegation. At the party convention that year, Nebraska's support proved critical in the selection of Woodrow Wilson as the Democratic presidential nominee. With Roosevelt leading a third-party ticket, Wilson easily won the election and made Bryan his secretary of state.

Elder Statesman and Lecturer

As secretary of state, Bryan advocated the signing of conciliation treaties, which created a one-year "cooling-off" period during which two countries could submit their differences to arbitration. The United States signed 30 such treaties with countries in Latin America and Europe during Bryan's tenure. Bryan was also instrumental in developing progressive laws on taxes, trusts, and banking. When World War I broke out in Europe in 1914, Bryan worked hard to maintain U.S. neutrality in the conflict. After a German submarine sank the British ocean liner *Lusitania* in 1915, killing 128 Americans, Wilson and Bryan disagreed over the appropriate U.S. response, and Bryan resigned in protest. Once the United States entered the war in 1917, however, Bryan gave Wilson his full support.

Bryan moved his family to Florida in 1916. In the 1920s he turned his attention to fighting the teaching of evolution. Bryan believed that Charles Darwin's theory of the origin of species undermined Christian teachings about Creation and threatened American morality. He agreed to assist the prosecution in the famous Scopes "Monkey" Trial, which charged biology teacher John Scopes with violating Tennessee's law against teaching evolution. In a trial that was broadcast nationwide on the radio, Bryan agreed to be cross-examined by defense attorney Clarence Darrow about his Creationist beliefs. Bryan became flustered on the witness stand, however, and Darrow was widely viewed as the winner of their showdown.

Four days later, on July 26, 1925, Bryan died in Dayton, Tennessee. His funeral train was visited by thousands of Americans, many of whom "believed him to be a godly hero who preached that the duty of a true Christian was to transform a nation and world plagued by the arrogance of wealth and the pain of inequality,"[3] according to one biographer. Bryan was buried at Arlington National Cemetery and had a library, park, church, hospital, and college named in his honor. According to progressive editor William Allen White, Bryan "influenced the thinking of the American people more profoundly than any other man of his generation."[4]

Sources:

Bryan, William Jennings, and Mary Baird Bryan. *The Memoirs of William Jennings Bryan.* Port Washington, NY: Kennikat Press, 1971. Originally published 1925.

Cherny, Robert W. *A Righteous Cause: The Life of William Jennings Bryan.* Boston: Little, Brown, 1985. Edition with new preface, Norman: University of Oklahoma Press, 1994.

Kazin, Michael. *A Godly Hero: The Life of William Jennings Bryan.* New York: Knopf, 2006.

Notes:

[1] Quoted in Kazin, Michael. *A Godly Hero: The Life of William Jennings Bryan.* New York: Knopf, 2006, p. 49.

[2] Quoted in Kazin, p. 141.

[3] Kazin, p. xiii.

[4] Quoted in Cherny, Robert W. *A Righteous Cause: The Life of William Jennings Bryan.* Boston: Little, Brown, 1985. Edition with new preface, Norman: University of Oklahoma Press, 1994, p. vii.

Andrew Carnegie (1835-1919)
Steel Magnate and Philanthropist

Andrew Carnegie was born on November 25, 1835, in Dunfermline, Scotland. His father, William Carnegie, was a skilled hand-weaver whose business suffered with the introduction of cheap manufactured linens. When Will Carnegie was forced to sell his hand loom, Carnegie's mother, the former Margaret Morrison, helped support the family by selling vegetables and sweets. In 1848 the couple took Andrew and his younger brother Tom to America to build a new life.

Living with relatives in Pennsylvania, Will Carnegie could only find a low-paying job in a cotton mill. Thirteen-year-old Andrew got a job there as well. Given the opportunity to work for the local telegraph company as a message boy, he memorized the streets of Pittsburgh. Before long he had taught himself Morse code and was filling in for telegraph operators on their breaks. Although Carnegie only had a few years of formal schooling, he continued his education by taking bookkeeping classes at night and making use of a local library. By the age of sixteen Carnegie had become a telegraph operator and the main provider for his family.

From Trains to Bridges

When Pennsylvania Railroad executive Thomas A. Scott sought a secretary and personal telegraph operator in 1853, Carnegie's bosses recommended him. Scott taught Carnegie about railroads and business, and he even loaned his young protégé the money to make his first investments. Carnegie advanced quickly at the Pennsylvania Railroad, taking Scott's position as Pittsburgh superintendent in 1859 after his mentor was promoted. During the first year of the Civil War Carnegie assisted Scott, who had been named an assistant secretary of war, in setting up the Union Army's telegraphs and railroads.

Carnegie's diverse investments, which included holdings in the oil, telegraph, iron, coal, and locomotive industries, were earning him $45,000 yearly by 1863. When the war ended in 1865 he left the Pennsylvania Railroad to focus on his own business ventures. His primary concerns were Keystone Bridge, which he helped found in 1863 as the country's first iron bridge company, and the Union Iron Mills, Keystone's principal supplier. Carnegie's railroad experience had taught him that iron made better bridges than wood; it also gave him many sales contacts. By delivering quality products on schedule, Carnegie grew his business. In 1870 he signed a contract to build the first steel bridge across the Mississippi River.

Between 1865 and 1870, Carnegie sold about $30 million in bonds to finance his St. Louis Bridge as well as various railway concerns. He earned commissions worth up to $1 million on these transactions. He moved to New York in 1867 and also took several trips to Europe, where he became fascinated by Britain's experiments with a new "Bessemer" process of steelmaking. "If this proved successful I knew that iron was destined to give place to steel; that the Iron Age would pass away and the Steel Age take its place,"[1] he later wrote.

A Pioneer in Steel

Carnegie built his first blast furnace for making pig iron, the raw material for steel, in 1870. In 1873 a severe economic depression hit the United States, but Carnegie was still able to find investors to help him build his first Bessemer steel rail plant. The Edgar Thomson Works—named after the president of the Pennsylvania Railroad—opened in 1875 in the Pittsburgh suburb of Braddock. Within two years it was returning 20 percent annually on Carnegie's original investment.

The company's success came from several innovations that Carnegie instituted. First was railroad-style accounting: by keeping track of every operating expense, managers could undercut competitors and still maximize profits. Second was investment: Carnegie put only 25 percent of profits into partner dividends, dedicating the other 75 percent to upgrading equipment and improving processes. Finally, Carnegie surrounded himself with talented associates. He hired Bessemer expert Alexander Holley to design his mills and patent holder "Captain" Bill Jones to manage them.

Carnegie also ruthlessly managed his partners, employees, and competitors. He bought a controlling interest in Henry Clay Frick's coke company and made Frick president of his steel company. He also bought or leased several iron ore fields and threatened to build his own railway when the Pennsylvania would not give him preferential rates. In depression years, Carnegie bought out faltering competitors or expanded his facilities, taking advantage of lower prices and labor costs.

Controversy and Philanthropy

By the late 1880s, Carnegie was spending half the year traveling to Europe, living in a Scottish castle, and writing. His first book was a modestly successful travelogue. His most notable book was 1886's *Triumphant Democracy,* arguing for the superiority of the American form of government. In the mid-1880s Carnegie also wrote essays about labor in which he argued that workers had the right to unionize, conflicts with management should be arbitrated, and the use of scab labor was unpardonable. These statements came back to haunt him in 1892, when a violent labor-management conflict at Carnegie Steel's plant in Homestead, Pennsylvania, brought him critical newspaper coverage in the United States and abroad. Carnegie blamed Frick for the unrest, even though he had expressly told his lieutenant to break the plant's union, whatever the cost.

By 1900, Carnegie was ready to retire. He sold out to a group organized by banker J. P. Morgan. Morgan paid almost $500 million for the company—with Carnegie pocketing $225 million—to create the billion-dollar U.S. Steel trust. Following his retirement, Carnegie devoted his energies to philanthropy. In his 1889 essay "The Gospel of Wealth" (see excerpt, p. 177), he had argued that the rich had a responsibility to give their money away. Remembering the important role a library had played in his youth, Carnegie donated some $50 million to build more than 2,800 public libraries in the United States and Great Britain. He was also an advocate for international peace efforts, founding the Carnegie Endowment for Peace in 1910. In all, he gave away $350 million to various charities and educational institutions during his lifetime. His legacies included New York City's Carnegie Hall (built in 1891), the Carnegie Institute of Technology (founded in 1900, now Carnegie-Mellon University), the Carnegie Institution for Science (founded in 1902), and the Carnegie Foundation for the Advancement of Teaching (founded in 1905).

Carnegie died on August 11, 1919, at Shadowbrook, his country home in Lenox, Massachusetts. He was buried in Sleepy Hollow Cemetery near Tarrytown, New York. He was survived by his wife, Louise Whitfield, whom he married in 1887, and his daughter Margaret, who was born in 1897. He is remembered today as one of the most talented businessmen in U.S. history. "There is no way to quantify the impact of Carnegie," said one historian. "There were other men of energy and invention in the nascent steel trade … but none had his drive, ambition, or subversive instincts."[2] Nevertheless, he remains best known in modern times for his charitable works. Whenever "the media evaluates benevolence," according to another writer, "it is measured against Carnegie."[3]

Sources:

Carnegie, Andrew. *Autobiography of Andrew Carnegie.* London: Constable & Co., 1920. Available online at Project Gutenberg, http://www.gutenberg.org/files/17976/17976-h/17976-h.htm.

Krass, Peter. *Carnegie.* Hoboken, NJ: John Wiley & Sons, 2002.

Morris, Charles R. *The Tycoons: How Andrew Carnegie, John D. Rockefeller, Jay Gould, and J. P. Morgan Invented the American Supereconomy.* New York: Times Books, 2005.

Nasaw, David. *Andrew Carnegie.* New York: The Penguin Press, 2006.

Notes:

[1] Carnegie, Andrew. *Autobiography of Andrew Carnegie.* London: Constable & Co., 1920, pp. 184-85.

[2] Morris, Charles R. *The Tycoons: How Andrew Carnegie, John D. Rockefeller, Jay Gould, and J. P. Morgan Invented the American Supereconomy.* New York: Times Books, 2005, p. 287.

[3] Krass, Peter. *Carnegie.* Hoboken, NJ: John Wiley & Sons, 2002, p. 539.

Grover Cleveland (1837-1908)
Democratic President of the United States

S tephen Grover Cleveland was born on March 18, 1837, in Caldwell, New Jersey. He was the fifth of nine children born to Presbyterian minister Richard Falley and Ann (Neal) Cleveland. Cleveland spent most of his youth in upstate New York, often taking odd jobs to help support the family. He spent his free time hunting and fishing in nearby woodlands and streams.

Cleveland received most of his formal education at Fayetteville Academy in New York. At fifteen he left school to work as a clerk. His college plans were derailed upon his father's death in 1853, which left him as the main source of support for his family. In 1855 an uncle in Buffalo, New York, found him a position in a local law office. Cleveland thus began intensive law studies. He was admitted to the bar in 1859 and took a job as a lawyer.

Swift Rise to the White House

Interested in Democratic politics, Cleveland was appointed Buffalo's assistant district attorney in 1863. Over the next few years he gained a reputation for dedication and thoroughness, and in 1870 he was asked to run for Erie County Sheriff. Cleveland easily won the job, which offered a steady income and better hours. When his term ended in 1873 Cleveland returned to private practice. Around this time he dropped his first name in favor of Grover. In 1881, local Democrats urged him to run for mayor, believing he could attract voters in Republican-dominated Buffalo. Cleveland agreed, but only if the campaign stressed reform. His strategy worked, and he ended up winning by almost 3,600 votes.

Cleveland soon became known as the "Veto Mayor." He rejected any city contracts or laws that carried any whiff of corruption. His reform credentials and independence from political machines led state Democrats to propose him as a candidate for governor. Bolstered by the support of many Republicans, Cleveland won by a record margin in 1882. The new governor vetoed eight laws in his first two weeks in office, including a popular bill to cut New York City transit fares in half. Cleveland argued that the bill broke the state's contract with the transit company, and even the bill's supporters admired his principled stand.

Cleveland's upright reputation and willingness to take on New York City's powerful but corrupt Tammany Hall political organization appealed to Democrats looking to win the White House in 1884. As one delegate observed at the convention, Cleveland's supporters "respect him not only for himself, for his character, for his integrity and judgment and iron will, but they love him most of all for the enemies he has made."[1] Despite Tammany Hall's efforts against him, Cleveland was nominated on the second ballot.

Cleveland's candidacy was nearly derailed by scandal, however. The bachelor was accused of fathering a son, Oscar Folsom Cleveland, with a widow named Maria Halpin in 1874. Cleveland discussed the matter openly, and his honesty and reform credentials created a contrast with his Republican opponent, Maine senator James G. Blaine, who had a history of profiting from his political position. With the aid of reformist Republican "Mugwumps," Cleveland won New York by barely 1,000 votes. His triumph in his home state gave him a 219-182 electoral college victory and made him the twenty-second president of the United States.

Experiences Political Ups and Downs

Cleveland named men of integrity and diligence to his cabinet and appointed several Southerners—who had been banished from high-level federal posts since the Civil War—to important positions in his administration. He also defied the patronage system (which rewarded political supporters with high-paying government jobs) by keeping several Republicans in federal posts. He vetoed a record number of bills, including ones that would have abused the Union veterans' pension system and required a literacy test for immigrants. He did sign several major pieces of legislation, though, including the Interstate Commerce Act, which regulated railroad rates; the Dawes Severalty Act, which attempted to assimilate Native Americans; and a bill limiting Chinese immigration. Cleveland's most popular act during his first term was to marry Frances Folsom, his late law partner's daughter, on June 2, 1886. The first White House wedding in U.S. history attracted attention from the media and fascinated the public.

Cleveland emphasized tariff reduction in his third address to Congress in 1887. He argued that high tariffs were no longer needed to protect U.S. industries from foreign competition or to raise revenue for the U.S. government, which had accumulated a budget surplus. He did not press the issue, however—he believed the president's job was to check Congress, not lead it—and his suggested reforms died in the GOP Senate. The Republicans ran against tariff reform in the 1888 election, uniting behind Benjamin Harrison. Cleveland refused to campaign for reelection, believing it beneath the dignity of the president. Although he won the popular vote by 100,000, he lost in the electoral college 233-168. When it was suggested that his tariff stand had cost him the election, he declared: "Perhaps I made a mistake from the party standpoint; but damn it, it was right."[2]

After leaving office Cleveland moved to New York City, where he worked part-time for a law firm. After public disgust at the high-tariff "Billion Dollar Congress" led to Republican losses in the 1890 midterm elections, Cleveland began giving speeches about tariff reform and monetary policy around the country. The birth in 1891 of his daughter, Ruth, also kept him in the public eye. In 1892 his fellow Democrats selected him as their presidential nominee on the first ballot. Despite a challenge from the Populist Party, Cleveland reclaimed the presidency from Harrison by nearly 400,000 popular votes and a 277-145 electoral majority. He thus became the first person ever elected to serve two non-consecutive terms as president. His Democratic Party also took control of both the House and Senate.

Second-Term Troubles

Shortly after Cleveland's inauguration as the twenty-fourth president of the United States, the Panic of 1893 led to a major depression. Cleveland's answer was to force Congress to repeal the Sherman Silver Act. The repeal succeeded, but the silver question split the Democratic Party. Silver advocates believed that using gold as the standard for U.S. currency favored wealthy bankers and industrialists. They believed that a switch to silver would benefit average Americans, including farmers and laborers. Cleveland's rejection of silver was thus viewed by many of his usual supporters as helping powerful business interests at the expense of working-class people.

In 1894 Cleveland ordered federal intervention in the Pullman railroad strike, further alienating him from his party. When he worked with banker J.

P. Morgan to issue gold bonds to replenish the U.S. Treasury in 1895, he was accused of being a tool of Wall Street investors. By 1896 Cleveland's own party was openly repudiating his policies. The Democrats subsequently nominated free-silver candidate William Jennings Bryan for president, but he lost to Republican William McKinley in the 1896 presidential election.

Cleveland retired to Princeton, New Jersey, and he became a trustee of Princeton University in 1903. He spent the next few years writing autobiographical articles and speeches, many of which were published as *Presidential Problems* in 1904 and *Fishing and Shooting Sketches* in 1906. Cleveland died of heart failure on June 24, 1908, at his home in Princeton. His dying words were "I have tried so hard to do right."[3] He left behind his wife and four surviving children, daughters Esther and Marion and sons Richard Folsom and Francis Grover. He was remembered for honoring his principles no matter the political cost. As fellow New Yorker Theodore Roosevelt said upon his death, Cleveland "showed signal powers as an administrator, coupled with entire devotion to the country's good, and a courage that quailed before no hostility once he was convinced where his duty lay."[4]

Sources:

Graff, Henry F. *Grover Cleveland*. New York: Times Books, 2002.
"Grover Cleveland." *The Presidents: A Reference History*. New York: Charles Scribner's Sons, 1996.
Jeffers, H. Paul, *An Honest President: The Life and Presidencies of Grover Cleveland*. New York: Morrow, 2000.

Notes:

[1] Quoted in Graff, Henry F. *Grover Cleveland*. New York: Times Books, 2002, p. 52.
[2] Quoted in Graff, p. 95.
[3] Quoted in Jeffers, H. Paul, *An Honest President: The Life and Presidencies of Grover Cleveland*. New York: Morrow, 2000, p. 8.
[4] Quoted in Jeffers, p. 1.

Eugene V. Debs (1855-1926)
Founder of the American Railway Union and the Socialist Party of America

Eugene Victor Debs was born on November 5, 1855, in Terre Haute, Indiana. His parents, Jean Daniel and Marguerite (Bettrich) Debs, had come to America from Alsace, France, in 1849. They eventually opened a grocery store in Terre Haute and raised six children. Debs attended local schools until age fourteen, when he left to work for the Terre Haute & Indianapolis Railway. His dangerous job as a fireman worried his mother, so in 1874 he found work as a billing clerk in a grocery warehouse. Debs furthered his studies by attending business college at night, joining a debating society, and reading widely.

Debs became a founding member and secretary of the local lodge of the Brotherhood of Locomotive Firemen (BLF) in 1875. Three years later he became associate editor of the BLF's *Locomotive Firemen's Magazine,* working at night to fulfill his duties. Debs also became involved in Democratic politics, and in the fall of 1879 he was elected city clerk, a post he held for four years. From then on he devoted all his time to political and union activities. In 1880 he became national secretary-treasurer of the BLF and editor of the magazine, and in 1885 he was elected to the Indiana House of Representatives. That year he also married Katherine Metzel.

Becomes Influential Union Leader

Debs quickly grew frustrated in the Indiana Assembly. Time after time he introduced bills to reform corporate practices and increase worker rights, only to see them defeated or watered down by special interests. He left after one term and spent much of his time traveling the country, helping organize local chapters for the BLF and other unions. He hoped to increase cooperation between trades and thus avoid the infighting that undermined negotiations with management. Debs was generally conservative as a union leader, favoring negotiation and arbitration over strikes, which frequently degenerated into violence. He also urged political action to improve working conditions for all laborers.

The struggles between and within various trade groups convinced Debs of the need for an industry-wide union for both skilled and unskilled railroad workers. He resigned as BFL secretary-treasurer in 1892 and the following year helped found the American Railway Union (ARU), becoming its first president. The new union had immediate success in a conflict with the Great Northern Railway, which announced multiple wage cuts in 1894. After over-seeing an eighteen-day strike that unfolded without a hint of violence, Debs convinced a coalition of businessmen to call for arbitration. The ARU received most of its wage demands in the ensuing settlement. This success led to rapid growth, as the ARU reached 150,000 members in its first year.

When workers in the Pullman Palace Car Company organized a strike to protest wage cuts in May 1894, it asked the ARU for a sympathy boycott of Pullman cars. Although Debs counseled against a strike, fearing that such an action might well lead to violence, rank-and-file members enthusiastically joined the boycott and refused to move trains carrying Pullman cars. Debs supported the union as work stoppages halted trains around the country. The federal government responded to the crisis by sending in troops and charging ARU leaders, including Debs, with conspiracy to obstruct the mails. The prosecutions continued even after the strike and boycott failed.

Moves to Socialism

Prosecutors ended up dropping the conspiracy charges against Debs and other union leaders in the middle of the trial. "The jury had been packed to convict. When our evidence began to come in, their eyes fairly bulged with astonishment," Debs recalled. "The jurors realized that they had been steeped in prejudice and grossly deceived."[1] Nevertheless, the ARU leader served six months in prison for contempt of court. He spent much of this time reading about labor problems and Socialist theory, which advocated giving workers greater control and ownership of factories, machinery, and other means of production. Disillusioned by the defeat of Democratic and Populist Party presidential candidate William Jennings Bryan in 1896, Debs met with rem-nants of the ARU and established the Social Democratic Party. In 1901 it became the Socialist Party of America (SPA).

While differing Socialist factions struggled to shape the goals of the movement, Debs remained the country's most popular and visible Socialist. He was the party's overwhelming choice to run for president in both 1900 and 1904. In the first election he received fewer than 88,000 votes, but in the second he earned over 400,000 votes, or around 3 percent of the popular vote. Debs also helped found the Industrial Workers of the World union in 1905, but he soon split with the group over its confrontational tactics. In 1908 Debs ran for president again, and this time his presidential campaign garnered almost 421,000 votes. As Progressive reform causes gained popularity, Debs's fourth campaign for the White House in 1912 earned him over 900,000 votes, almost 6 percent of the popular vote.

In declining health after 1912, Debs alternated occasional lecture tours with periods of recuperation at home and at sanitariums. He refused the SPA's presidential nomination in 1916, running unsuccessfully for a seat in the U.S. House instead. He spoke out against U.S. involvement in World War I, and in 1918 he was convicted of sedition under the recently passed Espionage Act after he gave an antiwar speech in Canton, Ohio. Debs did not mount a defense against the charges. Instead, he declared that "if it is a crime under the American law, punishable by imprisonment, for being opposed to human bloodshed, I am perfectly willing to be clothed in the stripes of a convict and to end my days in a prison cell."[2] The Supreme Court upheld his conviction in 1919 and Debs began a ten-year sentence in federal prison. Despite being stripped of his citizenship, Debs again received the SPA's nomination for president in 1920. Even as a prisoner, Debs earned almost 920,000 votes, or 3 percent of the total votes cast that year.

Debs's health further deteriorated in prison, but he refused to accept a conditional release. "While there is a lower class, I am in it," he said. "While there is a criminal element, I am of it; while there is a soul in prison, I am not free."[3] President Warren G. Harding commuted the activist's sentence on Christmas Day, 1921. Debs spent the next few years writing on prison reform, labor, and Socialist issues. The movement had fractured irreparably by then, however, and he refused to support the American Communist Party. Debs died on October 20, 1926, at a Chicago-area sanitarium. He is remembered as a major figure in the development of labor unions and the movement toward progressive reform of American industry. His leadership inspired millions of Americans to believe in his dream of "the emancipation of the working class and the brotherhood of all mankind."[4]

Sources:

Debs, Eugene V. *Debs: His Life, Writings and Speeches*. Girard, KS: The Appeal to Reason, 1908.
Ginger, Ray. *The Bending Cross: A Biography of Eugene Victor Debs*. Chicago: Haymarket Press, 2007.

Karsner, David. *Debs: His Authorized Life and Letters.* New York: Boni & Liveright, 1919.

Salvatore, Nick. *Eugene V. Debs: Citizen and Socialist.* Urbana: University of Illinois Press, 1982.

Zinn, Howard. "Eugene V. Debs and the Idea of Socialism." *The Progressive,* January 1999.

Notes:

[1] Debs, Eugene V. *Debs: His Life, Writings and Speeches.* Girard, KS: The Appeal to Reason, 1908, p. 236.

[2] Quoted in Karsner, David. *Debs: His Authorized Life and Letters.* New York: Boni & Liveright, 1919, p. 48.

[3] Quoted in Ginger, Ray. *The Bending Cross: A Biography of Eugene Victor Debs.* Chicago: Haymarket Press, 2007, p. 374.

[4] Debs, Eugene V. "The Canton, Ohio, Antiwar Speech." *The Call,* June 16, 1918. Available online at http://www.marxists.org/archive/debs/works/1918/canton.htm.

Samuel Gompers (1850-1924)
Founder and President of the American Federation of Labor

Samuel Gompers was born on January 27, 1850, in a poor neighborhood in London, England. He was the eldest of nine children born to Solomon and Sarah (Rood) Gompers, who were both Dutch-Jewish immigrants. Gompers entered a Jewish free school at age six but had to leave four years later to work. After a brief stint as an apprentice shoemaker, Gompers took up his father's trade of cigarmaking.

The family sought better opportunities in America and arrived in New York in 1863. Gompers continued working as a cigarmaker, taking night classes at Cooper Union to further his education. Regular readings and discussions in the factory taught Gompers about politics, economics, and labor. He joined the local cigarmakers' union as a teen, and at age seventeen he married Sophia Julian. They had twelve children, six of whom survived to adulthood.

Unifying the Unions

Gompers's involvement in union activity intensified in the 1870s, in part because his strong debating skills made him a natural representative for employees in negotiations with employers. In conjunction with Adolph Strasser, he set about reforming the Cigarmakers International Union (CIU). They raised dues so that the CIU could offer benefits to sick, unemployed, or traveling workers, as well as death benefits to workers' families. They also gave control over strike activity to the union's central office.

In 1881 Gompers and Strasser met with several other trade union leaders to create the Federation of Organized Trades and Labor Unions. This group evolved into the American Federation of Labor (AFL) in 1886. Unlike the politically oriented Knights of Labor, the AFL was dedicated to purely economic goals. The AFL was structured much like the CIU, with high dues to support worker programs and central control of strike actions. Although

141

Gompers tried to convince member unions to include women and African Americans in the AFL, he was forced to accommodate the segregationist policies of local chapters in the South.

Gompers was elected president of the new organization. He remained in that position every year until his death except for 1895, when he was defeated by a Socialist-backed candidate. Gompers spent his "sabbatical" year organizing for the United Garment Workers' Union and returned to the AFL presidency in 1896. From then on, the AFL followed Gompers's course of slow, steady growth that focused on economic action through the voluntary membership of skilled workers. He did not seek political reforms because he believed that wealthy corporate interests had the power to influence the government in their favor. He opposed the Sherman Antitrust Act, for instance, because he foresaw its use against labor unions.

Fostering Cooperation

Gompers was a conservative leader who believed in working within the capitalist system to aid the working class. In 1901 he helped found the National Civic Federation, an alliance designed to promote cooperation between business, labor, and government. During his tenure as vice-president of the organization, he endured criticism from other union leaders and Socialists, who claimed that he was not truly dedicated to championing the rights of workers. Gompers believed, however, that unions could achieve more through cooperation with industry. He realized it was fruitless to fight the introduction of labor-saving machinery, and he even came to accept it—as long as union men operated the new machinery and helped set production standards. He retained the loyalty of rank-and-file members by traveling up to 25,000 miles every year to give speeches and testify at government hearings and labor conferences. This busy schedule, combined with his leadership of the AFL, made him the country's most visible labor leader.

During the Progressive Era, Gompers gradually acknowledged that unions should support political candidates who favored pro-labor policies. In 1912 and 1916 the AFL was crucial in electing Democrat Woodrow Wilson to the presidency. Like many unionists, Gompers initially favored U.S. neutrality during World War I, but he eventually came to accept involvement in the conflict as inevitable. He then threw his support behind U.S. war efforts, serving on the Council for National Defense and organizing a War Committee on

Labor. After the war ended, Wilson appointed Gompers to the International Commission on Labor Legislation at the Versailles Peace Conference, where the treaty ending the war was crafted.

Despite suffering from kidney disease and diabetes in his later years, Gompers remained active in AFL business. He attended the 1924 AFL conference in El Paso, Texas, then went to Mexico to meet with labor and political leaders. Gompers fell ill on his return home, though, and died December 13 in San Antonio, Texas. He was buried in Tarrytown, New York. At his last AFL conference, he noted that his life's goal had been "to leave a better labor movement in America and in the world than I found in it when I entered."[1]

Sources:

Gompers, Samuel. *Seventy Years of Life and Labor: An Autobiography.* Edited with an introduction by Nick Salvatore. Ithaca, NY: ILR Press, 1984.

Mandel, Bernard. *Samuel Gompers: A Biography.* Yellow Springs, OH: Antioch Press, 1963.

Yellowitz, Irwin. "Samuel Gompers: A Half-Century in Labor's Front Rank." *Monthly Labor Review,* July 1989.

Notes:

[1] Quoted in Mandel, Bernard. *Samuel Gompers: A Biography.* Yellow Springs, OH: Antioch Press, 1963, p. 527.

Jay Gould (1836-1892)
Gilded Age Financier and Railroad Owner

Jason "Jay" Gould was born on May 27, 1836, in Roxbury, a rural town in the Catskill Mountains of New York. He was the first son born to John Burr and Mary (More) Gould. After Jay's mother died in 1841, his five older sisters helped raise him. Gould did not want to take over the family dairy farm, so he taught himself the trade of surveying. By age seventeen he was producing and selling his own maps. He enrolled at the college-preparatory Albany Academy but left to focus on his business.

By age twenty, Gould had already published several maps and a local history book. He also did some surveying for Zadock Pratt, a local farmer and tannery owner. Pratt took Gould as a partner for a new tannery in Pennsylvania. Gould surveyed the site and oversaw construction of tanning facilities and the surrounding town, which he named Gouldsboro. The tannery began production in 1857. When the partners had a falling out the following year, Gould created a partnership with hide brokers in order to gain the financing needed to buy Pratt's share of the business.

Making a Mark on Wall Street

In 1860 Gould sold off his stake in the tannery and moved to New York. He spent his time in the city's financial capital on Wall Street and learned various tricks to earn money by buying and selling stock in corporations. In January 1863 he married Helen Day Miller, who was the daughter of a prominent businessman. Gould's new father-in-law helped finance some of Gould's early speculative investments. He came to specialize in buying small railroads, improving them, and then selling or consolidating them for profit.

By 1867 Gould was a partner in his own trading firm and controlled enough Erie Railway stock to be named to its board of directors. When Cornelius Vanderbilt tried to buy control of Erie in 1868, Gould and board members Jim Fisk and Daniel Drew fought back. By manipulating the railroad's stock, obtaining favorable court rulings, and making payments to New York legislators—as much as $600,000 that spring and summer—Gould won the so-called Erie War and was named Erie's president. Afterwards, Vanderbilt grudgingly told a reporter that Gould was "the smartest man in America."[1] Gould bought smaller branch lines to extend the Erie's reach and issued bonds to obtain funds to upgrade the company's worn-down facilities. Gould was ousted in 1872, however, after Erie's British investors objected to the line's continued weak financial performance.

Gould continued his Wall Street speculations throughout this period. He often used insider information (which was legal at that time) to turn a profit on stock trades. In 1869, he schemed to buy enough gold to be able to manipulate its price—an action known as "cornering the market." His plan involved paying money to President Ulysses S. Grant's brother-in-law in an effort to influence U.S. government policy on gold sales. Gould's efforts did not succeed—in fact, his attempt to corner the gold market resulted in a widespread financial panic—but the incident cemented his reputation as the "Mephistopheles [devil] of Wall Street."

Creates Railroad and Telegraph Empire

In 1874 Gould took advantage of an economic depression to buy enough low-priced shares to gain control of the Union Pacific (UP) Railroad. He also invested heavily in steamship companies that had been competing with the UP for freight transport business. Gould promptly increased steamship transport charges, which convinced many industries to use UP instead. Within a year, Gould had increased the railroad's earnings 27 percent. He rode the entire railway line twice a year, brainstorming improvements, cost savings, mergers, and expansions. By 1881 he controlled almost 16,000 miles of track—one-ninth of the country's total mileage. Although financial difficulties forced him from the UP's board in 1883, he retook control of the company in 1890.

Because telegraph lines were built alongside railroad tracks, Gould used his railroad empire to gain control of that industry as well. He founded American Union Telegraph in 1879 and used it and the UP's Atlantic & Pacific Telegraph to undercut rival Western Union's business and raid its stock. By 1881 he had merged the companies to create a telegraph monopoly with himself at the head, earning $30 million in the process. Gould used similar methods to dominate New York City's elevated railway business. He often used the pages of the *New York World* newspaper, which he owned from 1879 to 1883, to attack the management of competing companies and build support for his own business deals.

Gould did not indulge in the ostentatious displays of wealth that were common among his peers during the Gilded Age. He preferred to spend his free time quietly at home with his wife and six children. Gould contracted tuberculosis in 1888, but he continued managing his business empire despite his growing illness. He died at his New York City home on December 2, 1892. Although the press vilified him on his death as cold-hearted and ruthless, he made many generous donations to charity during his lifetime on an anonymous basis. He is remembered today for his tremendous impact on the worlds of business management and high finance. As one historian concluded, "by any reckoning Gould must be counted among the two or three most important figures in the development of the American industrial economy."[2]

Sources:

Klein, Maury. *The Life and Legend of Jay Gould.* Baltimore, MD: Johns Hopkins University Press, 1986.

Morris, Charles R. *The Tycoons: How Andrew Carnegie, John D. Rockefeller, Jay Gould, and J. P. Morgan Invented the American Supereconomy.* New York: Times Books, 2005.

Renehan, Edward J., Jr. *Dark Genius of Wall Street: The Misunderstood Life of Jay Gould, King of the Robber Barons.* New York: Basic Books, 2005.

Notes:

[1] Quoted in Renehan, Edward J., Jr. *Dark Genius of Wall Street: The Misunderstood Life of Jay Gould, King of the Robber Barons.* New York: Basic Books, 2005, p. 151.

[2] Quoted in Klein, Maury. *The Life and Legend of Jay Gould.* Baltimore, MD: Johns Hopkins University Press, 1986, p. 496.

Mary Elizabeth Lease (1853-1933)
Reformist Speaker and Politician

Mary Elizabeth Clyens Lease was born on September 11, 1853, in Ridgeway, Pennsylvania. Her parents, Joseph P. and Mary Elizabeth (Murray) Clyens, had immigrated to the United States from Ireland. Mary grew up on the family farm in Ceres, New York. She was only ten when her father and two older half-brothers left home to serve in the Union Army during the Civil War. All three men were killed, leaving the remaining five family members in poverty. Nevertheless, Mary managed to graduate with honors from St. Elizabeth's Academy in Allegany, New York, in 1868. She then returned home to support her family as a teacher.

Dissatisfied with the low pay given to female teachers in New York, she founded a short-lived union in an effort to negotiate better wages. When this campaign failed, Mary moved in 1870 to a higher-paying position at St. Anne's Academy, a parochial school in Osage Mission, Kansas. Three years later she married Charles L. Lease, a druggist's clerk. They soon moved to sparsely settled Kingman County, where they hoped to establish a successful homestead farm. After two poor harvests, however, the couple could not afford their mortgage and the farm was repossessed.

From Farm Wife to Political Activist

The Leases moved to Denison, Texas, where Charles took another clerk position and Mary had the first of the couple's six children (two died in infancy). Denison was a rough town with many saloons, and Lease soon became involved in the temperance movement. When she gave her first public speech in support of the prohibition of alcohol, she discovered that her deep, rich voice captivated listeners.

In 1883 the Leases returned to Kansas for another homesteading attempt, but again the farm failed within two years. The family moved to Wichita, where Lease worked as a laundress to help support the family and

147

also began to study law. After passing the bar in 1885 she became politically active, serving as president of the local chapter of the Knights of Labor and speaking out about farm failures, women's suffrage, and Irish nationalism. Her popular speeches were peppered with literary quotes, sarcastic wit, and stories about her experiences as a farm wife. Lease also joined a new reformist party, the Kansas Union Labor Party, and in 1887 she spoke at the state convention. The party nominated her for superintendent of public instruction of Sedgwick County in 1888. Although she lost, she ran such a spirited campaign that the new People's Party, also known as the Populists, decided to hire her as a lecturer.

Lease gave more than 160 speeches during the 1890 campaign, using her own experience to relate how Populist issues affected women and families. Although her speeches were popular with audiences, she often met with sexism in the media. Newspaper critics tried to dismiss her as an "old harpy" and a "miserable caricature of womanhood."[1] Lease particularly targeted Kansas senator John J. Ingalls, who said women had no place in politics. Due in part to her efforts, voters turned him out of office in 1890 in favor of a Populist candidate.

Lease continued lecturing on behalf of the Populist Party during the 1892 campaign. After participating in the 1892 convention that nominated James B. Weaver for president, she toured the West and South with the candidate. She stirred the party faithful with her support for farmers and working-class Americans in an economy dominated by wealthy industrialists. "The people are at bay; let the bloodhounds of money who have dogged us thus far beware!" she declared. "What you farmers need is to raise less corn and more hell!"[2]

Leaves Populism Behind

Although Weaver made an impressive showing for a third-party candidate, polling over one million votes, he finished third in the 1892 presidential race. Women nationwide lobbied the Kansas legislature to name Lease to the U.S. Senate, but Populists did not control enough votes to make it happen. Instead, the governor made Lease president of the State Board of Charities, which was the highest post ever held by a Kansas woman at the time. In 1896 the Populist Party chose to support Democratic candidate William Jennings Bryan for president. Lease opposed the party's decision to fuse with the Democrats, but she campaigned for Bryan anyway. After one New York rally, a reporter called her "the foremost woman politician of the times."[3]

After Bryan lost the election, Lease moved with three of her children to New York City, where she wrote for Joseph Pulitzer's *New York World* newspaper. In 1902 she divorced her husband, who had never been pleased with her political activities. She made a living giving speeches supporting women's suffrage, prohibition, socialism, and birth control. Some of her ideas were published in the 1895 book *The Problem of Civilization Solved.* She also served on the board of the Business Women's League of New York, wrote for the New York Press Bureau, helped edit an encyclopedia, and gave literary lectures for the New York Board of Education.

As the United States entered the Progressive Era, Lease supported various progressive candidates, including Eugene Debs, Theodore Roosevelt, and Woodrow Wilson. She retired from public life in the 1920s and spent her remaining city years giving free legal advice to the poor. In 1931 she bought a farm in Callicoon, New York, where she died on October 29, 1933.

Sources:

McLeRoy, Sherrie S. "Lease, Mary Elizabeth Clyens." *Handbook of Texas Online.* Texas State Historical
    Association. Available online at http://www.tshaonline.org/handbook/online/articles/fle97.
Stiller, Richard. *Queen of the Populists: The Story of Mary Elizabeth Lease.* New York: Thomas Y.
    Crowell, 1970.

Notes:

[1] Quoted in Stiller, Richard. *Queen of the Populists: The Story of Mary Elizabeth Lease.* New York:
    Thomas Y. Crowell, 1970, pp. 126-27.
[2] Quoted in Stiller, p. 120.
[3] Quoted in Stiller, p. 206.

J. P. Morgan (1837-1913)
Leading Banker and Financier of the Gilded Age

John Pierpont Morgan was born on April 17, 1837, in Hartford, Connecticut, the eldest child of Juliet (Pierpont) and Junius S. Morgan. Pierpont, as he was known, had a privileged upbringing. His grandfather, Joseph Morgan, founded the Aetna Insurance Company, while his father had banking interests in London and the United States. After graduating from Boston English High School, Morgan spent two years learning French in a Swiss school and two years learning German at the University of Göttingen. He began his banking career in New York in 1857, eventually becoming the American agent for his father's London firm.

Morgan married Amelia Sturges in 1861. When she died of tuberculosis four months after the wedding, Morgan threw himself into his work. During the Civil War he dabbled in arms dealing, gold speculation, and short-term financing, earning up to $50,000 in yearly profits. In 1865 he married Frances Tracy, who bore him three daughters and a son.

Growing His Business

To reduce Morgan's risk-taking tendencies, his banker father set him up in business with experienced partners, creating Dabney, Morgan & Co. in 1864 and Drexel, Morgan & Co. in 1871. Morgan soon became the driving force behind both companies. His first major success came when he convinced the U.S. Treasury to allow him to sell a share of an 1873 government bond issue. Before this time, only rival financier Jay Cooke's bank had been allowed to sell treasury bonds. When Cooke's firm went bankrupt later that year, setting off the Panic of 1873, Morgan's steady guidance kept his company solvent and left Drexel, Morgan as one of the premier banks selling federal bonds overseas.

Morgan's access to European markets led William H. Vanderbilt to choose him to arrange the sale of the giant New York Central Railroad in 1879. The banker spent much of the 1880s trying to protect his clients' railroad investments by eliminating overbuilding and destructive competition within the industry. When Morgan's attempts to secure a "gentlemen's agreement" to regulate rates and settle disputes ended in failure, he began a program of consolidation. He bought control of railroads, reorganized and refinanced them, and put his people on their boards to ensure stability. His last attempt at "morganization"—uniting the Great Northern and Northern Pacific railroads under the banner of the Northern Securities holding company—was overturned by the Supreme Court in 1904 as a violation of the Sherman Antitrust Act.

Morgan's father died in 1890, leaving him $12 million and control of his London office. After his partner Anthony Drexel died in 1893, Morgan reorganized the firms as J. P. Morgan & Co. in 1895 and consolidated his control over American finance. During this period he put together several other major trusts that dominated entire industries. He merged Thomas Edison's electric company into General Electric in 1892, for instance, and he created International Harvester from competing farm equipment companies in 1902. His greatest achievement was merging Federal Steel with Andrew Carnegie's steel company in 1901 to create U.S. Steel, the world's first billion-dollar company. Morgan had less luck with his 1902 transatlantic shipping concern International Mercantile Marine, which ended up in receivership.

The Nation's Banker

Morgan's ability to forge and finance huge business deals gave him tremendous power and influence over the U.S. economy. After the financial panic of 1893 dangerously depleted the U.S. Treasury's gold reserves, President Grover Cleveland turned to Morgan to help resolve the situation. Morgan's syndicate sold $65 million in treasury bonds to move gold into the U.S. Treasury. Morgan also guaranteed that the gold would stay in the United States, and by closely managing the deal he kept his word. While Morgan was later criticized for the profit he made—he never disclosed the total—his actions did help stabilize the economy.

Morgan rescued the U.S. financial markets again during a 1907 banking panic. He gathered several major financiers together to assess which banks needed help, set up a fund to collect money, and demanded pledges for assistance. By essentially serving as a central bank, Morgan ended the panic. In this instance, however, his power over the economy alarmed Congress. Its

1912 investigation into the so-called "money trust" revealed that Morgan's 11 partners held 72 directorships on the boards of 47 major corporations. These findings contributed to public support for the 1913 passage of the Federal Reserve Act, which created a central banking system for the United States.

In the 1900s Morgan spent less time on business and more time on outside interests. He built several yachts and became involved in yacht racing. He also served the Episcopal Church as a lay delegate to national conventions. His greatest passion, however, was collecting art and manuscripts, on which he spent nearly $60 million during his lifetime. He served as president of the Metropolitan Museum of Art and co-founded the American Museum of Natural History, giving generously to both. Other gifts included over $1.4 million to build a maternity hospital for New York City's poor.

In 1913 Morgan fell ill while vacationing in Egypt. His party returned to Rome, Italy, where the banker died on March 31. He left a $68 million fortune, not including his art and manuscript collections, which were opened to the public at the Morgan Library and Museum. Although critics often complained that Morgan wielded too much power, supporters claimed that his financial dealings had a higher motivation. "He saw himself as the guardian of investors' wealth. If the enterprise went bad, Morgan intervened," one writer observed. "The point was to ensure that his investors got repaid. Morgan felt bound by moral obligation."[1]

Sources:

Brands, H. W. "Upside-Down Bailout." *American History,* August 2010.
Samuelson, Robert J. "J. P. Morgan Rises Again." *Newsweek,* August 12, 2002.
Strouse, Jean. *Morgan: American Financier.* New York: Random House, 1998.

Notes:

[1] Samuelson, Robert J. "J. P. Morgan Rises Again." *Newsweek,* August 12, 2002, p. 43.

Terence V. Powderly (1849-1924)
Leader of the Knights of Labor

Terence Vincent Powderly was born on January 22, 1849, in Carbondale, Pennsylvania. He was the eleventh of twelve children born to Terence and Margery (Walsh) Powderly, who were Irish-Catholic immigrants. He left school at thirteen to work for the Delaware & Hudson Railroad, working his way up from switchman to brakeman. At age seventeen he became an apprentice in the machinists' trade, and after three years he began working in the Delaware, Lackawanna, & Western Railroad's locomotive shop in Scranton, Pennsylvania. In 1872 he married Hannah Dever, a miner's daughter.

Powderly became intensely interested in the labor movement after seeing victims of the 1869 Avondale mine disaster, in which 110 miners were trapped and killed by a fire. "Working shoulder to shoulder in organization, not of one calling but all callings, appeared to me to be the only hope,"[1] he recalled. He joined the machinists' union in 1871 and three years later became an organizer for the International Brotherhood, a coalition of trade unions. In 1874 he was initiated into the Noble and Holy Order of the Knights of Labor, a secret organization for workers. He was elected master workman (chairman) of the Scranton local association and became an officer in the district association. Between anti-union blacklists and depression-related shutdowns, Powderly had trouble keeping machinist jobs. He became a full-time labor organizer and joined the Greenback-Labor Party, winning election as mayor of Scranton in 1878.

Becomes Leader of the Knights

Powderly served three two-year terms as Scranton's mayor. At the same time, he increased his work on behalf of the Knights of Labor. He helped write its constitution in 1878, and one year later he was elected Grand Master Workman of the Knights. Powderly immediately urged the group to abandon the secrecy and rituals that had led many churches to forbid their congregations to join. He also advocated an inclusive membership policy, opening the group to unskilled workers, African Americans, and women.

Powderly served as head of the Knights (his position was renamed General Master Workman in 1883) for the next fourteen years. His work included writing, lecturing, organizing new assemblies, and lobbying Congress to pass labor-related legislation. Powderly believed strikes should be used as a last resort, and then only with careful preparation. He did not have the authority to prevent local assemblies from striking, however, and was often called in to negotiate after the fact. One successful negotiation came in 1885 against Jay Gould's southwestern railroad interests. Workers clamored to join the Knights following the highly publicized victory, and membership jumped from around 100,000 in 1885 to over 700,000 in 1886.

This rapid growth ended up hurting the union, however. Many new assemblies formed with little knowledge of the Order's goals. Some workers joined and immediately went on strike without even consulting Powderly and the rest of the union's national leadership. The Knights did not have the funds to support all these strikes, and many of them failed. The 1886 Haymarket incident in Chicago, in which a bomb thrown by activists attending a labor rally killed several policemen, further tarnished the labor movement. As membership declined, internal strife grew within the Knights. In 1893 Powderly stepped down as General Master Workman when an executive board was elected that opposed his policies. By this time there were scarcely 75,000 members left in the union.

Moves into Public Service

Blacklisted from the machinists' trade because of his union activities, Powderly turned to studying law. He passed the bar in 1894 and built a practice serving mostly poor clients. He also spoke on the popular Chautauqua lecture circuit and published a history of his involvement with the labor movement, *Thirty Years of Labor, 1859 to 1889*. Powderly returned to the Republican Party he had favored as a youth to campaign for William McKinley, who as a congressman had frequently consulted the labor leader. After McKinley won the presidency in 1896, he rewarded Powderly with a post as commissioner-general of immigration. Powderly made enemies by investigating corruption among immigration officers at Ellis Island, many of whom were fired. In 1902 Powderly was accused of putting political pressure on

New York's commissioner of immigration, and President Theodore Roosevelt asked him to resign.

After learning that the accusations against Powderly had been false, Roosevelt sent him to Europe in 1906 to study the reasons why people emigrated. Upon Powderly's return, Roosevelt named him chief of the Division of Information in the Bureau of Immigration. Powderly served in that position from 1907 to 1921, then joined the Labor Department's Commission of Conciliation. He died at his Washington, D.C., home on June 24, 1924. He was survived by his second wife and former secretary, Emma Fickenscher. Calling Powderly "the first American working-class hero of national stature," one biographer noted that "in the eyes of many followers, Powderly epitomized the ideals of the movement he led—courage, manliness, honor, and unswerving dedication to the principle of solidarity."[2]

Sources:

Krynicki, Adam. "Powderly, Terence Vincent." *Pennsylvania Center for the Book,* Penn State University Libraries, Fall 2005. Available online at http://pabook.libraries.psu.edu/palitmap/bios/Powderly _Terence.html.

Phelan, Craig. *Grand Master Workman: Terence Powderly and the Knights of Labor.* Westport, CT: Greenwood Press, 2000.

Powderly, Terence V. *The Path I Trod: The Autobiography of Terence V. Powderly.* Edited by Harry J. Carman, Henry David, and Paul N. Guthrie. New York: AMS Press, 1968.

Notes:

[1] Powderly, Terence V. *The Path I Trod: The Autobiography of Terence V. Powderly.* New York: AMS Press, 1968.

[2] Phelan, Craig. *Grand Master Workman: Terence Powderly and the Knights of Labor.* Westport, CT: Greenwood Press, 2000, pp. 1-2.

John D. Rockefeller (1839-1937)
Founder of the Standard Oil Company

John Davison Rockefeller Sr. was born on July 8, 1839, in Richford, New York. He was the eldest son of William Rockefeller, a traveling salesman, and Eliza Davison Rockefeller. Although his father tended to be unreliable, his mother instilled in him a sense of morality, frugality, and hard work. The family relocated frequently before eventually settling near Cleveland in 1853. In 1855 Rockefeller graduated from high school and took a job as a bookkeeper for a local brokerage house. In 1859 he and a partner launched their own small trading company.

Rockefeller was a cautious, exacting accountant who tracked every penny his business spent. The first year his company grossed $450,000 and profits soared. In 1863 the partners expanded into oil refining. Two years later Rockefeller left his original business to focus on oil, which he sensed was key to America's industrial growth. He did so well the first year that he built a second refinery and sent his brother William to open a sales office in New York. Rockefeller's success allowed him to marry teacher Laura Spelman, the daughter of a Cleveland businessman, in 1864. They eventually had four children.

Dominating the Oil Industry

Rockefeller's refining interests grew as his reputation gained him new investors and partners. In 1870 he brought them all together into the Standard Oil Company, a sprawling corporation that owned warehouses, tank cars, and loading facilities as well as refineries. In an effort to offset fluctuating prices, Rockefeller agreed to join Pennsylvania Railroad president Thomas A. Scott's South Improvement Company (SIC), a pool of railroads and refiners that guaranteed traffic for the railroads and provided rebates for the refiners. "We had to do it in self-defense," the oilman explained. "The oil business was in confusion and daily growing worse. Someone had to make a stand."[1] The pooling scheme was uncovered in 1872, and the SIC was disbanded after a public outcry. Still, Rockefeller's involvement in the SIC gave him leverage to buy out all but four of his competitors in Cleveland, which was the center of America's oil refining industry at that time.

Standard Oil continued expanding as Rockefeller bought out refineries in New York, Pittsburgh, Philadelphia, and Baltimore. He convinced many competitors to join with the promise of greater profits. If they refused, however, he resorted to coercion or simply forced them out of business. By 1879 Standard Oil controlled 90 percent of U.S. oil refining. The company's ruthless business practices and monopoly power over the industry made Rockefeller a target of the investigative journalists known as muckrakers. An 1881 *Atlantic* exposé by Henry Demarest Lloyd revealed that the company routinely used rebates, predatory pricing, and political bribery to maintain its spot atop the oil industry. Nevertheless, Rockefeller and Standard Oil avoided serious penalties through careful legal maneuvering and application of pressure on lawmakers.

To circumvent Ohio laws against businesses owning out-of-state companies, for example, Standard Oil formed the first trust in 1882. Under this innovative form of business organization, a central board of trustees held controlling interest in the stock of various related corporations. After moving the Standard Oil offices to New York City the following year, Rockefeller tightened his grip on the industry: he obtained crude oil fields, developed methods to process previously unusable sulfur-based crude, built his own pipelines, created his own marketing and distribution system, and expanded sales overseas. Standard's control of all facets of industry operations became a model for other corporations. By the close of the 1890s, other commodities ranging from coal to beef were similarly controlled by giant corporate trusts.

Moves into Philanthropy

Rockefeller retired from active involvement in Standard Oil in 1897, although he retained the title of president. He was rarely seen in public during this period, in part because a bout with a medical condition called alopecia caused him to lose all of his hair. After retirement Rockefeller focused on philanthropy. With a net worth that peaked at $900 million in 1913, he was earning money as fast as he could donate it. Since his earliest days, Rockefeller had donated a tenth of his earnings to charity, mostly to the Baptist Church. He also supported various educational institutions, including Spelman Seminary (later College) for African American women, the University of Chicago (he gave $80 million over his lifetime), the Rockefeller Institute of

Medical Research (RIMR, now Rockefeller University), and the General Education Board. The latter two institutions supported the development of a meningitis vaccine in 1908 and an anti-hookworm campaign that started in the South and subsequently spread overseas.

Despite his charitable works, bad publicity continued to follow Rockefeller. Muckraker Ida Tarbell's 1904 *History of the Standard Oil Company* revealed that the company still indulged in illegal railroad rebates and other unlawful business practices. In 1906 the U.S. government charged that Standard was operating in clear violation of federal antitrust laws. In 1911 the Supreme Court found Standard Oil to be a monopoly that illegally restrained trade under the Sherman Antitrust Act and ordered the breakup of the company. Ironically, the dismantling of Standard Oil into smaller companies sent share prices soaring, increasing Rockefeller's wealth. He funneled more of it into the Rockefeller Foundation, which was chartered in 1913 to "promote the well-being of mankind throughout the world."[2] His lifetime gifts to the foundation totaled almost $245 million. By the 1920s it was the world's largest grant-making foundation and a leading sponsor of American medical research, education, and public health. As the Rockefeller Foundation approached the end of its first century, it had given away more than $14 billion (in 2011 dollars) worldwide. As Winston Churchill said shortly before Rockefeller's death: "When history passes its final verdict on John D. Rockefeller, it may well be that his endowment of research will be recognized as a milestone in the progress of the race."[3]

Rockefeller died at his Ormond, Florida, home on May 23, 1937. He was remembered as one of the most successful and innovative—as well as the most ruthless—business owners in American history. "Rockefeller was a unique hybrid in American business," one biographer noted: "both the instinctive, first-generation entrepreneur who founds a company and the second-generation manager who extends and develops it."[4]

Sources:

Chernow, Ron. *Titan: The Life of John D. Rockefeller, Sr.* New York: Random House, 1998.
Kelley, Timothy. "Breaking Up an Oil Giant." *New York Times Upfront*, April 10, 2000.
Nevins, Allan. *John D. Rockefeller: The Heroic Age of American Enterprise.* 2 volumes. New York: Charles Scribner's Sons, 1940.

Notes:

[1] Quoted in Chernow, Ron. *Titan: The Life of John D. Rockefeller, Sr.* New York: Random House, 1998, p. 148.

2   Quoted in Chernow, p. 564.
3   Quoted in Chernow, p. 479.
4   Chernow, p. 227.

PRIMARY SOURCES

Mark Twain Describes the Get-Rich-Quick Mining Culture

Although writer Mark Twain (born Samuel Clemens, 1835-1910) is best remembered today for classic novels like The Adventures of Huckleberry Finn, *he first gained acclaim as a travel writer and humorist. His 1872 book* Roughing It *is a semi-autobiographical account of the years he spent in the American West during and after the Civil War. In the excerpt below, Twain describes the "feverish" pursuit of wealth in the mining town of Virginia City, Nevada, where discovery of the huge Comstock Lode of silver ore created a boom town. Twain worked as a newspaper writer in the town, which gave him opportunities to cash in as well. Twain went on to satirize the American "get-rich-quick" mentality in his first novel,* The Gilded Age, *written with Charles Dudley Warner.*

Reporting was lucrative, and every man in the town was lavish with his money and his "feet." The city and all the great mountain side were riddled with mining shafts. There were more mines than miners. True, not ten of these mines were yielding rock worth hauling to a mill, but everybody said, "Wait till the shaft gets down where the ledge comes in solid, and then you will see!" So nobody was discouraged. These were nearly all "wild cat" mines, and wholly worthless, but nobody believed it then. The "Ophir," the "Gould & Curry," the "Mexican," and other great mines on the Comstock lead in Virginia and Gold Hill were turning out huge piles of rich rock every day, and every man believed that his little wild cat claim was as good as any on the "main lead" and would infallibly be worth a thousand dollars a foot when he "got down where it came in solid." Poor fellow, he was blessedly blind to the fact that he never would see that day. So the thousand wild cat shafts burrowed deeper and deeper into the earth day by day, and all men were beside themselves with hope and happiness. How they labored, prophesied, exulted! Surely nothing like it was ever seen before since the world began. Every one of these wild cat mines—not mines, but holes in the ground over imaginary mines—was incorporated and had handsomely engraved "stock" and the stock was salable, too. It was bought and sold with a feverish avidity in the boards every day. You could go up on the mountain side, scratch around and find a ledge (there was no lack of them), put up a "notice" with a grandiloquent name in it, start a shaft, get your stock printed, and with nothing whatever to prove that your mine was worth a straw, you could put your stock on the market and sell out for hundreds and even thousands of dollars. To make money, and make it fast, was as easy as it was to eat your dinner.

Every man owned "feet" in fifty different wild cat mines and considered his fortune made. Think of a city with not one solitary poor man in it! One would suppose that when month after month went by and still not a wild cat mine (by wild cat I mean, in general terms, any claim not located on the mother vein, i.e., the "Comstock") yielded a ton of rock worth crushing, the people would begin to wonder if they were not putting too much faith in their prospective riches; but there was not a thought of such a thing. They burrowed away, bought and sold, and were happy.

New claims were taken up daily, and it was the friendly custom to run straight to the newspaper offices, give the reporter forty or fifty "feet," and get them to go and examine the mine and publish a notice of it. They did not care a fig what you said about the property so you said something. Consequently we generally said a word or two to the effect that the "indications" were good, or that the ledge was "six feet wide," or that the rock "resembled the Comstock" (and so it did—but as a general thing the resemblance was not startling enough to knock you down). If the rock was moderately promising, we followed the custom of the country, used strong adjectives and frothed at the mouth as if a very marvel in silver discoveries had transpired. If the mine was a "developed" one, and had no pay ore to show (and of course it hadn't), we praised the tunnel; said it was one of the most infatuating tunnels in the land; driveled and driveled about the tunnel till we ran entirely out of ecstasies—but never said a word about the rock. We would squander half a column of adulation on a shaft, or a new wire rope, or a dressed pine windlass, or a fascinating force pump, and close with a burst of admiration of the "gentlemanly and efficient Superintendent" of the mine—but never utter a whisper about the rock. And those people were always pleased, always satisfied. Occasionally we patched up and varnished our reputation for discrimination and stern, undeviating accuracy, by giving some old abandoned claim a blast that ought to have made its dry bones rattle—and then somebody would seize it and sell it on the fleeting notoriety thus conferred upon it.

There was nothing in the shape of a mining claim that was not salable. We received presents of "feet" every day. If we needed a hundred dollars or so, we sold some; if not, we hoarded it away, satisfied that it would ultimately be worth a thousand dollars a foot. I had a trunk about half full of "stock." When a claim made a stir in the market and went up to a high figure, I searched through my pile to see if I had any of its stock—and generally found it.

The prices rose and fell constantly; but still a fall disturbed us little, because a thousand dollars a foot was our figure, and so we were content to let it fluctuate as much as it pleased till it reached it. My pile of stock was not all given to me by people who wished their claims "noticed." At least half of it was given me by persons who had no thought of such a thing, and looked for nothing more than a simple verbal "thank you;" and you were not even obliged by law to furnish that. If you are coming up the street with a couple of baskets of apples in your hands, and you meet a friend, you naturally invite him to take a few. That describes the condition of things in Virginia in the "flush times." Every man had his pockets full of stock, and it was the actual custom of the country to part with small quantities of it to friends without the asking.

Very often it was a good idea to close the transaction instantly, when a man offered a stock present to a friend, for the offer was only good and binding at that moment, and if the price went to a high figure shortly afterward the procrastination was a thing to be regretted. Mr. [William M.] Stewart (Senator, now, from Nevada) one day told me he would give me twenty feet of "Justis" stock if I would walk over to his office. It was worth five or ten dollars a foot. I asked him to make the offer good for next day, as I was just going to dinner. He said he would not be in town; so I risked it and took my dinner instead of the stock. Within the week the price went up to seventy dollars and afterward to a hundred and fifty, but nothing could make that man yield. I suppose he sold that stock of mine and placed the guilty proceeds in his own pocket.…

These are actual facts, and I could make the list a long one and still confine myself strictly to the truth. Many a time friends gave us as much as twenty-five feet of stock that was selling at twenty-five dollars a foot, and they thought no more of it than they would of offering a guest a cigar. These were "flush times" indeed! I thought they were going to last always, but somehow I never was much of a prophet.

Source:

Twain, Mark. *Roughing It.* Hartford, CT: American Publishing Co., 1872, pp. 231-34.

The Glitter of Gilded Age High Society

The economic free-for-all of the Gilded Age created hundreds of new millionaires, many of whom aspired to reach the peak of American high society in New York City. Society events were occasions for these millionaires to display their newfound wealth in hopes of impressing the country's most prominent "old-money" families. In 1883 Mrs. William K. Vanderbilt, wife of the grandson of railroad tycoon Cornelius, planned the most extravagant ball New York society had ever seen. The costume ball was held in the Vanderbilts' brand-new, $3 million mansion on Fifth Avenue, with the festivities costing at least $250,000. The ball was the talk of the town and produced ostentatious displays of wealth, as this article from the New York Times *makes clear.*

The Vanderbilt ball has agitated New York society more than any social event that has occurred here in many years. Since the announcement that it would take place, which was made about a week before the beginning of Lent, scarcely anything else has been talked about. It has been on every tongue and a fixed idea in every head. It has disturbed the sleep and occupied the waking hours of social butterflies, both male and female, for over six weeks, and has even, perhaps, interfered to some extent with that rigid observance of Lenten devotions which the Church exacts. Amid the rush and excitement of business men have found their minds haunted by uncontrollable thoughts as to whether they should appear as Robert Le Diable, Cardinal Richelieu, Otho the barbarian, or the Count of Monte Cristo, while the ladies have been driven to the verge of distraction in the effort to settle the comparative advantages of ancient, medieval, and modern costumes, or the relative superiority, from an effective point of view, of such characters and symbolic representations as a Princess de Croy, Rachel, Marie Stuart, Marie Antoinette, the Four Seasons, Night, Morning, Innocence, and the Electric Light. Invitations have, of course, been in great demand, and in all about 1,200 were issued.

As Lent drew to a close, everybody having decided what he or she was going to wear, the attention of the select few turned from the question of costumes to the settlement of the details of the ball itself and the practicing of the parts assigned to them in the various fancy quadrilles [dances] decided on to make the most conspicuous features of the entertainment. The drilling in these quadrilles have been going on assiduously in Mrs. William Astor's and other private residences for more than a week, while prospective guests not so favored as to be able to witness these preliminary entertainments have had to content themselves with recounting such items of information as could be extracted from the initiated....

Inside, long before the ball commenced, the house was in a blaze of light, which shown upon profuse decorations of flowers. These, which were by Klunder, were at once novel and imposing. They were confined chiefly to the second floor, although throughout the hall and parlors on the first floor, were distributed vases and gilded baskets filled with natural roses of extraordinary size, such as the dark crimson Jacqueminot, the deep pink Glorie de Paris, the pale pink Baroness de Rothschild and Adolphe de Rothschild, the King of Morocco; the Dutchess of Kent and the new and beautiful Marie Louise Vassey. But a delightful surprise greeted the guests upon the second floor, as they reached the head of the grand stairway. Grouped around the clustered columns which ornament either side of the stately hall were tall palms overtopping a dense mass of ferns and ornamental grasses, while suspended between the capitals of the columns were strings of variegated Japanese lanterns. Entered through this hall is the gymnasium, a spacious apartment, where supper was served on numerous small tables. But it had not the appearance of an apartment last night; it was like a garden in a tropical forest. The walls were nowhere to be seen, but in their places an impenetrable thicket of fern above fern and palm above palm, while from the branches of the palms hung a profusion of lovely orchids, displaying a rich variety of color and an almost endless variation of fantastic forms. In the centre of the room was a gigantic palm, upon whose umbrageous [shade-providing] head rested a thick cluster of that beautiful Cuban vine, vougen villa, which trailed from the dome in the centre of the ceiling. To make the resemblance to a garden more complete, two beautiful fountains played in opposite corners of the apartment. The doors of the apartment, thrown back against the walls, were completely covered with roses and lilies of the valley....

The guests on arriving found themselves in a grand hall about 65 feet long, 16 feet in height, and 20 feet in width. Under foot was a floor of polished and luminous Echallion stone, and above them a ceiling richly paneled in oak. Over a high wainscoting of Caen stone, richly carved, are antique Italian tapestries, beautifully worked by hand. Out of this hall to the right rises the grand stairway, which is not only the finest piece of work of its kind in this country, but one of the finest in the world. The stairway occupies a space 30 feet square, the whole structure of the stairway being of the finest Caen stone, carved with wonderful delicacy and vigor. It climbs by ample easy stages to a height of 50 feet, ending in a pendentive dome. Another stairway, also in Caen stone, leading from the second to the third story, is seen through a rampant arch, with an effect which recalls the unique and glorious stairway of the Chateau of Chambord. In the gymnasium, on the third floor, a most beautiful apartment, 50 feet in length by 35 in width, the members of the six organized quadrilles of the evening gradually assembled before 11 o'clock....

Winding through the motley crowd of princes, monks, cavaliers, highlanders, queens, kings, dairy-maids, bull-fighters, knights, brigands, and nobles, the procession passed down the grand stairway and through the ball into a noble room on the front of the house in the style of Francois Premier, 25 feet in width by 40 in length, wainscoted richly and heavily in carved French walnut and hung in dark red plush. Vast carved cabinets and an immense, deep fire-place give an air of antique grandeur to this room, from which the procession passed into a bright and charming *salon* of the style of Louis XV, 30 feet in width by 35 in length, wainscoted in oak and enriched with carved work and gilding. The whole wainscoting of this beautiful apartment was brought from a château in France. On the walls hang three French Gobelin tapestries a century old, but in the brilliance and freshness of their coloring seemingly the work of yesterday, and over the chimney-piece hangs a superb portrait of Mrs. Vanderbilt by Madrázo, full of spirit, character, and grace. The ceiling, exquisitely painted by Paul Bandry, represents the marriage of Cupid and Psyche, and the furniture is of the bright and gracious style of that age of airy arrogance and perfumed coquetry [flirtation] which preceded the tragedy of the great Revolution. Thence the procession swept on into the grand dining-hall, converted last night into a ball-room, and the dancing began....

In the "Hobby-horse Quadrille," with which the ball began, the horses were the most wonderful things of the kind ever constructed in this country. The workmen were two months in finishing them. They were of life-size, covered with genuine hides; had large, bright eyes, and flowing manes and tails, but were light enough to be easily and comfortably attached to the waists of the wearers, whose feet were concealed by richly embroidered hangings. False legs were represented on the outside of the blankets, so the deception was quite perfect. The costumes were red hunting-coats, white satin vests, yellow satin knee-breeches, white satin stockings. The ladies wore red hunting-coats and white satin skirts, elegantly embroidered. All the dresses were in the style of Louis XIV....

Mrs. Vanderbilt's irreproachable taste was seen to perfection in her costume as a Venetian Princess taken from a picture by Cabanel. The underskirt was of white and yellow brocade, shading from the deepest orange to the lightest canary, only the highlights being white. The figures of flowers and leaves were outlined in gold, white, and iridescent beads; light-blue satin train embroidered magnificently in gold and lined with Roman red. Almost the entire length of the train was caught up at one side, forming a large puff. The waist was of blue satin covered with gold embroidery—the dress was cut square in the neck, and the flowing sleeves were of transparent gold tissue. She wore a Venetian cap, covered with magnificent jewels, the most noticeable of these being a superb peacock in many colored gems.

Source:

"All Society in Costume; Mrs. W. K. Vanderbilt's Great Fancy Dress Ball." *New York Times,* March 27, 1883, p. 1.

Exposing the Price-Fixing Schemes of the "Lords of Industry"

A forerunner of the investigative journalists known as the muckrakers, Henry Demarest Lloyd (1847-1903) was a progressive reformer who served as the editorial writer for the Chicago Tribune. *He also wrote antitrust and pro-labor pieces for various periodicals. In 1884 he published "Lords of Industry," an investigation of the growing tendency of businesses to enter into pools and trusts. In this excerpt, Lloyd quotes economist Adam Smith on price-fixing conspiracies, then argues that uncontrolled business combinations run counter to American ideals of freedom and equality by stifling competition in favor of higher prices.*

Adam Smith said in 1776: "People of the same trade hardly meet together even for merriment and diversion but the conversation ends in a conspiracy against the public or in some contrivance to raise prices." The expansive ferment [activity] of the New Industry, coming with the new science, the new land, and the new liberties of our era, broke up these "conspiracies," and for a century we have heard nothing of them; but the race to overrun is being succeeded by the struggle to divide, and combinations are reappearing on all sides. This any one may see from the reports of the proceedings of the conventions and meetings of innumerable associations of manufacturers and dealers and even producers, which are being held almost constantly. They all do something to raise prices, or hold them up, and they wind up with banquets for which we pay....

Combinations, more or less successful, have been made by ice-men of New York, fish dealers of Boston, Western millers, copper miners, manufacturers of sewer pipe, lamps, pottery, glass, hoop-iron, shot, rivets, sugar, candy, starch, preserved fruits, glucose, vapor stoves, chairs, lime, rubber, screws, chains, harvesting machinery, pins, salt, type, brass tubing, hardware, silk, and wire cloth, to say nothing of the railroad, labor telegraph, and telephone pools with which we are so familiar. On the third of April the largest and most influential meeting of cotton manufacturers ever held in the South came together at Augusta to take measures to cure the devastating plague of too much cotton cloth. A plan was unanimously adopted for the organization of a Southern Manufacturers' Association for the same general purposes as the New England Manufacturers' Association. The convention recommended its members to imitate the action of the Almighty in making a short crop of cotton by making a short crop of yarns and cloth, and referred to a committee the preparation of plans for a more thorough pool.

Such are some of the pools into which our industry is eddying [moving]. They come and go, but more come than go, and those that stay grow. All are "voluntary," of course, but if the milk farmer of Orange County, the iron moulder of Troy, the lumber dealer of San Francisco, the Lackawanna Railroad, or any other individual or corporate producer, show any backwardness about accepting the invitation to join "the pool" they are whipped in with all the competitive weapons at command, from assault and battery to boycotting and conspiracy. The private wars that are ravaging our world of trade give small men their choice between extermination and vassalage [submission]. Combine or die! The little coke burner of Connellsville works or stops work, the coal dealer of Chicago raises his prices or lowers them, the type-setter takes up his stick or lays it down, as the master of the pool directs. Competitors swear themselves on the Bible into accomplices, and free and equal citizens abandon their business privacy to pool commissioners vested with absolute power, but subject to human frailties. Commerce is learning the delights of universal suffrage, and in scores of trades supply and demand are adjusted by a majority vote. In a society which has the wherewithal to cover, fatten, and cheer every one, Lords of Industry are acquiring the power to pool the profits of scarcity and to decree famine. They cannot stop the brook that runs the mill, but they can chain the wheel; they cannot hide the coal mine, but they can close the shaft three days every week. To keep up gold-digging rates of dividends, they declare war against plenty. On all that keeps him alive the workman must pay them their prices, while they lock him out of the mill in which alone his labor can be made to fetch the price of life. Only society can compel a social use of its resources; the man is for himself.

On the theory of "too much of everything," our industries, from railroads to working men, are being organized to prevent milk, nails, lumber, freights, labor, soothing syrup, and all these other things from becoming too cheap. The majority have never yet been able to buy enough of anything. The minority have too much of everything to sell. Seeds of social trouble germinate fast in such conditions. Society is letting these combinations become institutions without compelling them to adjust their charges to the cost of production, which used to be the universal rule of price. Our laws and commissions to regulate the railroads are but toddling steps in a path in which we need to walk like men. The change from competition to combination is nothing less than one of those revolutions which march through history with giant strides. It is not likely that this revolution will go backward. Nothing goes backward in this country except reform. When [engineer George] Stephenson said of railroads that where combination was possible competition was impossible, he was unconsciously declaring the law of all industry.

Man, the only animal which forgets, has already in a century or two forgotten that the freedom, the independence of his group, of the state, and even of the family, which he has enjoyed for a brief interval, have been unknown in most of the history of our race, and in all the history of most races. The livery companies of London, with their gloomy guildhalls, their wealth, their gluttony and wine-bibbing, their wretched Irish estates, exist to-day, vain reminders to us of a time when the entire industry of Europe was regimented into organizations, voluntary at first, afterward adopted by the law, which did what our pools of railroads, laborers, manufacturers, and others are trying to do. Not only prices but manners were pooled.... This system existed for centuries. It is so unlike our own that the contemplation of it may well shake us out of our conceit that the transitions, displacements, changes, upheavals, struggles, exterminations—from Indians to sewing women—of the last two hundred and fifty years were the normal condition of the race.

Those were not exceptional times. Our day of free competition and free contract has been the exceptional era in history. Explorer, pioneer, protestant, reformer, captain of industry, could not move in the harness of the guild brother, the vassal, the monk, and were allowed to throw away mediaeval uniforms. But now "the individual withers; the world is more and more." Society having let the individual overrun the new worlds to be conquered, is re-establishing its lines of communication with him. Literary theorists still repeat the cant of individualism in law, politics, and morals; but the world of affairs is gladly accepting in lieu of the liberty of each to do as he will with his own, all it can get of the liberty given by laws that let no one do as he might with his own. The dream of the French Revolution, that man was good enough to be emancipated from the bonds of association and government by the simple proclamation of Liberty, Fraternity, and Equality, was but the frenzied expression of what was called Freedom of Self-interest in a quieter but not less bloody revolution, if the mortality of the factories, the mines, and the tenements be charged to its account. A rope cannot be made of sand; a society cannot be made of competitive units.

We have given competition its own way, and have found that we are not good enough or wise enough to be trusted with this power of ruining ourselves in the attempt to ruin others. Free competition could be let run only in a community where every one had learned to say and act "I am the state." We have had an era of material inventions. We now need a renaissance of moral inventions, contrivances to tap the vast currents of moral magnetism flowing uncaught over the face of society. Morals and values rise and fall together. If our combinations have no morals, they can have no values. If the tendency to combination is irresistible, control of it is imperative. Monopoly and anti-monopoly, odious as these words have become to the literary ear, represent the two great tendencies of our time: monopoly, the tendency to combination; anti-monopoly, the demand for social control of it. As the man is bent towards business or patriotism, he will negotiate combinations or agitate for laws to regulate them. The first is capitalistic, the second is social. The first, industrial; the second, moral. The first promotes wealth; the second, citizenship. These combinations are not to be waved away as fresh pictures of folly or total depravity. There is something in them deeper than that....

Our young men can no longer go West; they must go up or down. Not new land, but new virtue must be the outlet for the future. Our halt at the shores of the Pacific is a much more serious affair than that which brought our ancestors to a pause before the barriers of the Atlantic, and compelled them to practise living together for a few hundred years. We cannot hereafter, as in the past, recover freedom by going to the prairies; we must find it in the society of the good. In the presence of great combinations in all departments of life, the moralist and patriot have work to do of a significance never before approached during the itinerant phases of our civilization. It may be that the coming age of combination will issue in a nobler and fuller liberty for the individual than has yet been seen, but that consummation will be possible, not in a day of competitive trade, but in one of competitive morals.

Source:

Lloyd, Henry Demarest. *Lords of Industry.* New York: Knickerbocker Press, 1910, pp. 116-147. Originally published in *North American Review,* June 1884.

An Anarchist Protests His Haymarket Death Sentence

In May 1886, labor activists and anarchists (people who sought a free society with no govern-ment) organized a peaceful protest against police brutality in Chicago's Haymarket Square. The rally was uneventful until an unknown agitator threw a bomb, killing several policemen and set-ting off panicky exchanges of gunfire. The people of Chicago were appalled by the so-called Haymarket Riot and demanded that those responsible be brought to justice. Authorities quickly responded by charging eight anarchist leaders with murder, including publisher August Spies and his typesetter, Adolph Fischer. Although Fischer had attended the rally, he had already left by the time the bomb was thrown. Nevertheless, he was convicted of murder and hanged in November 1887. His last words were "Hurray for Anarchy! This is the happiest moment of my life!" The document below is Fischer's final statement avowing his innocence but acknowledging his willingness to die for his principles.

YOUR HONOR: You ask me why sentence of death should not be passed upon me. I will not talk much. I will only say that I protest against my being sentenced to death, because I have committed no crime. I was tried here in this room for murder, and I was convicted of Anarchy. I protest against being sentenced to death, because I have not been found guilty of murder. But, however, if I am to die on account of being an Anarchist, on account of my love for liberty, fraternity and equality, then I will not remon-strate. If death is the penalty for our love of the freedom of the human race, then I say openly I have forfeited my life; but a murderer I am not.

Although being one of the parties who arranged the Haymarket meeting, I had no more to do with the throwing of that bomb, I had no more connec-tion with it than State's Attorney Grinnell had, perhaps. I do not deny that I was present at the Haymarket meeting but that meeting … was not called for the purpose of committing violence and crime. No; but the meeting was called for the purpose of protesting against the outrages and crimes commit-ted by the police on the day previous, out at McCormick's. The State's wit-ness, Waller, and others have testified here, and I only need to repeat it, that we had a meeting on Monday night, and in this meeting—the affair at McCormick's taking place just a few hours previous—took action and called a mass-meeting for the purpose of protesting against the brutal outrages of the police. Waller was chairman of this meeting, and he himself made the motion to hold the meeting at the Haymarket. It was he also who appointed me as a committee to have handbills printed and to provide for speakers; that I did, and nothing else. The next day I went to Wehrer & Klein, and had 25,000 handbills printed, and I invited Spies to speak at the Haymarket meeting. In the original of the "copy" I had the line "Workingmen, appear armed!" and I had my reason too for putting those words in, because I didn't want the workingmen to be shot down in that meeting as on other occasions. But as those circulars were printed, or as a few of them were printed and brought over to me at the Arbeiter-Zeitung office, my comrade Spies saw one of them. I had invited him to speak before that. He showed me the circular, and said: "Well, Fischer, if those circulars are distributed, I won't speak." I admitted it would be better to take the objectionable words out, and Mr. Spies spoke. And that is all I had to do with that meeting. Well, I went to the Haymarket about 8:15 o'clock, and stayed there until Parsons interrupted Fielden's speech. Parsons stepped up to the stand, and said that it looked like it was going to rain, and that the assembly had better adjourn to Zepf's Hall. At that moment a friend of mine who testified on the witness stand, went with me to Zepf's Hall, and we sat down at a table and had a glass of beer. At the moment I was going to sit down, my friend Parsons came in with some other persons, and after I was sitting there about five minutes the explosion occurred. I had no idea that anything of the kind would happen, because, as the State's witnesses testified, themselves, there was no agreement to defend ourselves that night. It was only a meeting called to protest.

Now, as I said before, this verdict, which was rendered by the jury in this room, is not directed against murder, but against Anarchy. I feel that I am sentenced, or that I will be sentenced, to death because of being an Anarchist, and not because I am a murderer. I have never been a murderer. I have never yet committed a crime in my life; but I know a certain man who is on the way to becoming a murderer, an assassin, and that man is Grinnell—the State's Attorney Grinnell—because he brought men on the witness stand who he knew would swear falsely; and I publicly denounce Mr. Grinnell as being a murderer and an assassin if I should be executed. But if the ruling class thinks that by hanging us, hanging a few Anarchists, they can crush out Anarchy, they will be badly mistaken, because the Anarchist loves his principles more than his life.

An Anarchist is always ready to die for his principles; but in this case I have been charged with murder, and I am not a murderer. You will find it impossible to kill a principle, although you may take the life of men who confess these principles. The more the believers in just causes are persecuted, the

175

quicker will their ideas be realized. For instance, in rendering such an unjust and barbarous verdict, the twelve "honorable men" in the jury-box have done more for the furtherance of Anarchism than the convicted could have accomplished in a generation. This verdict is a death-blow against free speech, free press, and free thought in this country, and the people will be conscious of it, too. This is all I care to say.

Source:

Fischer, Adolph. "Speech of Adolph Fischer." In *The Accused, the Accusers: The Famous Speeches of the Eight Chicago Anarchists in Court When Asked if They Had Anything to Say Why Sentence Should Not Be Passed upon Them. On October 7th, 8th and 9th, 1886, Chicago, Illinois.* Chicago: Socialistic Publishing Society, 1886, pp. 36-38. Available online at Chicago Historical Society, Haymarket Affair Digital Collection, http://www.chicagohistory.org/hadc/books/b01/B01S004.htm.

Andrew Carnegie's "Gospel of Wealth"

By the time Andrew Carnegie sold his steel company in 1901, his share was worth $225 million, making him one of the richest men in America. Even before he retired to devote his remaining years to philanthropy, Carnegie had made it a practice to donate much of his personal fortune to worthy causes. In 1889 he presented his philosophy of giving in an essay entitled "The Gospel of Wealth." In the excerpt below, Carnegie argues that the concentration of wealth in the hands of a few is a natural outgrowth of the industrial age. He rejects the idea that the United States should attempt to balance the distribution of wealth by abandoning capitalism in favor of a radically different system. Instead, Carnegie suggests that successful men serve as "trustees" for the poor by giving their riches to causes that benefit society. Carnegie donated over $350 million during his lifetime, and his example inspired many of his fellow corporate titans—most notably Standard Oil's John D. Rockefeller—to follow suit.

The problem of our age is the proper administration of wealth, so that the ties of brotherhood may still bind together the rich and poor in harmonious relationship. The conditions of human life have not only been changed, but revolutionized, within the past few hundred years. In former days there was little difference between the dwelling, dress, food, and environment of the chief and those of his retainers. The Indians are to-day where civilized man then was. When visiting the Sioux, I was led to the wigwam of the chief. It was just like the others in external appearance, and even within the difference was trifling between it and those of the poorest of his braves. The contrast between the palace of the millionaire and the cottage of the laborer with us to-day measures the change which has come with civilization.

This change, however, is not to be deplored, but welcomed as highly beneficial. It is well, nay, essential for the progress of the race, that the houses of some should be homes for all that is highest and best in literature and the arts, and for all the refinements of civilization, rather than that none should be so. Much better this great irregularity than universal squalor. Without wealth there can be no Mæcenas [patrons of the arts]. The "good old times" were not good old times. Neither master nor servant was as well situated then as to-day. A relapse to old conditions would be disastrous to both—not the least so to him who serves— and would sweep away civilization with it. But whether the change be for good or ill, it is upon us, beyond our power to alter, and, therefore, to be accepted and made the best of. It is a waste of time to criticise the inevitable.

It is easy to see how the change has come. One illustration will serve for almost every phase of the cause. In the manufacture of products we have the whole story. It applies to all combinations of human industry, as stimulated and enlarged by the inventions of this scientific age. Formerly, articles were manufactured at the domestic hearth or in small shops which formed part of the household. The master and his apprentices worked side by side, the latter living with the master, and therefore subject to the same conditions. When these apprentices rose to be masters, there was little or no change in their mode of life, and they, in turn, educated in the same routine succeeding apprentices. There was, substantially, social equality, and even political equality, for those engaged in industrial pursuits had then little or no political voice in the State.

But the inevitable result of such a mode of manufacture was crude articles at high prices. To-day the world obtains commodities of excellent quality at prices which even the generation preceding this would have deemed incredible. In the commercial world similar causes have produced similar results, and the race is benefited thereby. The poor enjoy what the rich could not before afford. What were the luxuries have become the necessaries of life. The laborer has now more comforts than the landlord had a few generations ago. The farmer has more luxuries than the landlord had, and is more richly clad and better housed. The landlord has books and pictures rarer, and appointments more artistic, than the King could then obtain.

The price we pay for this salutary change is, no doubt, great. We assemble thousands of operatives in the factory, in the mine, and in the counting-house, of whom the employer can know little or nothing, and to whom the employer is little better than a myth. All intercourse between them is at an end. Rigid castes are formed, and, as usual, mutual ignorance breeds mutual distrust. Each caste is without sympathy for the other, and ready to credit anything disparaging in regard to it. Under the law of competition, the employer of thousands is forced into the strictest economies, among which the rates paid to labor figure prominently, and often there is friction between the employer and the employed, between capital and labor, between rich and poor. Human society loses homogeneity.

The price which society pays for the law of competition, like the price it pays for cheap comforts and luxuries, is also great; but the advantage of this law are also greater still, for it is to this law that we owe our wonderful material development, which brings improved conditions in its train. But, whether the law be benign or not, we must say of it, as we say of the change in the conditions of men to which we have referred: It is here; we cannot evade it; no substitutes for it have been found; and while the law may be sometimes hard for the individual, it is best for the race, because it insures the survival of the fittest in every department. We accept and welcome therefore, as conditions to which we must accommodate ourselves, great inequality of environment, the concentration of business, industrial and commercial, in the hands of a few, and the law of competition between these, as being not only beneficial, but essential for the future progress of the race. Having accepted these, it follows that there must be great scope for the exercise of special ability in the merchant and in the manufacturer who has to conduct affairs upon a great scale.... Such men become interested in firms or corporations using millions; and estimating only simple interest to be made upon the capital invested, it is inevitable that their income must exceed their expenditures, and that they must accumulate wealth. Nor is there any middle ground which such men can occupy, because the great manufacturing or commercial concern which does not earn at least interest upon its capital soon becomes bankrupt. It must either go forward or fall behind: to stand still is impossible. It is a condition essential for its successful operation that it should be thus far profitable, and even that, in addition to interest on capital, it should make profit. It is a law, as certain as any of the others named, that men possessed of this peculiar talent for affair, under the free play of economic forces, must, of necessity, soon be in receipt of more revenue than can be judiciously expended upon themselves; and this law is as beneficial for the race as the others....

We start, then, with a condition of affairs under which the best interests of the race are promoted, but which inevitably gives wealth to the few. Thus far, accepting conditions as they exist, the situation can be surveyed and pronounced good. The question then arises,—and, if the foregoing be correct, it is the only question with which we have to deal,—What is the proper mode of administering wealth after the laws upon which civilization is founded have thrown it into the hands of the few? And it is of this great question that I believe I offer the true solution. It will be understood that fortunes are here spoken of, not moderate sums saved by many years of effort, the returns on which are required for the comfortable maintenance and education of families. This is not wealth, but only competence which it should be the aim of all to acquire.

There are but three modes in which surplus wealth can be disposed of. It can all be left to the families of the decedents; or it can be bequeathed for public purposes; or, finally, it can be administered during their lives by its possessors. Under the first and second modes most of the wealth of the world that has reached the few has hitherto been applied. Let us in turn consider each of these modes. The first is the most injudicious. ... Why should men leave great fortunes to their children? If this is done from affection, is it not misguided affection? Observation teaches that, generally speaking, it is not well for the children that they should be so burdened. Neither is it well for the state. Beyond providing for the wife and daughters moderate sources of income, and very moderate allowances indeed, if any, for the sons, men may well hesitate, for it is no longer questionable that great sums bequeathed oftener work more for the injury than for the good of the recipients. Wise men will soon conclude that, for the best interests of the members of their families and of the state, such bequests are an improper use of their means....

As to the second mode, that of leaving wealth at death for public uses, it may be said that this is only a means for the disposal of wealth, provided a man is content to wait until he is dead before it becomes of much good in the world. Knowledge of the results of legacies bequeathed is not calculated to inspire the brightest hopes of much posthumous good being accomplished. The cases are not few in which the real object sought by the testator is not attained, nor are they few in which his real wishes are thwarted. In many cases the bequests are so used as to become only monuments of his folly. It is well to remember that it requires the exercise of not less ability than that which acquired the wealth to use it so as to be really beneficial to the community. Besides this, it may fairly be said that no man is to be extolled for doing what he cannot help doing, nor is he to be thanked by the community to which he only leaves wealth at death. Men who leave vast sums in this way may fairly be thought men who would not have left it at all, had they been able to take it with them. The memories of such cannot be held in grateful remembrance, for there is no grace in their gifts. It is not to be wondered at that such bequests seem so generally to lack the blessing.

The growing disposition to tax more and more heavily large estates left at death is a cheering indication of the growth of a salutary change in public opinion....

This policy would work powerfully to induce the rich man to attend to the administration of wealth during his life, which is the end that society should always have in view, as being that by far most fruitful for the people. Nor need it be feared that this policy would sap the root of enterprise and render men less anxious to accumulate, for to the class whose ambition it is to leave great fortunes and be talked about after their death, it will attract even more attention, and, indeed, be a somewhat nobler ambition to have enormous sums paid over to the state from their fortunes.

There remains, then, only one mode of using great fortunes; but in this we have the true antidote for the temporary unequal distribution of wealth, the reconciliation of the rich and the poor—a reign of harmony—another ideal, differing, indeed, from that of the Communist in requiring only the further evolution of existing conditions, not the total overthrow of our civilization. It is founded upon the present most intense individualism, and the race is projected to put it in practice by degree whenever it pleases. Under its sway we shall have an ideal state, in which the surplus wealth of the few will become, in the best sense the property of the many, because administered for the common good, and this wealth, passing through the hands of the few, can be made a much more potent force for the elevation of our race than if it had been distributed in small sums to the people themselves. Even the poorest can be made to see this, and to agree that great sums gathered by some of their fellow-citizens and spent for public purposes, from which the masses reap the principal benefit, are more valuable to them than if scattered among them through the course of many years in trifling amounts....

This, then, is held to be the duty of the man of Wealth: First, to set an example of modest, unostentatious living, shunning display or extravagance; to provide moderately for the legitimate wants of those dependent upon him; and after doing so to consider all surplus revenues which come to him simply as trust funds, which he is called upon to administer, and strictly bound as a matter of duty to administer in the manner which, in his judgment, is best calculated to produce the most beneficial results for the community—the man of wealth thus becoming the mere agent and trustee for his poorer brethren, bringing to their service his superior wisdom, experience and ability to administer, doing for them better than they would or could do for themselves....

These who would administer wisely must, indeed, be wise, for one of the serious obstacles to the improvement of our race is indiscriminate charity. It were better for mankind that the millions of the rich were thrown in to the sea than so spent as to encourage the slothful, the drunken, the unworthy. Of every thousand dollars spent in so called charity to-day, it is probable that $950 is unwisely spent; so spent, indeed as to produce the very evils which it proposes to mitigate or cure....

In bestowing charity, the main consideration should be to help those who will help themselves; to provide part of the means by which those who desire to improve may do so; to give those who desire to use the aids by which they may rise; to assist, but rarely or never to do all. Neither the individual nor the race is improved by alms-giving. Those worthy of assistance, except in rare cases, seldom require assistance…. He is the only true reformer who is as careful and as anxious not to aid the unworthy as he is to aid the worthy, and, perhaps, even more so, for in alms-giving more injury is probably done by rewarding vice than by relieving virtue.

The rich man is thus almost restricted to following the examples of Peter Cooper, Enoch Pratt of Baltimore, Mr. Pratt of Brooklyn, Senator Stanford, and others, who know that the best means of benefiting the community is to place within its reach the ladders upon which the aspiring can rise—parks, and means of recreation, by which men are helped in body and mind; works of art, certain to give pleasure and improve the public taste, and public institutions of various kinds, which will improve the general condition of the people;—in this manner returning their surplus wealth to the mass of their fellows in the forms best calculated to do them lasting good.

Thus is the problem of Rich and Poor to be solved. The laws of accumulation will be left free; the laws of distribution free. Individualism will continue, but the millionaire will be but a trustee for the poor; intrusted for a season with a great part of the increased wealth of the community, but administering it for the community far better than it could or would have done for itself. The best minds will thus have reached a stage in the development of the race in which it is clearly seen that there is no mode of disposing of surplus wealth creditable to thoughtful and earnest men into whose hands it flows save by using it year by year for the general good. This day already dawns. But a little while, and although, without incurring the pity of their fellows, men may die sharers in great business enterprises from which their capital cannot be or has not been withdrawn, and is left chiefly at death for public uses, yet the man who dies leaving behind many millions of available wealth, which was his to administer during life, will pass away "unwept, unhonored, and unsung," no matter to what uses he leaves the dross which he cannot take with him. Of such as these the public verdict will then be: "The man who dies thus rich dies disgraced."

Such, in my opinion, is the true Gospel concerning Wealth, obedience to which is destined some day to solve the problem of the Rich and the Poor, and to bring "Peace on earth, among men Good-Will."

Source:

Carnegie, Andrew. "The Gospel of Wealth." *North American Review,* June 1889.

"The Problem of the Children" in New York City

While the movers and shakers of Gilded Age society were staging extravagant balls in New York City, thousands of workers and immigrants were enduring unspeakable living conditions in nearby tenement buildings. Photojournalist Jacob Riis, another pioneering muckraker, documented the city's overcrowding, lack of sanitation, and general squalor in his 1890 book How the Other Half Lives. *In this excerpt from the chapter "The Problem of the Children," Riis relates the various hazards facing America's youngest citizens inside its greatest city.*

I counted the other day the little ones, up to ten years or so, in a Bayard Street tenement that for a yard has a triangular space in the centre with sides fourteen or fifteen feet long, just room enough for a row of ill-smelling closets at the base of the triangle and a hydrant at the apex. There was about as much light in this "yard" as in the average cellar. I gave up my self-imposed task in despair when I had counted one hundred and twenty-eight in forty families. Thirteen I had missed, or not found in. Applying the average for the forty to the whole fifty-three [apartments in the building], the house contained one hundred and seventy children. It is not the only time I have had to give up such census work. I have in mind an alley—an inlet rather to a row of rear tenements—that is either two or four feet wide according as the wall of the crazy old building that gives on it bulges out or in. I tried to count the children that swarmed there, but could not. Sometimes I have doubted that anybody knows just how many there are about. Bodies of drowned children turn up in the rivers right along in summer whom no one seems to know anything about. When last spring some workmen, while moving a pile of lumber on a North River pier, found under the last plank the body of a little lad crushed to death, no one had missed a boy, though his parents afterward turned up. The truant officer assuredly does not know, though he spends his life trying to find out, somewhat illogically, perhaps, since the department that employs him admits that thousands of poor children are crowded out of the schools year by year for want of room. There was a big tenement in the Sixth Ward, now happily appropriated by the beneficent spirit of business that blots out so many foul spots in New York—it figured not long ago in the official reports as "an out-and-out hogpen"—that had a record of one hundred and two arrests in four years among its four hundred and seventy-eight tenants, fifty-seven of them for drunken and disorderly conduct. I do not know how many children there were in it, but the inspector reported that he found only seven in the whole house who owned that they went to school. The rest gathered all the instruction they received running for beer for their elders. Some of them claimed the "flat" as their home as a mere matter of form. They slept in the streets at night. The official came upon a little party of four drinking beer out of the cover of a milk-can in the hallway. They were of the seven good boys and proved their claim to the title by offering him some.

The old question, what to do with the boy, assumes a new and serious phase in the tenements. Under the best conditions found there, it is not easily answered. In nine cases out of ten he would make an excellent mechanic, if trained early to work at a trade, for he is neither dull nor slow, but the short-sighted despotism of the trades unions has practically closed that avenue to him. Trade-schools, however excellent, cannot supply the opportunity thus denied him, and at the outset the boy stands condemned by his own to low and ill-paid drudgery, held down by the hand that of all should labor to raise him. Home, the greatest factor of all in the training of the young, means nothing to him but a pigeon-hole in a coop along with so many other human animals. Its influence is scarcely of the elevating kind, if it have any. The very games at which he takes a hand in the street become polluting in its atmosphere. With no steady hand to guide him, the boy takes naturally to idle ways. Caught in the street by the truant officer, or by the agents of the Children's Societies, peddling, perhaps, or begging, to help out the family resources, he runs the risk of being sent to a reformatory, where contact with vicious boys older than himself soon develop the latent possibilities for evil that lie hidden in him. The city has no Truant Home in which to keep him, and all efforts of the children's friends to enforce school attendance are paralyzed by this want. The risk of the reformatory is too great. What is done in the end is to let him take chances—with the chances all against him. The result is the rough young savage, familiar from the street. Rough as he is, if any one doubt that this child of common clay have in him the instinct of beauty, of love for the ideal of which his life has no embodiment, let him put the matter to the test. Let him take into a tenement block a handful of flowers from the fields and watch the brightened faces, the sudden abandonment of play and fight that go ever hand in hand where there is no elbow-room, the wild entreaty for "posies," the eager love with which the little messengers of peace are shielded, once possessed; then let him change his mind. I have seen an armful of daisies keep the peace of a block better than a policeman and his club, seen instincts awaken under their gentle appeal, whose very existence the soil in which they grew made seem a mockery. I have not forgotten the deputation of ragamuffins from a Mulberry Street alley that knocked at my office door one morning on a mysterious expedition for flowers, not for themselves, but for "a lady," and having obtained what they wanted, trooped off to bestow them, a ragged and dirty little band, with a solemnity that was quite unusual. It was not until an old man called the next day to thank me for the flowers that I found out they had decked the bier of a pauper, in the dark rear room where she lay waiting in her pine-board coffin for the city's hearse. Yet, as I knew, that dismal alley with its bare brick walls, between which no sun ever rose or set, was the world of those children. It filled their young lives. Probably not one of them had ever been out of the sight of it. They were too dirty, too ragged, and too generally disreputable, too well hidden in their slum besides, to come into line with the Fresh Air summer boarders.

Source:

Riis, Jacob A. *How the Other Half Lives: Studies among the Tenements of New York.* New York: Charles Scribner's Sons, 1890, pp. 179-182.

The Sherman Antitrust Act

In 1890 Congress passed a law intended to limit the power of the huge corporations that held monopoly control over several industries in the United States. The Sherman Antitrust Act— named for its principal author, Ohio senator John Sherman—prohibited combinations, conspiracies, or other actions "in restraint of trade or commerce." By using such inexact phrasing, and by leaving enforcement of the law in the hands of the courts, Congress undermined the effectiveness of the Sherman Act. Not only would it fail to prevent illegal business monopolies and pooling arrangements over the next decade, it would be most often used to prevent labor actions such as strikes and boycotts. The full text of the act is reprinted below.

An act to protect trade and commerce against unlawful restraints and monopolies.

Be it enacted by the Senate and House of Representatives of the United States of America in Congress assembled,

Sec. 1. Every contract, combination in the form of trust or other-wise, or conspiracy, in restraint of trade or commerce among the several States, or with foreign nations, is hereby declared to be illegal. Every person who shall make any such contract or engage in any such combination or conspiracy, shall be deemed guilty of a misdemeanor, and, on conviction thereof, shall be punished by fine not exceeding five thousand dollars, or by imprisonment not exceeding one year, or by both said punishments, at the discretion of the court.

Sec. 2. Every person who shall monopolize, or attempt to monopolize, or combine or conspire with any other person or persons, to monopolize any part of the trade or commerce among the several States, or with foreign nations, shall be deemed guilty of a misdemeanor, and, on conviction thereof; shall be punished by fine not exceeding five thousand dollars, or by imprisonment not exceeding one year, or by both said punishments, in the discretion of the court.

Sec. 3. Every contract, combination in form of trust or otherwise, or conspiracy, in restraint of trade or commerce in any Territory of the United States or of the District of Columbia, or in restraint of trade or commerce between any such Territory and another, or between any such Territory or Territories and any State or States or the District of Columbia, or with foreign nations, or between the District of Columbia and any State or States or foreign nations, is hereby declared illegal. Every person who shall make any such contract or engage in any such combination or conspiracy, shall be deemed guilty of a misdemeanor, and, on conviction thereof, shall be punished by fine not exceeding five thousand dollars, or by imprisonment not exceeding one year, or by both said punishments, in the discretion of the court.

Sec. 4. The several circuit courts of the United States are hereby invested with jurisdiction to prevent and restrain violations of this act; and it shall be the duty of the several district attorneys of the United States, in their respective districts, under the direction of the Attorney-General, to institute proceedings in equity to prevent and restrain such violations. Such proceedings may be by way of petition setting forth the case and praying that such violation shall be enjoined or otherwise prohibited. When the parties complained of shall have been duly notified of such petition the court shall proceed, as soon as may be, to the hearing and determination of the case; and pending such petition and before final decree, the court may at any time make such temporary restraining order or prohibition as shall be deemed just in the premises.

Sec. 5. Whenever it shall appear to the court before which any proceeding under section four of this act may be pending, that the ends of justice require that other parties should be brought before the court, the court may cause them to be summoned, whether they reside in the district in which the court is held or not; and subpoenas to that end may be served in any district by the marshal thereof.

Sec. 6. Any property owned under any contract or by any combination, or pursuant to any conspiracy (and being the subject thereof) mentioned in section one of this act, and being in the course of transportation from one State to another, or to a foreign country, shall be forfeited to the United States, and may be seized and condemned by like proceedings as those provided by law for the forfeiture, seizure, and condemnation of property imported into the United States contrary to law.

Sec. 7. Any person who shall be injured in his business or property by any other person or corporation by reason of anything forbidden or declared to be unlawful by this act, may sue therefor in any circuit court of the United States in the district in which the defendant resides or is found, without respect to the amount in controversy, and shall recover three fold the damages by him sustained, and the costs of suit, including a reasonable attorney's fee.

Sec. 8. That the word "person," or "persons," wherever used in this act shall be deemed to include corporations and associations existing under or authorized by the laws of either the United States, the laws of any of the Territories, the laws of any State, or the laws of any foreign country.

Approved, July 2, 1890.

Source:

National Archives and Records Administration. "Our Documents: Transcript of Sherman Antitrust Act (1890)." Available online at http://ourdocuments.gov/doc.php?flash=true&doc=51&page=transcript.

The Populists Articulate Their Principles

The People's Party, also known as the Populists, grew out of the Farmers' Alliances of the 1880s. Its main goal was to protect "producers"—including farmers and factory workers—against the economic power and political influence of wealthy capitalists. In 1892, two years after electing its first U.S. senators and congressmen, the party held its first presidential nominating convention. The Preamble to the Populist Platform, written by former Minnesota congressman Ignatius Donnelly, is excerpted below. It explains the party's case against the current capitalist-dominated system and calls for the return of political and economic power to average citizens.

The conditions which surround us best justify our co-operation; we meet in the midst of a nation brought to the verge of moral, political, and material ruin. Corruption dominates the ballot-box, the Legislatures, the Congress, and touches even the ermine of the bench. The people are demoralized; most of the States have been compelled to isolate the voters at the polling places to prevent universal intimidation and bribery. The newspapers are largely subsidized or muzzled, public opinion silenced, business prostrated, homes covered with mortgages, labor impoverished, and the land concentrating in the hands of capitalists. The urban workmen are denied the right to organize for self-protection; imported pauperized labor beats down their wages, a hireling standing army, unrecognized by our laws, is established to shoot them down, and they are rapidly degenerating into European conditions. The fruits of the toil of millions are boldly stolen to build up colossal fortunes for a few, unprecedented in the history of mankind; and the possessors of these, in turn despise the Republic and endanger liberty. From the same prolific womb of governmental injustice we breed the two great classes—tramps and millionaires.

The national power to create money is appropriated to enrich bondholders; a vast public debt payable in legal tender currency has been funded into gold-bearing bonds, thereby adding millions to the burdens of the people.

Silver, which has been accepted as coin since the dawn of history, has been demonetized to add to the purchasing power of gold by decreasing the value of all forms of property as well as human labor, and the supply of currency is purposely abridged to fatten usurers [people who lend money at unreasonably high rates of interest], bankrupt enterprise, and enslave industry. A vast conspiracy against mankind has been organized on two continents, and it is rapidly taking possession of the world. If not met and overthrown at once, it forebodes terrible social convulsions, the destruction of civilization, or the establishment of an absolute despotism [a system of government in which the leader holds complete power].

We have witnessed for more than a quarter of a century the struggles of the two great political parties for power and plunder, while grievous wrongs have been inflicted upon the suffering people. We charge that the controlling influence dominating both these parties have permitted the existing dreadful conditions to develop without serious effort to prevent or restrain them. Neither do they now promise us any substantial reform. They have agreed together to ignore, in the coming campaign, every issue but one. They propose to drown the outcries of a plundered people with the uproar of a sham battle over the tariff, so that capitalists, corporations, national banks, rings, trusts, watered stock, the demonetization of silver and the oppressions of the usurers may all be lost sight of. They propose to sacrifice our homes, lives, and children on the altar of mammon [material wealth]; to destroy the multitude in order to secure corruption funds from the millionaires.

Assembled on the anniversary of the birthday of the nation, and filled with the spirit of the grand general and chief who established our independence, we seek to restore the government of the Republic to the hands of "the plain people," with which class it originated. We assert our purposes to be identical with the purposes of the National Constitution, to form a more perfect union and establish justice, insure domestic tranquillity, provide for the common defense, promote the general welfare, and secure the blessings of liberty for ourselves and our posterity.

We declare that this Republic can only endure as a free government while built upon the love of the whole people for each other and for the nation; that it cannot be pinned together by bayonets; that the civil war is over and that every passion and resentment which grew out of it must die with it, and that we must be in fact, as we are in name, one united brotherhood of free men.

Our country finds itself confronted by conditions for which there is no precedent in the history of the world; our annual agricultural productions amount to billions of dollars in value, which must, within a few weeks or months be exchanged for billions of dollars' worth of commodities consumed in their production; the existing currency supply is wholly inadequate to make this exchange; the results are falling prices, the formation of combines and rings, the impoverishment of the producing class. We pledge ourselves that, if given power, we will labor to correct these evils by wise and reasonable legislation, in accordance with the terms of our platform.

We believe that the power of government—in other words, of the people—should be expanded (as in the ease of the postal service) as rapidly and as far as the good sense of an intelligent people and the teachings of experience shall justify, to the end that oppression, injustice and poverty, shall eventually cease in the land.

While our sympathies as a party of reform are naturally upon the side of every proposition which will tend to make men intelligent, virtuous and temperate, we nevertheless regard these questions, important as they are, as secondary to the great issues now pressing for solution, and upon which not only our individual prosperity, but the very existence of free institutions depend; and we ask all men to first help us to determine whether we are to have a republic to administer, before we differ as to the conditions upon which it is to be administered, believing that the forces of reform this day organized will never cease to move forward, until every wrong is remedied, and equal rights and equal privileges securely established for all the men and women of this country.

Source:

Donnelly, Ignatius. "Preamble to the Populist Party Platform," July 4, 1892. From Populist Party Platform of 1892. John T. Woolley and Gerhard Peters, *The American Presidency Project* [online]. Santa Barbara, CA. Available online at http://www.presidency.ucsb.edu/ws/index.php?pid=29616.

William Jennings Bryan's "Cross of Gold" Speech

On July 9, 1896, former Nebraska congressman William Jennings Bryan made his famous "Cross of Gold" speech at the Democratic Convention in Chicago. At the time, the delegates were engaged in a heated debate about whether the party should continue to support the gold standard for U.S. currency, or whether it should adopt a free-silver plank in its official platform. Bryan emerged as a strong advocate for silver, arguing that the gold standard favored wealthy bankers and industrialists, while silver benefited "the struggling masses who produce the wealth and pay the taxes." On the strength of this speech, which is excerpted below, Bryan won the Democratic nomination for president, making him the youngest candidate (at thirty-six) ever nominated. Although Bryan lost the 1896 presidential election, his leadership helped shift the Democratic Party toward a more activist brand of politics.

Never before in the history of this country has there been witnessed such a contest as that through which we have passed. Never before in the history of American politics has a great issue been fought out as this issue has been by the voters themselves....

When you come before us and tell us that we shall disturb your business interests, we reply that you have disturbed our business interests by your action. We say to you that you have made too limited in its application the definition of a businessman. The man who is employed for wages is as much a businessman as his employer. The attorney in a country town is as much a businessman as the corporation counsel in a great metropolis. The merchant at the crossroads store is as much a businessman as the merchant of New York. The farmer who goes forth in the morning and toils all day, begins in the spring and toils all summer, and by the application of brain and muscle to the natural resources of this country creates wealth, is as much a business-man as the man who goes upon the Board of Trade and bets upon the price of grain. The miners who go 1,000 feet into the earth or climb 2,000 feet upon the cliffs and bring forth from their hiding places the precious metals to be poured in the channels of trade are as much businessmen as the few financial magnates who in a backroom corner the money of the world.

We come to speak for this broader class of businessmen. Ah, my friends, we say not one word against those who live upon the Atlantic Coast; but those hardy pioneers who braved all the dangers of the wilderness, who have made the desert to blossom as the rose—those pioneers away out there, rearing their children near to nature's heart, where they can mingle their voices with the voices of the birds—out there where they have erected schoolhouses for the education of their children and churches where they praise their Creator, and the cemeteries where sleep the ashes of their dead—are as deserving of the consideration of this party as any people in this country.

It is for these that we speak. We do not come as aggressors. Our war is not a war of conquest. We are fighting in the defense of our homes, our families, and posterity. We have petitioned, and our petitions have been scorned. We have entreated, and our entreaties have been disregarded. We have begged, and they have mocked when our calamity came.

We beg no longer; we entreat no more; we petition no more. We defy them!...

They tell us that this platform was made to catch votes. We reply to them that changing conditions make new issues; that the principles upon which rest Democracy are as everlasting as the hills; but that they must be applied to new conditions as they arise. Conditions have arisen and we are attempting to meet those conditions. They tell us that the income tax ought not to be brought in here; that is not a new idea. They criticize us for our criticism of the Supreme Court of the United States. My friends, we have made no criticism. We have simply called attention to what you know. If you want criticisms, read the dissenting opinions of the Court. That will give you criticisms.

They say we passed an unconstitutional law. I deny it. The income tax was not unconstitutional when it was passed. It was not unconstitutional when it went before the Supreme Court for the first time. It did not become unconstitutional until one judge changed his mind; and we cannot be expected to know when a judge will change his mind.

The income tax is a just law. It simply intends to put the burdens of government justly upon the backs of the people. I am in favor of an income tax. When I find a man who is not willing to pay his share of the burden of the government which protects him, I find a man who is unworthy to enjoy the blessings of a government like ours.

He says that we are opposing the national bank currency. It is true.... We say in our platform that we believe that the right to coin money and issue money is a function of government. We believe it. We believe it is a part of sovereignty and can no more with safety be delegated to private individuals than can the power to make penal statutes or levy laws for taxation.

Mr. Jefferson, who was once regarded as good Democratic authority, seems to have a different opinion from the gentleman who has addressed us on the part of the minority. Those who are opposed to this proposition tell us that the issue of paper money is a function of the bank and that the government ought to go out of the banking business. I stand with Jefferson rather than with them, and tell them, as he did, that the issue of money is a function of the government and that the banks should go out of the governing business....

Now, my friends, let me come to the great paramount issue. If they ask us here why it is we say more on the money question than we say upon the tariff question, I reply that if protection has slain its thousands the gold standard has slain its tens of thousands. If they ask us why we did not embody all these things in our platform which we believe, we reply to them that when we have restored the money of the Constitution, all other necessary reforms will be possible, and that until that is done there is no reform that can be accomplished.

Why is it that within three months such a change has come over the sentiments of the country? Three months ago, when it was confidently asserted that those who believed in the gold standard would frame our platforms and nominate our candidates, even the advocates of the gold standard did not think that we could elect a President; but they had good reasons for the suspicion, because there is scarcely a state here today asking for the gold standard that is not within the absolute control of the Republican Party.

But note the change. Mr. McKinley was nominated at St. Louis upon a platform that declared for the maintenance of the gold standard until it should be changed into bimetallism [both gold and silver] by an international agreement. Mr. McKinley was the most popular man among the Republicans; and everybody three months ago in the Republican Party prophesied his election. How is it today?...

Ah, my friends, is not the change evident to anyone who will look at the matter? It is because no private character, however pure, no personal popularity, however great, can protect from the avenging wrath of an indignant people the man who will either declare that he is in favor of fastening the gold standard upon this people, or who is willing to surrender the right of self-government and place legislative control in the hands of foreign potentates and powers....

We go forth confident that we shall win. Why? Because upon the paramount issue in this campaign there is not a spot of ground upon which the enemy will dare to challenge battle. Why, if they tell us that the gold standard is a good thing, we point to their platform and tell them that their platform pledges the party to get rid of a gold standard and substitute bimetallism. If the gold standard is a good thing, why try to get rid of it? If the gold standard, and I might call your attention to the fact that some of the very people who are in this convention today and who tell you that we ought to declare in favor of international bimetallism and thereby declare that the gold standard is wrong and that the principles of bimetallism are better—these very people four months ago were open and avowed advocates of the gold standard and telling us that we could not legislate two metals together even with all the world.

I want to suggest this truth, that if the gold standard is a good thing we ought to declare in favor of its retention and not in favor of abandoning it; and if the gold standard is a bad thing, why should we wait until some other nations are willing to help us to let it go?

Here is the line of battle. We care not upon which issue they force the fight. We are prepared to meet them on either issue or on both. If they tell us that the gold standard is the standard of civilization, we reply to them that this, the most enlightened of all nations of the earth, has never declared for a gold standard, and both the parties this year are declaring against it. If the gold standard is the standard of civilization, why, my friends, should we not have it? So if they come to meet us on that, we can present the history of our nation. More than that, we can tell them this, that they will search the pages of history in vain to find a single instance in which the common people of any land ever declared themselves in favor of a gold standard. They can find where the holders of fixed investments have.

[Treasury secretary] Carlisle said in 1878 that this was a struggle between the idle holders of idle capital and the struggling masses who produce the wealth and pay the taxes of the country; and my friends, it is simply a question that we shall decide upon which side shall the Democratic Party fight. Upon the side of the idle holders of idle capital, or upon the side of the struggling masses? That is the question that the party must answer first; and then it must be answered by each individual hereafter. The sympathies of the Democratic Party, as described by the platform, are on the side of the struggling masses, who have ever been the foundation of the Democratic Party.

There are two ideas of government. There are those who believe that if you just legislate to make the well-to-do prosperous, that their prosperity will leak through on those below. The Democratic idea has been that if you legislate to make the masses prosperous their prosperity will find its way up and through every class that rests upon it.

You come to us and tell us that the great cities are in favor of the gold standard. I tell you that the great cities rest upon these broad and fertile prairies. Burn down your cities and leave our farms, and your cities will spring up again as if by magic. But destroy our farms and the grass will grow in the streets of every city in the country.

My friends, we shall declare that this nation is able to legislate for its own people on every question without waiting for the aid or consent of any other nation on earth, and upon that issue we expect to carry every single state in the Union.

… Our ancestors, when but 3 million, had the courage to declare their political independence of every other nation upon earth. Shall we, their descendants, when we have grown to 70 million, declare that we are less independent than our forefathers? No, my friends, it will never be the judgment of this people. Therefore, we care not upon what lines the battle is fought. If they say bimetallism is good but we cannot have it till some nation helps us, we reply that, instead of having a gold standard because England has, we shall restore bimetallism, and then let England have bimetallism because the United States have.

If they dare to come out in the open field and defend the gold standard as a good thing, we shall fight them to the uttermost, having behind us the producing masses of the nation and the world. Having behind us the commercial interests and the laboring interests and all the toiling masses, we shall answer their demands for a gold standard by saying to them, you shall not press down upon the brow of labor this crown of thorns. You shall not crucify mankind upon a cross of gold.

Source:

Bryan, William Jennings. Official Proceedings of the Democratic National Convention Held in Chicago, Illinois, July 7, 8, 9, 10, and 11, 1896. Logansport, IN: 1896, pp. 226-234. Reprinted in *The Annals of America, Vol. 12, 1895-1904: Populism, Imperialism, and Reform*. Chicago: Encyclopedia Britannica, 1968, pp. 100-105.

A Second Gilded Age? The Income Gap Says Yes

As the income gap between the top 1 percent and bottom 95 percent of wage earners grew during the economically volatile 1990s and 2000s, many writers and economists wondered whether the United States was entering a second Gilded Age. Chuck Collins, the great-grandson of processed-meat pioneer Oscar Mayer, donated his nearly half-million-dollar inheritance to charity at the age of twenty-six. Since then he has been an advocate for the use of government policies and corporate philanthropy to reduce economic inequality. In the following essay, Collins claims that the United States has in effect entered another Gilded Age. He argues that frank discussions about the origins of wealth are needed before the government can address the problems caused by wealth inequality in America.

Sixty of us gathered recently in a Chicago church basement for a program about the precarious U.S. economy. For almost two hours, we sat on clanky metal chairs discussing rising gas and food prices, home foreclosures, declining wages, increasing personal debt, and our fears for the future. Everyone knew the story: The economy is squeezing low-wage workers and pushing once-secure middle-class households into deep distress.

The discussion turned to solutions: living wage laws, expanded unionization, and increasing security and opportunity through low-cost college, matching savings programs, and assistance to first-time homebuyers. Then a woman wearing a colorful shawl commented that the problem was deeper, that "the wealthiest 1 percent now had a greater share of the nation's wealth and yet were paying less taxes."

A young man in a Chicago Cubs baseball cap responded, "All this talk about the rich getting richer is a distraction. The key is to help everyone have the same opportunities. We shouldn't be attacking the wealthy, especially with all the generous donations to charity."

A lively exchange ensued. Can we reduce poverty, the group debated, without addressing inequality? Is the common good undermined by vast wealth concentrated in a few hands? Can we reduce unequal wealth without demonizing "rich people"? All good questions. All need answers—because our nation's extreme inequality has become too staggering to go unexamined.

Most of the wealth and income gains of the last three decades, economists tell us, have flowed up to the wealthiest 1 percent of households, those

Reprinted with permission from *Sojourners*, (800) 714-7474, www.sojo.net.

with more than $5 million in assets. And within that affluent group, most gains have gone to the tiptop of the wealth pyramid, the 100,000 households that comprise our richest one-tenth of 1 percent. Last year, 7,500 households in the U.S. actually had annual incomes over $20 million.

Meanwhile, after several decades of unprecedented economic growth and wealth expansion, the U.S. poverty rate is virtually unchanged and the gap between black and white household net worth has improved barely at all. The U.S. has entered, in effect, a second Gilded Age. We live in an epoch that mirrors the horrific inequalities of wealth and opportunity of a century ago. That was the last time that the wealthiest 1 percent of households owned more wealth than all the families in the bottom 95 percent combined.

These facts go largely uncontested in our national political discourse. Even conservative politicians and think tanks concede that income inequality has accelerated. The dispute lies over whether this inequality matters—and what to do about it.

The Inequality Burden. The evidence that inequality does matter has been steadily mounting. The corrosive and growing concentration of wealth and power sits at the root of many of our most urgent societal problems. Extreme inequality is bad for our democracy, bad for our culture, and bad for our economy.

As Louis Brandeis, later a Supreme Court justice, observed during the first Gilded Age, "We can have a democratic society or we can have great concentrated wealth in the hands of a few. We cannot have both." Today, Barbara Ehrenreich notes, "We live in a society where many people cannot afford to buy groceries, while others are able to buy congressmen."

Extreme wealth generates extreme power—the power to shape political priorities and cultural norms. Our electoral system more and more resembles nothing so much as legalized bribery, with multiple avenues for the very wealthy to influence elections, legislation, and government operations. Movements for social change—efforts to expand health care, reduce poverty, and adequately fund education—find themselves continually stalled by this monetary might.

Inequality undermines our culture and civic life, breaking down the social cohesion and solidarity required for healthy communities. In societies with narrower divides between rich, poor, and middle, public health officials

198

tell us, people at all economic levels enjoy better health. Last spring's PBS series *Unnatural Causes: Why Inequality Is Making Us Sick* dramatically portrayed this.

Too much inequality also undermines economic health and well-being. After three decades of stagnant wages, average families struggle to maintain their buying power by working more hours and taking on additional debt. Neither course is sustainable over the long haul. At the top of the economic ladder, the desire by wealth-holders to maximize financial returns has led to massive speculation—in technology, housing, and now commodities such as food. These trends make our economy deeply unstable.

Why are we becoming more unequal? The title of a book by former *BusinessWeek* economist William Wolman and reporter Anne Colamosea offers an apt capsule description: *The Judas Economy: The Triumph of Capital and the Betrayal of Work.* The rules of the economy, simply put, have been tilted to favor asset-owners at the expense of people who work for wages.

Silence about Inequality. Today, especially in religious circles, we are hesitant to discuss class and wealth inequality. We don't want to be considered antagonistic or divisive, or be accused of fomenting "class war." The goal of alleviating poverty, we tell each other, can unite people across political differences. But addressing unequal wealth exposes deeper differences in values and worldview.

Still, if we want to make serious progress against poverty, we need to face these differences. A group of veteran anti-poverty advocates, for instance, recently announced a new campaign to cut poverty in half in 10 years via a combination of tax credits, child care assistance, and higher education grants. The effort will cost an estimated $90 billion a year. The campaign proposes to raise that money by reversing the "excessive tax cuts" that have gone to households with incomes over $200,000. The activists behind this campaign understand that their effort, to succeed, must focus on the top, not just the floor.

That same lesson jumps out at us from the movements to reduce the inequalities of the first Gilded Age. Labor leaders, rural populists, and adherents of the social gospel stressed the vital importance of not ignoring the dangers of concentrated wealth. They warned against the "anti-democratic perils of plutocracy." Among these critics: the patrician president Theodore Roosevelt, who railed against the "malefactors of great wealth" and urged Congress to pass progressive income and inheritance taxes.

Between 1915 and 1955, a broad "anti-inequality" movement succeeded in reducing vast disparities. In 40 short years, the U.S. ended an age of excess and Newport mansions and created the first mass middle class in world history. That movement taxed the wealthy and made public investments in shared prosperity, from infrastructure to free higher education to affordable access to homeownership.

Like their predecessors a century ago, religious leaders today must talk unflinchingly about the wealth gap and the need for redistribution. They need to personally engage those who control vast resources in our society and amplify the prophetic voices that do indeed exist among the privileged. As billionaire superinvestor Warren Buffett observed, "There is a class war—and my class is winning."

Tackling Inequality or Attacking Rich People? As Christians, we rightfully are uncomfortable demonizing anyone, including the rich. We prefer to talk about abstract "structures of inequality." Sinful social structures perpetuate economic injustice and can only be altered by changing institutional and governmental rules and values. Yet individual choices and behaviors also matter. There is a difference between attacking someone and holding them responsible—as we all are—for contributing to or diminishing the common good.

Some individuals bear disproportionate responsibility for worsening inequality because of how they unabashedly use their money and power to expand their privilege and wealth. For example, hedge fund manager Bruce Kovner of Caxton Associates collected an income of $715 million in 2006. He donates millions to think tanks and consultants who oppose campaigns that seek living wages, policies that would directly improve the lives of the security workers who protect his Manhattan office building and have no health insurance. Similarly, during the 1990s, 18 high-net-worth families, including the Waltons of Wal-Mart and the heirs to the Mars candy and Blethen newspaper empires, contributed millions toward a campaign to abolish the federal estate tax, our nation's only levy on inherited wealth.

Fortunately, the wealthiest 1 percent is not a monolith. Significant numbers of wealthy people work for economic justice as donors, activists, and campaigners. In 2001, more than 2,500 multimillionaires and billionaires signed a public petition sponsored by Responsible Wealth, a national network of affluent people concerned about inequality, to preserve the estate tax. Many of these high-net-worth individuals personally lobbied Congress to retain a tax that they would eventually pay.

But the vast majority of wealthy people are as disengaged as other citizens in matters of public policy. They unwittingly benefit from the current rules of the game, which reward wealth, undermine wages, and perpetuate injustice. Like all potential allies, they need to be enlisted into a movement for greater fairness that is in everyone's long-term interest.

Prophetic Christian witness can help us navigate the politics of class, race, inequality, and mutual responsibility. Our churches can be and should be places where we care for one another, nurture a vision of a just economy, and take action together. We must make clear that this growing economic divide is bad for everyone, including the wealthy. As Rev. Charles Demere, a member of Responsible Wealth, observes: "I don't want my grandchildren to grow up in an apartheid society. We can't build walls high enough to protect them or any child." A movement to reverse extreme inequality can create a moral common ground across divisions of race and class.

The Myth of Individual Wealth. Progressive taxation is key to any program to reduce extreme inequality. For three decades, we've reduced taxes on the wealthy, dismantled public investments in opportunity, and shifted our tax responsibilities onto the next generation by racking up $9 trillion in federal debt. We have, in effect, redistributed wealth up the economic ladder.

Yet "redistribution" remains a forbidden word in our political lexicon. Organized anti-tax and antigovernment groups frame progressive taxes as confiscatory "takings" from "virtuous wealth creators." They focus on what a faceless government demands of us through taxation, while ignoring the "givings" we get from government—the public investments and institutions that make our communities healthy and individual wealth possible.

I co-wrote a book with Bill Gates Sr., the father of Microsoft's founder, about the need to preserve the federal estate tax. Gates Sr. eloquently describes the estate tax as a "gratitude tax," a mechanism that enables individuals to "pay back" the society that made their wealth possible. Individual creativity and effort matter, he argues, and should be rewarded.

"But when someone has accumulated $10 million or $50 million," Gates points out, "they have benefited disproportionately from society's investments in education, public infrastructure, scientific research, and other forms of society's common wealth. Show me a first-generation fortune and I'll show you a successful partnership between a talented individual and society's invisible venture capitalist, the commons." Progressive taxation, he argues, "recy-

201

cles common wealth" so others have an opportunity for a decent life. With this refreshing analysis of the origins of wealth, Gates unpacks our national narratives about individual wealth and success and turns what he calls the "great man theory of individual wealth creation" on its head. Our religious congregations are places where this unpacking can continue.

Prophetic religious voices can also press for rules to ensure that the economy works for everyone, not just the very wealthy. These rules need to cover trade, tax, and wage policies and address questions of government spending priorities—whether, for instance, to close corporate loopholes or invest in education.

Instead of being fearful, we should directly engage the taboo issues of class that divide us. This means talking about the true origins of wealth and how it ends up in the hands of a few.

Whatever the social concern we are working on—poverty, climate crisis, local food systems—we face the same problem. The critical changes our society needs are being blocked by the power of concentrated wealth. As long as so much wealth and power resides in the hands of a few, we will be tethered to an economic system more focused on perpetuation of privilege than strengthening the common good.

Source:

Collins, Chuck. "A Problem of Riches: How the Growing Gap between the Very Wealthy and Everyone Else Is Destroying Our Society from Within." *Sojourners Magazine,* September-October 2008, p. 24. Available online at http://www.sojo.net/2008/09/problem-riches.

A New Gilded Age? Living Standards Say No

Tyler Cowen, a professor of economics at George Mason University, is the author of the 2011 e-book The Great Stagnation, *which examines the recent slowdown in the American economy. In the article excerpted below, Cowen explores the growing income inequality of the early twenty-first century. He argues that although the disparity in incomes between rich and poor in the United States may resemble the Gilded Age, there is no similar disparity in living conditions. The author claims that most modern working-class Americans have access to necessities like health care, education, and leisure time that were not available to their Gilded Age counterparts. He says that this difference explains why the early twenty-first century has not seen the type of widespread political protests that characterized the late nineteenth century.*

Does growing wealth and income inequality in the United States presage the downfall of the American republic? Will we evolve into a new Gilded Age plutocracy [control of government by the wealthy], irrevocably split between the competing interests of rich and poor? Or is growing inequality a mere bump in the road, a statistical blip along the path to greater wealth for virtually every American? Or is income inequality partially desirable, reflecting the greater productivity of society's stars?

There is plenty of speculation on these possibilities, but a lot of it has been aimed at elevating one political agenda over another rather than elevating our understanding. As a result, there's more confusion about this issue than just about any other in contemporary American political discourse. The reality is that most of the worries about income inequality are bogus, but some are probably better grounded and even more serious than even many of their heralds realize. If our economic churn is bound to throw off political sparks, whether alarms about plutocracy or something else, we owe it to ourselves to seek out an accurate picture of what is really going on. Let's start with the subset of worries about inequality that are significantly overblown.

In terms of immediate political stability, there is less to the income inequality issue than meets the eye. Most analyses of income inequality neglect two major points. First, the inequality of personal well-being is

Excerpted from "The Inequality that Matters" by Tyler Cowen, *The American Interest*, January/February 2011. Reprinted by permission of the author and *The American Interest*. © 2011. All rights reserved. To view the full text of this article, visit http://www.the-americaninterest.com/article.cfm?piece=907.

sharply down over the past hundred years and perhaps over the past twenty years as well. Bill Gates is much, much richer than I am, yet it is not obvious that he is much happier if, indeed, he is happier at all. I have access to penicillin, air travel, good cheap food, the Internet and virtually all of the technical innovations that Gates does. Like the vast majority of Americans, I have access to some important new pharmaceuticals, such as statins to protect against heart disease. To be sure, Gates receives the very best care from the world's top doctors, but our health outcomes are in the same ballpark. I don't have a private jet or take luxury vacations, and—I think it is fair to say—my house is much smaller than his. I can't meet with the world's elite on demand. Still, by broad historical standards, what I share with Bill Gates is far more significant than what I don't share with him.

Compare these circumstances to those of 1911, a century ago. Even in the wealthier countries, the average person had little formal education, worked six days a week or more, often at hard physical labor, never took vacations, and could not access most of the world's culture. The living standards of Carnegie and Rockefeller towered above those of typical Americans, not just in terms of money but also in terms of comfort. Most people today may not articulate this truth to themselves in so many words, but they sense it keenly enough. So when average people read about or see income inequality, they don't feel the moral outrage that radiates from the more passionate egalitarian quarters of society. Instead, they think their lives are pretty good and that they either earned through hard work or lucked into a healthy share of the American dream. (The persistently unemployed, of course, are a different matter, and I will return to them later.) It is pretty easy to convince a lot of Americans that unemployment and poverty are social problems because discrete examples of both are visible on the evening news, or maybe even in or at the periphery of one's own life. It's much harder to get those same people worked up about generalized measures of inequality.

This is why, for example, large numbers of Americans oppose the idea of an estate tax even though the current form of the tax, slated to return in 2011, is very unlikely to affect them or their estates. In narrowly self-interested terms, that view may be irrational, but most Americans are unwilling to frame national issues in terms of rich versus poor. There's a great deal of hostility toward various government bailouts, but the idea of "undeserving" recipients is the key factor in those feelings. Resentment against Wall Street gamesters hasn't spilled over much into resentment against the wealthy more generally. The bailout for General Motors' labor unions wasn't so popular either—again, obviously not because of any bias against the wealthy but because a basic sense of fairness was violated. As of November 2010, congressional Democrats are of a mixed mind as to whether the Bush tax cuts should expire for those whose annual income exceeds $250,000; that is in large part because their constituents bear no animus toward rich people, only toward undeservedly rich people.

A neglected observation, too, is that envy is usually local. At least in the United States, most economic resentment is not directed toward billionaires or high-roller financiers—not even corrupt ones. It's directed at the guy down the hall who got a bigger raise. It's directed at the husband of your wife's sister, because the brand of beer he stocks costs $3 a case more than yours, and so on. That's another reason why a lot of people aren't so bothered by income or wealth inequality at the macro level. Most of us don't compare ourselves to billionaires. Gore Vidal put it honestly: "Whenever a friend succeeds, a little something in me dies."

Occasionally the cynic in me wonders why so many relatively well-off intellectuals lead the egalitarian charge against the privileges of the wealthy. One group has the status currency of money and the other has the status currency of intellect, so might they be competing for overall social regard? The high status of the wealthy in America, or for that matter the high status of celebrities, seems to bother our intellectual class most. That class composes a very small group, however, so the upshot is that growing income inequality won't necessarily have major political implications at the macro level.

… All that said, income inequality does matter—for both politics and the economy. To see how, we must distinguish between inequality itself and what causes it. But first let's review the trends in more detail.

The numbers are clear: Income inequality has been rising in the United States, especially at the very top. The data show a big difference between two quite separate issues, namely income growth at the very top of the distribution and greater inequality throughout the distribution. The first trend is much more pronounced than the second, although the two are often confused.

When it comes to the first trend, the share of pre-tax income earned by the richest 1 percent of earners has increased from about 8 percent in 1974 to more than 18 percent in 2007. Furthermore, the richest 0.01 percent (the 15,000 or so richest families) had a share of less than 1 percent in 1974 but more than 6 percent of national income in 2007. As noted, those figures are from pre-tax income, so don't look to the George W. Bush tax cuts to explain the pattern. Furthermore, these gains have been sustained and have evolved over many years, rather than coming in one or two small bursts between 1974 and today.[1]

These numbers have been challenged on the grounds that, since various tax reforms have kicked in, individuals now receive their incomes in different and harder to measure ways, namely through corporate forms, stock options and fringe benefits. Caution is in order, but the overall trend seems robust. Similar broad patterns are indicated by different sources, such as studies of executive compensation. Anecdotal observation suggests extreme and unprecedented returns earned by investment bankers, fired CEOs, J.K. Rowling and Tiger Woods.

At the same time, wage growth for the median earner has slowed since 1973. But that slower wage growth has afflicted large numbers of Americans, and it is conceptually distinct from the higher relative share of top income earners. For instance, if you take the 1979-2005 period, the average incomes of the bottom fifth of households increased only 6 percent while the incomes of the middle quintile [fifth] rose by 21 percent. That's a widening of the spread of incomes, but it's not so drastic compared to the explosive gains at the very top.

The broader change in income distribution, the one occurring beneath the very top earners, can be deconstructed in a manner that makes nearly all of it look harmless. For instance, there is usually greater inequality of income among both older people and the more highly educated, if only because there is more time and more room for fortunes to vary. Since America is becoming both older and more highly educated, our measured income inequality will increase pretty much by demographic fiat. Economist Thomas Lemieux at the University of British Columbia estimates that these demographic effects explain three-quarters of the observed rise in income inequality for men, and even more for women.[2]

Attacking the problem from a different angle, other economists are challenging whether there is much growth in inequality at all below the super-rich. For instance, real incomes are measured using a common price index, yet poorer people are more likely to shop at discount outlets like Wal-Mart, which have seen big price drops over the past twenty years.[3] Once we take this behavior into account, it is unclear whether the real income gaps between the poor and middle class have been widening much at all. Robert J. Gordon, an economist from Northwestern University who is hardly known as a right-wing apologist, wrote in a recent paper that "there was no increase of inequality after 1993 in the bottom 99 percent of the population," and that whatever overall change there was "can be entirely explained by the behavior of income in the top 1 percent."[4]

And so we come again to the gains of the top earners, clearly the big story told by the data. It's worth noting that over this same period of time, inequality of work hours increased too. The top earners worked a lot more and most other Americans worked somewhat less. That's another reason why high earners don't occasion more resentment: Many people understand how hard they have to work to get there. It also seems that most of the income gains of the top earners were related to performance pay—bonuses, in other words—and not wildly out-of-whack yearly salaries.[5]

It is also the case that any society with a lot of "threshold earners" is likely to experience growing income inequality. A threshold earner is someone who seeks to earn a certain amount of money and no more. If wages go up, that person will respond by seeking less work or by working less hard or less often. That person simply wants to "get by" in terms of absolute earning power in order to experience other gains in the form of leisure—whether spending time with friends and family, walking in the woods and so on. Luck aside, that person's income will never rise much above the threshold.

It's not obvious what causes the percentage of threshold earners to rise or fall, but it seems reasonable to suppose that the more single-occupancy households there are, the more threshold earners there will be, since a major incentive for earning money is to use it to take care of other people with whom one lives. For a variety of reasons, single-occupancy households in the United States are at an all-time high. There are also a growing number of late odyssey years [a transitional period in early adulthood] graduate students who try to cover their own expenses but otherwise devote their time to study. If the percentage of threshold earners rises for whatever reasons, however, the aggregate gap between them and the more financially ambitious will widen. There is nothing morally or practically wrong with an increase in inequality from a source such as that....

If we are looking for objectionable problems in the top 1 percent of income earners, much of it boils down to finance and activities related to financial markets. And to be sure, the high incomes in finance should give us all pause....

There is an unholy dynamic of short-term trading and investing, backed up by bailouts and risk reduction from the government and the Federal Reserve. This is not good. "Going short on volatility" is a dangerous strategy from a social point of view. For one thing, in so-called normal times, the finance sector attracts a big chunk of the smartest, most hard-working and most talented individuals. That represents a huge human capital opportunity cost to society and the economy at large. But more immediate and more important, it means that banks take far too many risks and go way out on a limb, often in correlated fashion. When their bets turn sour, as they did in 2007-09, everyone else pays the price....

Is the overall picture a shame? Yes. Is it distorting resource distribution and productivity in the meantime? Yes. Will it again bring our economy to its knees? Probably. Maybe that's simply the price of modern society. Income inequality will likely continue to rise and we will search in vain for the appropriate political remedies for our underlying problems.

Notes:

[1] See Jacob S. Hacker and Paul Pierson, "Winner-Take-All Politics: Public Policy, Political Organization, and the Precipitous Rise of Top Incomes in the United States," *Politics & Society* (June 2010). For one criticism of those numbers, see Scott Winship, "Hacker-mania!," ScottWinshipWeb, September 19, 2010.

[2] Lemieux, "Increasing Residual Wage Inequality: Composition Effects, Noisy Data, or Rising Demand for Skill?" *American Economic Review,* June 2006.

[3] See Christian Broda and John Romalis, "Shattering the Conventional Wisdom on Growing Inequality," *New York Times* Freakonomics blog, May 19, 2008.

[4] Gordon, "Misperceptions About the Magnitude and Timing of Changes in American Income Inequality," National Bureau of Economic Research, NBER Working Paper No. 15351 (September 2009).

[5] See Thomas Lemieux, W. Bentley Macleod and Daniel Parent, "Performance Pay and Wage Inequality," *Quarterly Journal of Economics* (February 2009).

Source:

Cowen, Tyler. "The Inequality That Matters." *The American Interest,* January/February 2011. Available online at http://www.the-american-interest.com/article.cfm?piece=907.

IMPORTANT PEOPLE, PLACES, AND TERMS

AAISW
See Amalgamated Association of Iron and Steel Workers (AAISW)

Adams, Charles Francis, Jr. (1835-1915)
Grandson of President John Quincy Adams who was an early advocate of railroad regulation and author of the 1869 book *A Chapter of Erie*.

AFL
See American Federation of Labor (AFL)

Amalgamated Association of Iron and Steel Workers (AAISW)
The nation's largest trade union until 1892, when a strike at Carnegie Steel's Homestead Plant ended in violence and broke the union.

American Federation of Labor (AFL)
A group of trade unions founded in 1886 by Samuel Gompers.

American Railway Union (ARU)
An industrial union for both skilled and unskilled railway workers, founded in 1893 by Eugene V. Debs.

Ames, Oakes (1804-1873)
Tool manufacturer, Massachusetts congressman, and head of the Crédit Mobilier railroad construction company who was censured (formally reprimanded) by Congress for bribing public officials.

Anarchism
A political movement that arose during the nineteenth century and advocated the elimination of government and big business.

Arthur, Chester A. (1830-1886)
Twenty-first president of the United States (1881-1885) who took office following the assassination of President James Garfield.

ARU
> *See* American Railway Union (ARU)

Big Four
> California businessmen and chief financiers of the Central Pacific Railroad, including president Leland Stanford, vice-president Collis P. Huntington, treasurer Mark Hopkins, and construction supervisor Charles Crocker.

Black Friday
> Nickname for September 24, 1869, the day that New York's Gold Exchange and stock market crashed following Jay Gould's attempt to corner the gold market.

Blaine, James G. (1830-1893)
> Leader of the "Half-Breed" reformist section of the Republican Party who served as Speaker of the House of Representatives (1869-1875), senator from Maine (1876-1881), secretary of state (1881 and 1889-1892), and GOP candidate for president in 1884.

Bond
> An investment instrument that is a guarantee by a government or corporation to repay a loan, usually with interest, at the end of a specified period. Bonds can be traded and thus can fluctuate in value.

Boycott
> A form of political protest in which workers voluntarily refuse to deal with a company or consumers voluntarily refuse to buy from or patronize a company.

Bryan, William Jennings (1860-1925)
> Three-time Democratic candidate for president and Populist Party candidate in 1896.

Capital
> Wealth in the form of money or property that is accumulated by an individual or business and can be used to generate more wealth; also sometimes used in reference to the world of business.

Carnegie, Andrew (1835-1919)
> Founder of Carnegie Steel who revolutionized and dominated the American steel industry and became a pioneering philanthropist.

Central Pacific Railroad

The western branch of the first transcontinental railroad, founded by the "Big Four" California businessmen.

Charter

A document granting rights, usually issued by a government.

Civil War

The war over states' rights and slavery that split the United States between North (Union) and South (Confederacy) and was fought from 1861 to 1865.

Clemens, Samuel Langhorne (1835-1910)

Author of travelogues, humor, and fiction under the pseudonym Mark Twain. His first novel, *The Gilded Age,* written with Charles Dudley Warner, lent its name to the post-Civil War era.

Cleveland, Grover (1837-1908)

The only Democrat elected president during the Gilded Age, he served two nonconsecutive terms as the twenty-second and twenty-fourth president of the United States (1885-1889 and 1893-1897).

CNLU

See Colored National Labor Union (CNLU)

Coke

A type of coal that has been heated to eliminate waste elements and increase its carbon content; it is used to turn iron into steel.

Collateral

Something of value that is promised as security for a loan.

Colored National Labor Union (CNLU)

Union for African-American trade workers organized by Isaac Myers after black members were denied admission into the National Labor Union.

Company town

A settlement established by a company for its employees that includes housing, retail stores, schools, and entertainment venues; residents of company towns are dependent on the company for their living arrangements as well as their jobs.

Confederacy
 The eleven Southern states that split from the Union during the Civil War (1861-1865).

Conkling, Roscoe (1829-1888)
 Leader of the "Stalwart" section of the Republican Party who served as U.S. representative (1859-1863 and 1865-67) and Senator (1867-1881) from New York.

Cooke, Jay (1821-1905)
 Major financier of federal bonds during and after the Civil War; the failure of his bank in 1873 led to a nationwide panic and depression.

Corbin, Abel R. (1808-1881)
 Businessman who married President Ulysses S. Grant's sister Virginia and became involved in Jay Gould's attempt to corner the gold market.

Corner
 An attempt to control a commodity or stock in order to manipulate its price, or any attempt to control an area of business so that others cannot be successful in it.

Corporation
 A business organization, chartered by a state, that is authorized to act as a single entity on behalf of its owners, called shareholders. A corporation has legal rights and responsibilities as a person, a centralized board to manage affairs, stock (shares of partial ownership) that can be sold or transferred, and limited liability for individual members.

Craft union
 See Trade union

Crédit Mobilier of America
 Construction and finance company set up to build the Union Pacific Railway that charged the government millions of dollars in inflated expenses and bribed public officials.

Debs, Eugene V. (1855-1926)
 Founder of the American Railway Union and the American Socialist Party and five-time Socialist candidate for president.

Democratic Party

One of the two dominant political parties of the Gilded Age, the Democrats favored low tariffs and limited government involvement in business.

Depreciate

To lower in value over time.

Dividend

A portion of a corporation's profits that is distributed to shareholders in proportion to the number of stock shares they own.

Drawback

A rebate on competitors' shipments given by a railroad to preferred customers.

Drew, Daniel (1797-1879)

Financier and member of the Erie Railroad board of directors who manipulated the company's stock for profit and was ousted after the Erie War.

Duty

A tax or fee charged by a government, usually on imported goods.

Electoral college

A body of electors chosen by voters in each state that formally elects the president and vice president of the United States; each state is allocated a number of electors equal to its number of representatives in the U.S. Congress.

Erie Railroad

One of the great trunk lines serving New York City, it was the subject of stock speculation and financial maneuverings during the 1868 Erie War.

Erie War

The 1868 battle between Cornelius Vanderbilt and Daniel Drew, Jim Fisk, and Jay Gould for control of the Erie Railroad.

Farmers' Alliances

Social and political organizations formed to represent the interests of farmers; they were a successor to the Grange movement and forerunner of the Populist (People's) Party.

Federal Reserve System
Established by Congress in 1913, this central-banking system of the United States consists of twelve regional banks governed by a board; it regulates interest rates and the availability of bank credit and sets other monetary policies.

Federation of Organized Trades and Labor Unions (FOTLU)
An alternative to the Knights of Labor and predecessor to the AFL.

Financial panic
A sudden demand to sell stocks or acquire currency that results in a run on stock exchanges or banks; panics were frequent during the Gilded Age and often resulted in economic depressions.

Fischer, Adolph (1858-1887)
Labor activist and anarchist convicted of murder and executed after the Haymarket Square Riot in 1886.

Fisk, Jim (1834-1872)
Jay Gould's flamboyant business partner who was involved in the 1868 Erie War and the 1869 attempt to corner the market on gold.

Foreclosure
The legal process through which ownership of property is terminated, usually due to nonpayment of a loan.

FOTLU
See Federation of Organized Trades and Labor Unions (FOTLU)

Free silver
The idea that silver should be added to U.S. currency at a ratio of 16:1 to gold; it was advocated by farmers, laborers, and other debtors who believed that the measure would reduce the value of the dollar.

Frick, Henry Clay (1849-1919)
President of Frick Coke and later of Carnegie Steel who survived an assassination attempt during the Homestead conflict of 1892.

Garfield, James A. (1831-1881)
Twentieth president of the United States (1881) who was assassinated only six months after taking office.

George, Henry (1839-1897)

Economist, reformer, author of the 1886 study *Progress and Poverty*, advocate of a single tax on land values, and third-party candidate for New York City mayor in 1886.

Gilded Age

An era of American history, extending roughly from 1865 to 1901, that was characterized by unchecked economic development, political corruption, extreme income disparities between rich and poor, and the transformation from a rural, farming culture to an urban, industrial society.

Gold standard

A monetary policy in which national currency is backed by gold at a fixed rate; it was advocated by bankers, businessmen, and other lenders hoping to maintain the value of the dollar.

Gompers, Samuel (1850-1924)

Founder and president of the American Federation of Labor.

GOP

Short for "Grand Old Party," an alternative name for the Republican Party.

Gould, Jay (1836-1892)

Financier and railroad baron who was involved in the Erie War and gold speculation; he later served as president of Western Union telegraph and Union Pacific and Missouri Pacific railroads.

Grange

Social and political organization for farmers founded in 1867; also known as the Order of the Patrons of Husbandry.

Grant, Ulysses S. (1822-1885)

Eighteenth president of the United States (1869-1877) and commander of the Union Army during the Civil War.

Great Northern Railway

The northernmost U.S. transcontinental railroad and the first built without government aid, running from Minneapolis, Minnesota, to Seattle, Washington.

Greenback

Slang term for paper money issued by the U.S. federal government that was backed by government guarantees, not specie (silver or gold coin); the name originated from the green ink used to print the notes.

Greenback Party

Third party dedicated to increasing the number of greenbacks in circulation and adding silver coins to the currency; at various times it was also called the Greenback-Labor or National Party.

Half-Breeds

Faction of the Republican Party in the 1870s and 1880s dedicated to civil service reform.

Harriman, Edward (1848-1909)

President of the Union Pacific Railroad who secretly tried to buy a majority of the Northern Pacific Railway in 1901 and was thwarted by J. P. Morgan.

Harrison, Benjamin (1833-1901)

Twenty-third President of the United States (1889-1893) who was elected by a considerable electoral margin in 1888 despite losing the popular vote.

Hayes, Rutherford B. (1822-1893)

Nineteenth president of the United States (1877-1881) who was elected in 1876 by a margin of one electoral vote.

Haymarket Square

Public park in Chicago that was the site of an infamous 1886 labor rally that ended with a bombing and riot.

Hill, James J. (1838-1916)

Founder and president of the transcontinental Great Northern Railway.

Holding company

A company that is established to purchase and hold enough shares of stock in other companies to control their management and operations.

Homestead, Pennsylvania

Site of a Carnegie Steel plant where a strike of steel workers turned violent, necessitating federal intervention.

Homesteading

The idea that public lands should be given away or sold at low cost to people willing to settle and develop them. The Homestead Act of 1862 allowed Americans to claim 160 acres of public land for ten dollars after living on or cultivating it for five years.

Horizontal integration

Domination of an industry through mergers or buyouts of companies involved in the same line of business.

ICC

See Interstate Commerce Commission (ICC)

Imperialism

The idea that the United States should seek to acquire territory and expand its influence overseas.

Interstate Commerce Clause

The section of the U.S. Constitution that gives Congress the power to regulate commerce between states; it was often used by the Supreme Court during the Gilded Age to overturn various regulatory laws.

Interstate Commerce Commission (ICC)

Created by the Interstate Commerce Act in 1887, the ICC reviewed railroad rates, investigated abuses, and enforced safety regulations.

Johnson, Andrew (1808-1875)

Seventeenth president of the United States (1865-1869) who promoted homesteading during his tenure as a Tennessee congressman.

Jones, Mary Harris (1830-1930)

Labor organizer and progressive activist.

Kickback

A secret, illegal payment made in return for arranging a business transaction or contract.

Knights of Labor

Originally founded in 1869 as a secret lodge, the Noble and Holy Order of the Knights of Labor became the largest, most inclusive union in American history.

Labor union
An organization of workers created to negotiate with employers for better wages and working conditions and to provide benefits.

Land grant
A gift of public lands made by the government to encourage development; during the Gilded Age, grants were often given to railroad companies as an incentive to spread lines across the country.

Lease, Mary Elizabeth (1853-1933)
Populist speaker and progressive activist noted for her oratorical ability.

Liberal Republican Party
Short-lived reform-minded splinter group of Republicans who unsuccessfully ran a candidate against incumbent Republican president Ulysses S. Grant in the 1872 presidential election.

Lincoln, Abraham (1809-1865)
Sixteenth president of the United States (1861-1865) who led the Union to victory during the Civil War and promoted policies that developed the American frontier.

Lockout
An industrial action in which an employer shuts down factories and keeps employees from their jobs in order to force them to meet the employer's demands. *See also* Strike.

Margin buying
Buying stock by putting as little as 1 percent down and borrowing the rest in the future, using the stock as collateral.

McKinley, William A. (1843-1901)
Twenty-fifth president of the United States (1897-1901) whose assassination marked the end of the Gilded Age; as a congressman, he was noted for the bill increasing tariffs that bore his name.

Monopoly
A single company (or group of companies working together) that controls an entire industry, often resulting in high prices for consumers.

Morgan, John Pierpont (1837-1913)

Leading banker and financier of the Gilded Age and founder of the investment bank J. P. Morgan & Company.

Muckrakers

Journalists who investigate social problems and political corruption and publish books and articles intended to raise public awareness and generate calls for reform.

Munn v. Illinois

A Supreme Court decision that affirmed states' rights to regulate businesses in the public interest.

National Labor Union (NLU)

An early organization of trade unions founded by William Sylvis in 1866 that remained active until around 1872.

New York Central Railroad

One of the country's great trunk lines serving New York City; it was owned by Cornelius Vanderbilt and sold in 1879 through J. P. Morgan's bank.

NLU

See National Labor Union (NLU)

Nonpartisan

Without regard to political beliefs or party affiliations.

Northern Pacific Railway

A transcontinental railroad from Duluth, Minnesota, to Puget Sound in Washington that was completed in 1883.

Northern Securities Company

A holding company created by J. P. Morgan to pool the interests of the competing Union Pacific, Northern Pacific, and Great Northern railroads; it was broken up by a 1904 Supreme Court ruling.

Panic

See Financial panic

Parsons, Albert (1848-1887)

Labor activist and anarchist convicted of murder and executed after the Haymarket Square Riot in 1886.

Patronage system
> The practice of giving government jobs to political supporters as a reward for loyalty.

Pendleton Civil Service Reform Act
> Pioneering legislation requiring candidates for government jobs to pass a merit-based exam and forbidding political assessments on government workers.

People's Party
> *See* Populist Party

Philanthropy
> An effort to promote the well-being of others through charitable acts or monetary donations.

Pinkerton National Detective Agency
> A private security agency frequently hired by businesses to infiltrate unions, protect scab workers, and serve as a private army in labor disputes.

Pool
> A group of corporations that come together to set prices or divide business to their common advantage; railroad pools were made illegal by the Interstate Commerce Act in 1887.

Populist Party
> A third party founded in the late 1880s out of the belief that the two major political parties (Democrats and Republicans) failed to represent the interests of common people because they were largely controlled by wealthy bankers and business owners; the Populist message found a ready audience among farmers, miners, small ranchers, and railroad workers.

Powderly, Terence V. (1849-1924)
> Grand Master Workman of the Knights of Labor from 1879 to 1893; under his leadership, the group grew into the largest, most inclusive union in American history.

Primary election
> A preliminary election in which party members vote to select candidates to run in a general election.

Progressive Era

A period of American history, extending roughly from 1901 to the 1910s, that saw significant reforms in various social, political, and economic institutions that had been affected by Gilded Age industrialization.

Prohibition Party

Third party dedicated to prohibition, a ban on the manufacture and sale of alcohol.

Pullman, Illinois

A "company town" established by the Pullman Palace Car Company for its workers; a nationwide railroad strike began there in 1894.

Rebate

A refund of a portion of the price of goods or services by the seller to the purchaser; during the Gilded Age, railroads gave rebates to customers who guaranteed a minimum amount of business (this practice was made illegal in 1903).

Republican Party

One of the two dominant political parties of the Gilded Age, the Republicans favored protective tariffs and other policies that promoted American business interests.

Riis, Jacob (1849-1914)

A Danish-born American journalist who exposed the horrifying conditions in New York City's tenements in his 1890 book *How the Other Half Lives*.

Robber baron

Disparaging term used to describe wealthy business owners who used shady deals, bribery, and ruthless business practices to monopolize industries and earn excess profits.

Rockefeller, John D. (1839-1937)

Founder and president of the Standard Oil trust and major philanthropist.

Roosevelt, Theodore (1858-1919)

Twenty-sixth president of the United States (1901-1909) who assumed office upon the assassination of William McKinley and ushered in the Progressive Era of reform.

Scab worker
Disparaging term used to refer to a replacement worker hired to do the job of a union member, especially during a strike or labor stoppage.

Scott, Thomas A. (1823-1881)
President of the Pennsylvania Railroad, mentor to Andrew Carnegie, and conspirator with John D. Rockefeller and others in the South Improvement Company.

Scrip
A private currency that only has value to the company that issues it; many Gilded Age companies paid workers in scrip that could only be used at company stores, which overcharged for goods.

Share
A unit of ownership in a company that entitles the holder to a claim on company profits and obligates the holder to meet the company's losses. *See also* Stock.

Sherman Antitrust Act
Pioneering antimonopoly legislation passed in 1890 to prohibit business practices that represented an "illegal restraint of trade."

Sherman Silver Purchase Act
Legislation passed in 1890 that required the federal government to purchase a specified amount of silver every month for coinage; it was repealed after the depression of 1893.

SIC
See South Improvement Company (SIC)

Sinclair, Upton (1878-1968)
Muckraking journalist whose fictionalized account of conditions in Chicago's meatpacking industry, *The Jungle* (1906), spurred federal regulation of the food and drug industries.

Social Darwinism
A theory that explains the gulf between wealthy and impoverished Americans by claiming that rich people are innately superior in terms of intelligence and ambition.

Socialism

An economic system that emphasizes collective ownership of businesses and other property as a means to distribute wealth fairly among all members of a society.

South Improvement Company (SIC)

A proposed alliance of Standard Oil with the Pennsylvania, Erie, and New York Central railroads to pool business and give preferred shipping rates.

Spanish-American War

An 1898 conflict between Spain and the United States that ended in a decisive American victory and resulted in U.S. control over former Spanish colonies in Puerto Rico, Guam, and the Philippines.

Specie

A type of currency that has intrinsic value, such as gold or silver coins.

Spies, August (1855-1887)

Anarchist and labor journalist convicted of murder and executed after the Haymarket Square Riot in 1886.

Splinter group

A political party or organization that forms by breaking off from a larger group, usually over differences of opinion on specific issues.

Spoils system

See Patronage system

Stalwarts

A faction of the Republican Party in the 1870s and 1880s dedicated to maintaining the patronage system.

Standard Oil Company

Pioneering oil conglomerate founded by John D. Rockefeller.

Stanford, Leland (1824-1893)

President of the Central Pacific Railroad, governor of California (1862-1863), U.S. senator (1885-93), and founder of Stanford University.

Stock

An investment instrument that represents part-ownership in a corporation, in proportion to the number of shares owned, and gives the holder a claim on profits and assets. Stocks can be bought, sold, and traded and thus can fluctuate in value.

Stock shorting
Promising to deliver stock for a set price in the future, in the belief that prices will fall and the seller can pocket the difference between the purchase price and promised delivery price.

Stock watering
Releasing more shares of stock in a company in order to artificially inflate the company's value; it also reduces the value of each individual share of stock.

Strike
A labor action in which workers walk off the job until specific demands, such as higher wages or better working conditions, are met. *See also* Lockout.

Subsidy
Financial aid given by the government to encourage a particular business or economic outcome; common types of subsidies include cash, low-cost loans, or land grants.

Subtreasury plan
A proposal by the Farmers' Alliance for the government to establish warehouses (called subtreasuries) where farmers could deposit crops in return for low-interest loans.

Suffrage
The right to vote.

Sylvis, William (1828-1869)
Iron molder and founder of the National Labor Union.

Taft, William Howard (1857-1930)
Twenty-seventh president of the United States (1909-1913). Personally chosen by Theodore Roosevelt to run to succeed him, Taft was defeated in his bid for a second term by Woodrow Wilson when Roosevelt ran against him as a third-party candidate.

Tammany Hall

The Democratic headquarters in New York City; also used to refer to the political machine that controlled New York's city and state governments during the Gilded Age.

Tarbell, Ida (1857-1944)

Muckraking journalist who exposed John D. Rockefeller's monopolistic business practices in her 1904 work *A History of Standard Oil*.

Tariff

A tax, usually on goods imported into the country, that provided the U.S. government's main source of revenue during the Gilded Age.

Third party

A political party that forms outside of the mainstream political parties in a two-party system.

Tompkins Square

A park in New York City that was the site of an 1874 labor rally that ended in police violence against workers.

Trade union

A type of labor union limited to skilled workers; sometimes also called a craft union.

Transcontinental railroad

A railroad that spans the American continent from coast to coast; often used to refer to the first such railroad, a combination of the Union Pacific and Central Pacific lines.

Trust

A type of holding company that consolidates and controls the assets of several businesses; used more generally during the Gilded Age to refer to any business monopoly.

Turner, Frederick Jackson (1861-1932)

Historian who first suggested the importance of the American frontier in the development of American politics, culture, and character.

Twain, Mark

See Clemens, Samuel Langhorne

Tweed, William M. "Boss" (1823-1878)
Leader of New York City's Tammany Hall political machine and symbol of political corruption.

UMW
See United Mine Workers (UMW)

United Mine Workers (UMW)
Coal miners' union founded in 1890 that was involved in important labor actions during the Gilded Age and Progressive Era.

Union
The mostly Northern states that remained part of the United States after the Confederate states seceded during the Civil War (1861-1865). *See also* Labor union.

Union Pacific Railroad
The eastern branch of the first transcontinental railroad, chartered and supported by the U.S. government in the Pacific Railway Act of 1862.

U.S. Steel
The world's first billion-dollar corporation, put together in 1901 by J. P. Morgan by combining interests in Federal Steel and Carnegie Steel.

Vanderbilt, Cornelius (1794-1877)
Pioneering shipping and railroad owner, president of the New York Central Railroad during the 1868 Erie War, and America's richest man at the time of his death.

Vertical integration
Expanding a company's business operations to include all aspects of the production process through the acquisition of input suppliers (backward integration) and distribution channels (forward integration).

Warner, Charles Dudley (1829-1900)
Editor and essayist whose novel with Samuel Clemens, *The Gilded Age*, lent its name to the post-Civil War era.

Weaver, James B. (1833-1913)
Iowa congressman (1879-81 and 1885-89), Greenback Party candidate for president in 1880, and People's (Populist) Party candidate for president in 1892.

Workers' compensation

A system, mandated by law, to provide financial support to workers who become ill or are injured or killed on the job.

CHRONOLOGY

1859

The Comstock Lode of silver is discovered in Nevada. *See p. 19.*

1860

Abraham Lincoln is elected president of the United States. *See p. 11.*

1861

The American Civil War begins. *See p. 13.*

1862

The Homestead Act opens federal lands in the West for settlement. *See p. 11.*

The Pacific Railway Act provides support for building the first transcontinental railroad. *See p. 13.*

The Legal Tender Act creates paper currency ("greenbacks") backed by government guarantees, not specie (coin money). *See p. 27.*

1865

The Civil War ends, making funds and workers available for transcontinental railroad construction. *See p. 10.*

1866

William Sylvis founds the National Labor Union. *See p. 74.*

Native Americans and U.S. Army troops engage in a series of clashes for control of the West that becomes known as the Great Sioux War. *See p. 17.*

1867

The Grange (the Order of the Patrons of Husbandry) is founded by a U.S. Department of Agriculture official. *See p. 59.*

1868

Former Union Army general Ulysses S. Grant is elected president. *See p. 31.*

The "Erie War" for control of the Erie Railroad is waged between Cornelius Vanderbilt and Daniel Drew, Jim Fisk, and Jay Gould. *See p. 28.*

1869

May 10—The final spike linking the Central Pacific and Union Pacific railroad lines is driven at Promontory Point, Utah, completing America's first transcontinental railroad. *See p. 16.*

September 24—In an event known as "Black Friday," New York City's Gold Exchange and stock market crash following Jay Gould's attempt to corner the gold market. *See p. 32.*

J. P. Morgan repels an attempt by Jay Gould and Jim Fisk to take over a regional New York railroad.

The Noble and Holy Order of the Knights of Labor is founded by Philadelphia garment cutters. *See p. 80.*

1870

John D. Rockefeller incorporates Standard Oil in Ohio. *See p. 42.*

The Miners' Benevolent Association (MBA) signs the first contract between coal miners and mine operators. *See p. 76.*

1871

Congress declares Native Americans wards of the state, no longer recognizing them as independent tribes. *See p. 17.*

The South Improvement Company is created, joining the Pennsylvania, New York Central, and Erie railroads with Standard Oil. *See p. 42.*

1872

Grant is elected to a second term as president. *See p. 57.*

The South Improvement Company's rate schedule is published and its charter is revoked. *See p. 42.*

1873

September 18—Jay Cooke's bank fails, setting off the Panic of 1873. *See p. 37.*

November—William M. "Boss" Tweed of New York City's Tammany Hall political machine is convicted of embezzlement and sentenced to prison. *See p. 58.*

Following an investigation of the Crédit Mobilier railroad financing scandal, Congress censures two members for accepting bribes. *See p. 35.*

Congress passes the Coinage Act, removing silver coins from circulation. *See p. 61.*

1874

January 13—Mounted police beat a group of 7,000 workers rallying in New York City's Tompkins Square. *See p. 77.*

American voters learn of a scandal in which delinquent tax collections were kicked back to Republican campaign coffers. *See p. 57.*

1875

Andrew Carnegie opens his first Bessemer steel plant, the J. Edgar Thomson Works near Pittsburgh, Pennsylvania. *See p. 47.*

The Whiskey Ring scandal, in which distillers and public officials worked together to defraud the federal government of liquor taxes, results in 230 indictments. *See p. 57.*

Ten leaders of the Miners' Benevolent Association (MBA) are executed on trumped-up charges. *See p. 76.*

1876

June 25 and 26—U.S. forces are routed by Lakota Sioux Indians and their allies at the Battle of Little Big Horn. *See p. 17.*

Rutherford B. Hayes loses the popular vote but wins the presidency by one electoral vote. *See p. 61.*

Secretary of War William Belknap is forced to resign in a bribery scandal. *See p. 58.*

1877

March 1—The Supreme Court decides in *Munn v. Illinois* that states have the right to regulate businesses that affect the public interest. *See p. 59.*

Baltimore & Ohio railroad workers strike in West Virginia, setting off labor strikes and riots nationwide. *See p. 78.*

1878

Congress passes the Bland-Allison Act, temporarily halting the United States' move back to the gold standard.

1879

J. P. Morgan arranges the sale of the New York Central Railroad for William H. Vanderbilt. *See p. 50.*

1880

James A. Garfield is elected president after winning the popular vote by only 8,355 votes. *See p. 62.*

1881

July 2—President Garfield is shot by a disappointed federal office-seeker. *See p. 63.*

September 19—President Garfield dies and Chester A. Arthur is sworn in as president the following day. *See p. 63.*

1882

John D. Rockefeller creates a holding company or trust to unite Standard Oil and his various other oil interests. *See p. 46.*

Congress passes the Chinese Exclusion Act after intense lobbying by labor unions. *See p. 81.*

The first federal workers' compensation law is passed, but it applies only to employees in life-saving jobs. *See p. 112.*

1883

Andrew Carnegie buys half of Frick Coke, adding the company to his steel holdings. *See p. 48.*

President Arthur signs the Pendleton Civil Service Reform Act. *See p. 64.*

1884

Democrat Grover Cleveland is elected president, winning both the popular and electoral votes. *See p. 65.*

1885

A strike by Terence Powderly's Knights of Labor against Jay Gould's southwest railroad interests forces the first meeting between a major industrialist and a labor leader. *See p. 82.*

1886

May 4—A bomb is thrown during a labor rally in Chicago's Haymarket Square, leading to a battle between police and demonstrators that ends in eleven deaths. *See p. 83.*

October 25—The Supreme Court decides in *Wabash v. Illinois* that states cannot regulate businesses that operate across state lines, such as railroads. *See p. 65.*

Samuel Gompers helps found the American Federation of Labor. *See p. 85.*

Knights of Labor membership peaks at more than 700,000. *See p. 82.*

Congress initiates an antitrust investigation of Standard Oil. *See p. 46.*

1887

November 11—Four anarchists are executed for their supposed involvement in the Haymarket bombing. *See p. 84.*

The Dawes Severalty Act splits Native American reservation lands into homesteads and sells any "excess" land to white settlers. *See p. 18.*

The Interstate Commerce Act creates the Interstate Commerce Commission (ICC), the first federal regulatory agency. *See p. 66.*

1888

Benjamin Harrison narrowly loses the popular vote but easily wins enough electoral votes to become president. *See p. 67.*

Massachusetts is the first state to implement the secret ballot. *See p. 109.*

1889

April 22—In Oklahoma, 50,000 homesteaders claim 12,000 tracts of former Indian Territory lands in a few hours.

National Farmers' Alliance leader Charles Macune proposes a government subtreasury financing plan for farmers. *See p. 69.*

1890

Farmers' Alliance and People's (Populist) Party candidates begin winning local and federal political offices. *See p. 69.*

A U.S. Census report declares the western frontier settled. *See p. 18.*

The Sherman Silver Purchase Act is passed, postponing conflicts over currency issues.

The Sherman Antitrust Act prohibits corporations from forming combinations or using monopolistic business practices that amount to an "illegal restraint of trade." *See p. 67.*

Wyoming becomes the first state to grant women the right to vote. *See p. 111.*

Jacob Riis publishes an exposé of urban poverty entitled *How the Other Half Lives. See p. 105.*

December 29—U.S. troops massacre Lakota Sioux at Wounded Knee Creek in South Dakota, effectively ending Native American resistance to white expansion. *See p. 18.*

1892

June 29—Carnegie Steel locks out employees from its plant in Homestead, Pennsylvania. *See p. 90.*

July 4—The People's (Populist) Party holds its first presidential convention. *See p. 92.*

July 6—Shots are exchanged between workers and armed guards at Homestead. *See p. 90.*

July 17—Homestead is placed under martial law. *See p. 91.*

July 23—Anarchist Alexander Berkman attacks and wounds Henry Clay Frick, president of Carnegie Steel. *See p. 91.*

November—The Homestead conflict ends with the capitulation of the union. *See p. 91.*

Grover Cleveland reclaims the White House. *See p. 93.*

1893

May—The National Cordage Company declares bankruptcy, setting off a financial panic that turns into a lengthy economic depression. *See p. 93.*

Spurred by President Cleveland, Congress repeals the Sherman Silver Purchase Act.

1894

May 1—"Coxey's Army" of protesters reaches Washington, D.C., and is arrested for trespassing. *See p. 95.*

Employees of the Pullman Palace Car Company in Illinois go on strike to protest wage cuts. *See p. 95.*

Democrats lose over 120 House seats in the biggest mid-term election swing in history. *See p. 96.*

1895

January 21—In *United States v. E.C. Knight and Co.*, the Supreme Court rules that the Sherman Antitrust Act does not apply to manufacturing operations. *See p. 99.*

J. P. Morgan heads a syndicate to restore the U.S. Treasury's gold supply. *See p. 52.*

1896

July 7—William Jennings Bryan wins the Democratic nomination for president. *See p. 97.*

Republican William McKinley defeats Bryan in what becomes known as the first modern presidential election. *See p. 98.*

1897

March 22—In *United States v. Trans-Missouri Freight Association*, the Supreme Court rules that a railroad industry association's attempt to regulate rates violates the Sherman Antitrust Act. *See p. 100.*

1898

February 15—The USS *Maine* explodes under mysterious circumstances in the harbor at Havana, Cuba. *See p. 103.*

February 28—In *Holden v. Hardy,* the Supreme Court upholds a Utah law regulating working hours for miners. *See p. 101.*

April 25—The United States declares war against Spain. *See p. 103.*

May 31—In *Smyth v. Ames,* also called the *Maximum Freight Case,* the Supreme Court rules that the Interstate Commerce Commission does not have the authority to set railroad rates. *See p. 100.*

August 12—The United States and Spain sign a peace treaty ending the Spanish-American War that establishes U.S. control over former Spanish colonies in Puerto Rico, Guam, and the Philippines. *See p. 103.*

J. P. Morgan creates the Federal Steel trust. *See p. 52.*

South Dakota is the first state to adopt the voter initiative and referendum. *See p. 111.*

1900

McKinley, with Theodore Roosevelt as his vice-presidential running mate, is re-elected by a wide margin over Bryan. *See p. 103.*

1901

March—J. P. Morgan announces the formation of U.S. Steel, the world's first billion-dollar corporation. *See p. 52.*

May 9—On "Blue Thursday," a bidding war for Northern Pacific shares nearly causes a stock panic.

September 5—President McKinley is shot while visiting the Pan-American Expo in Buffalo, New York. *See p. 103.*

September 14—McKinley dies, and Theodore Roosevelt is sworn in as president. *See p. 103.*

J. P. Morgan creates the Northern Securities Company to pool the interests of the Northern Pacific, Great Northern, and Union Pacific railroads. *See p. 107.*

1902

May—The United Mine Workers (UMW) go on strike for higher wages and an eight-hour work day. *See p. 107.*

October—President Roosevelt forces the mine owners into arbitration to settle the strike. *See p. 107.*

1903

The Department of Commerce and Labor is established as a cabinet-level agency. *See p. 108.*

Congress gives the ICC the ability to assess fines and issue injunctions, and it also makes railroad rebates illegal. *See p. 108.*

1904

March 14—The Supreme Court holds in *Northern Securities Co. v. United States* that the railway pool is a monopoly and must be split up. *See p. 108.*

Ida Tarbell publishes a muckraking exposé of John D. Rockefeller's business empire entitled *The History of the Standard Oil Company. See p. 106.*

1906

Upton Sinclair publishes *The Jungle*, an exposé of unsanitary conditions in Chicago's meatpacking industry. *See p. 106.*

Congress gives the ICC the ability to set railroad rates. *See p. 109.*

The Federal Employers Liability Act becomes the first national workers' compensation law. *See p. 113.*

The Pure Food and Drug Act regulates U.S. food and drug production. *See p. 109.*

1907

J. P. Morgan rescues New York banks from a financial panic. *See p. 115.*

1908

Oregon becomes the first state to institute voter recalls of public officials. *See p. 110.*

1911

March 25—A fire at the Triangle Shirtwaist Factory kills 146 mostly young, female garment workers and leads to calls for workplace safety regulations. *See p. 111.*

May 15—The Supreme Court orders the breakup of Standard Oil as an illegal monopoly in *Standard Oil Co. of New Jersey v. United States. See p. 116.*

1912

Democrat Woodrow Wilson is elected president over Progressive Party candidate Theodore Roosevelt and Republican president William Howard Taft. *See p. 115.*

1913

February 13—The 16th Amendment to the Constitution gives the federal government the authority to collect income taxes. *See p. 115.*

May 31—The 17th Amendment to the Constitution provides for the direct election of U.S. senators by popular vote. *See p. 110.*

The Federal Reserve Act establishes a central-banking system of twelve regional banks, ruled by a Federal Reserve Board that sets interest rates and regulates bank credit. *See p. 115.*

1914

The Clayton Antitrust Act bans price discrimination, exclusive selling agreements, and holding companies if pursued in restraint of trade. *See p. 116.*

The Federal Trade Commission is established to investigate trusts and advise businesses on violations. *See p. 116.*

1916

The Federal Employees' Compensation Act provides workers' compensation to all federal workers regardless of position. *See p. 113.*

The Adamson Act establishes an eight-hour work day for national railroad workers. *See p. 114.*

Congress passes the Keating-Owen Child Labor Act banning child labor. *See p. 114.*

The Federal Farm Loan Act creates twelve district banks to give low-interest loans to farmers. *See p. 115.*

The Bonded Warehouse Act allows farmers to use crops as collateral for low-interest loans. *See p. 115.*

1917

March 19—The Supreme Court decides in *Wilson v. New* that Congress can regulate working hours. *See p. 114.*

1918

June 3—In *Hammer v. Dagenhart,* the Supreme Court overturns Congress' ban on child labor. *See p. 114.*

1920

August 18—The 19th Amendment to the Constitution gives women the right to vote. *See p. 111.*

1932

The Norris-LaGuardia Act limits the use of injunctions against labor actions. *See p. 116.*

1938

The Fair Labor Standards Act bans child labor, establishes a minimum wage, and sets a maximum work week with overtime at one-and-a-half times the regular pay rate. *See p. 114.*

1941

February 3—In *United States v. Darby,* the Supreme Court upholds the Fair Labor Standards Act, overturning its 1918 *Hammer v. Dagenhart* decision. *See p. 114.*

2011

The top 1 percent of American earners accounts for almost 25 percent of the country's pre-tax income and 40 percent of the nation's wealth, creating an income disparity between rich and poor that some analysts compare to the Gilded Age. *See p. 117.*

The "Occupy Wall Street" movement organizes a series of demonstrations in major cities to demand reform of the financial industry and social justice for the 99 percent of Americans who are not extremely wealthy.

SOURCES FOR
FURTHER STUDY

Beatty, Jack. *Age of Betrayal: The Triumph of Money in America, 1865-1900.* New York: Knopf, 2007. This engaging popular history explains how corporations came to rule America during the Gilded Age.

Calhoun, Charles W. *From Bloody Shirt to Full Dinner Pail: The Transformation of Politics and Governance in the Gilded Age.* New York: Hill and Wang, 2010. Written by a historian for a popular audience, this book provides a detailed and interesting survey of the political landscape of the Gilded Age.

Cashman, Sean Dennis. *America in the Gilded Age: From the Death of Lincoln to the Rise of Theodore Roosevelt.* 3rd edition. New York: New York University Press, 1993. This thorough account is considered one of the first comprehensive histories of the Gilded Age.

Clark, Judith Freeman. *The Gilded Age.* Revised edition. New York: Facts on File, 2006. This general survey of the era, which contains a varied collection of primary sources and a liberal selection of photographs, is especially recommended for younger students.

Josephson, Matthew. *The Robber Barons.* New York: Harcourt, 1934. This pioneering economic history of the Gilded Age, written in vivid prose, focuses on industrialists like John D. Rockefeller and Andrew Carnegie.

"The Richest Man in the World: Andrew Carnegie." *The American Experience,* PBS-TV. Available online at http://www.pbs.org/wgbh/amex/carnegie/index.html. This multimedia presentation explores the life and times of steel magnate Andrew Carnegie through a documentary film, gallery of photographs, and timeline of historic events.

Summers, Mark Wahlgren. *The Gilded Age, or, the Hazard of New Functions.* Upper Saddle River, NJ: Prentice Hall, 1997. Written by a historian, this book offers a broad survey of the era, covering politics, economics, and social and cultural movements.

Trachtenberg, Alan. *The Incorporation of America: Culture and Society in the Gilded Age.* 25th anniversary edition. New York: Hill and Wang, 2007. Using an interesting interdisciplinary approach, this volume explores how the corporate structures developed during the Gilded Age came to affect political and cultural life.

Wall, James T. *Wall Street and the Fruited Plain: Money, Expansion, and Politics in the Gilded Age*. Lanham, MD: University Press of America, 2008. This survey of the era is organized by topic and includes sidebars highlighting lesser-known events and people.

BIBLIOGRAPHY

Books

Ackerman, Kenneth D. *The Gold Ring: Wall Street's Swindle of the Century and Its Most Scandalous Crash—Black Friday, 1869.* New edition. New York: Carroll & Graf, 2005.

Ambrose, Stephen. *Nothing Like It in the World: The Men Who Built the Transcontinental Railroad, 1863-1869.* New York: Simon & Schuster, 2000.

Bain, David Haward. *Empire Express: Building the First Transcontinental Railroad.* New York: Viking, 1999.

Billington, Ray Allen, and Martin Ridge. *Westward Expansion: A History of the American Frontier.* 6th edition. Albuquerque: University of New Mexico Press, 2001.

Borneman, Walter R. *Rival Rails: The Race to Build America's Greatest Transcontinental Railroad.* New York: Random House, 2010.

Bruce, Robert V. *1877: Year of Violence.* New York: Bobbs-Merrill, 1959.

Calhoun, Charles W., editor. *The Gilded Age: Perspectives on the Origins of Modern America.* 2nd edition. Lanham, MD: Rowman & Littlefield, 2007.

Carnegie, Andrew. *Autobiography of Andrew Carnegie.* London: Constable & Co., 1920.

Cashman, Sean Dennis. *America in the Age of the Titans: The Progressive Era and World War I.* New York: New York University Press, 1988.

Chambers, John Whiteclay II. *The Tyranny of Change: America in the Progressive Era, 1900-1917.* New York: St. Martin's Press, 1980.

Chernow, Ron. *Titan: The Life of John D. Rockefeller, Sr.* New York: Random House, 1998.

Daniels, Roger. *Coming to America: A History of Immigration and Ethnicity in American Life.* 2nd edition. New York: HarperPerennial, 2002.

Davis, William C. *The American Frontier: Pioneers, Settlers, and Cowboys 1800-1899.* New York: Salamander Books, 1992.

Dray, Philip. *There Is Power in a Union: The Epic Story of Labor in America.* New York: Doubleday, 2010.

Fink, Leon, editor. *Major Problems in the Gilded Age and the Progressive Era: Documents and Essays.* 2nd ed. Boston, MA: Houghton Mifflin, 2001.

Folsom, Burton W., Jr. *The Myth of the Robber Barons.* 3rd edition. Herndon, VA: Young America's Foundation, 1996.

George, Henry. *Progress and Poverty.* New York: D. Appleton & Co., 1886.

Goodwyn, Lawrence. *The Populist Moment: A Short History of the Agrarian Revolt in America.* New York: Oxford University Press, 1978.

Gordon, John Steele. *The Scarlet Woman of Wall Street: Jay Gould, Jim Fisk, Cornelius Vanderbilt, the Erie Railway Wars, and the Birth of Wall Street.* New York: Weidenfeld & Nicolson, 1988.

Green, James. *Death in the Haymarket: A Story of Chicago, the First Labor Movement, and the Bombing That Divided Gilded Age America.* New York: Anchor Books, 2007.

Himmelberg, Robert F., editor. *The Rise of Big Business and the Beginnings of Antitrust and Railroad Regulation, 1870-1900.* New York: Garland Publishing, 1994.

Jeffers, H. Paul. *An Honest President: The Life and Presidencies of Grover Cleveland.* New York: Morrow, 2000.

Krass, Peter. *Carnegie.* Hoboken, NJ: John Wiley & Sons, 2002.

Krause, Paul. *The Battle for Homestead, 1880-1892: Politics, Culture, and Steel.* Pittsburgh: University of Pittsburgh Press, 1992.

Lubetkin, M. John. *Jay Cooke's Gamble: The Northern Pacific Railroad, the Sioux, and the Panic of 1873.* Norman: University of Oklahoma Press, 2006.

McGrath, Robert C. *American Populism: A Social History, 1877-1898.* New York: Farrar, Straus, & Giroux, 1992.

McKee, Thomas Hudson. *The National Conventions and Platforms of All Political Parties, 1789 to 1904: Convention, Popular, and Electoral Vote.* 5th edition. Baltimore, MD: Friedenwald Company, 1904.

Meltzer, Milton. *Bread—and Roses: The Struggle of American Labor, 1865-1915.* New York: Facts on File, 1991.

Morris, Charles R. *The Tycoons: How Andrew Carnegie, John D. Rockefeller, Jay Gould, and J. P. Morgan Invented the American Supereconomy.* New York: Times Books, 2005.

Nasaw, David. *Andrew Carnegie.* New York: Penguin Press, 2006.

Nicholson, Philip Yale. *Labor's Story in the United States.* Philadelphia: Temple University Press, 2004.

Phelan, Craig. *Grand Master Workman: Terence Powderly and the Knights of Labor.* Westport, CT: Greenwood Press, 2000.

Powderly, Terence V. *Thirty Years of Labor, 1859 to 1889.* Columbus, OH: Excelsior Publishing House, 1889.

Renehan, Edward J., Jr. *Dark Genius of Wall Street: The Misunderstood Life of Jay Gould, King of the Robber Barons.* New York: Basic Books, 2005.

Stiles, T. J. *The First Tycoon: The Epic Life of Cornelius Vanderbilt.* New York: Knopf, 2009.

240

Stiles, T. J., collector and editor. *Robber Barons and Radicals*. New York: Perigee, 1997.

Stowell, David O., editor. *The Great Strikes of 1877*. Urbana: University of Illinois Press, 2008.

Strouse, Jean. *Morgan: American Financier*. New York: Random House, 1998.

Wexler, Sanford. *Westward Expansion: An Eyewitness History*. New York: Facts on File, 1991.

Wicker, Elmus. *Banking Panics of the Gilded Age*. New York: Cambridge University Press, 2000.

Williams, R. Hal. *Realigning America: McKinley, Bryan, and the Remarkable Election of 1896*. Lawrence: University Press of Kansas, 2010.

Periodicals

Billington, Monroe. "Susanna Madora Salter—First Woman Mayor." *Kansas Historical Quarterly*, Autumn 1954. Available online at http://www.kancoll.org/khq/1954/54_3_billington.htm.

Brookhiser, Richard. "1886: The Men Who Would Be Mayor." *City Journal*, Autumn 1993. Available online at http://www.city-journal.org/article02.php?aid=1464.

Cassedy, James Gilbert. "African Americans and the American Labor Movement." *Prologue Magazine*, Summer 1997. Available online at http://www.archives.gov/publications/prologue/1997/summer/american-labor-movement.html.

Gross, Daniel, et al. "Split By Decision." *Newsweek International*. November 12, 2007.

Grossman, Jonathan. "The Coal Strike of 1902—Turning Point in U.S. Policy." *Monthly Labor Review*, October 1975. Available online from the U.S. Department of Labor, http://www.dol.gov/oasam/programs/history/coalstrike.htm.

Grossman, Jonathan. "Fair Labor Standards Act of 1938: Maximum Struggle for a Minimum Wage." *Monthly Labor Review*, June 1978. Available online from the U.S. Department of Labor, http://www.dol.gov/oasam/programs/history/flsa1938.htm.

Hill, Herbert. "The Problem of Race in American Labor History." *Reviews in American History*, Vol. 24, Issue 2, 1996.

Kaufman, Jason. "Rise and Fall of a Nation of Joiners: The Knights of Labor Revisited." *Journal of Interdisciplinary History*, Volume 31, Number 4, Spring 2001.

Krugman, Paul. "Making Banking Boring." *New York Times*, April 10, 2009.

Mead, Walter Russell. "American Dreams, American Resentments." *The American Interest*, January-February, 2011.

Moody, John, and George Kibbe Turner. "The Masters of Capital in America: Morgan: The Great Trustee." *McClure's Magazine*, November 1910.

Nordlund, Willis J. "The Federal Employees' Compensation Act." *Monthly Labor Review*, September 1991. Available online at http://www.bls.gov/opub/mlr/1991/09/art1full.pdf.

Norgren, Jill. "Belva Lockwood: Blazing the Trail for Women in Law." *Prologue Magazine,* Spring 2005. Available online at http://www.archives.gov/publications/prologue/2005 /spring/belva-lockwood-1.html.

Stiglitz, Joseph E. "Of the 1%, by the 1%, for the 1%." *Vanity Fair,* May 2011.

Williams-Searle, John. "Risk, Disability, and Citizenship: U.S. Railroaders and the Federal Employers' Liability Act." *Disability Studies Quarterly,* Summer 2008. Available online at http://www.dsq-sds.org/article/view/113/113.

Winerman, Marc. "The Origins of the FTC: Concentration, Cooperation, Control and Competition." *Antitrust Law Journal,* Volume 71, 2003. Available online at http:// www.ftc.gov/ftc/history/docs/origins.pdf.

Online

The American Experience, PBS-TV. "The Progressive Movement (1900-1918)." Available online at "http://www.pbs.org/wgbh/americanexperience/features/general-article/ eleanor-progressive/.

The American Experience, PBS-TV. "The Richest Man in the World: Andrew Carnegie." Available online at http://www.pbs.org/wgbh/amex/carnegie/index.html.

Biographical Directory of the United States Congress, 1774 to Present. Available online at http://bioguide.congress.gov.

Kennedy, Robert C. "Reform—By George!" *On This Day,* New York Times Learning Network, October 23, 2001. Available online at http://www.nytimes.com/learning/general/ onthisday/harp/1023.html.

Legal Information Institute, Cornell University Law School. "CRS Annotated Constitution." Available online at http://www.law.cornell.edu/anncon.

Office of the Comptroller of the Currency, U.S. Department of the Treasury. "History." Available online at http://www.occ.treas.gov/about/history.html.

U.S. Department of Labor, Office of Workers' Compensation Programs. "History of OWCP." Available online at http://www.dol.gov/owcp/owcphist.htm.

U.S. National Archives and Records Administration. "Historical Election Results: Electoral College Box Scores, 1789-1996." Available online at http://www.archives.gov/federal- register/electoral-college/scores.html.

"U.S. Supreme Court Opinions." Available online at FindLaw, http://www.findlaw.com/case code/supreme.html.

Utley, Robert M., and Francis A. Ketterson, Jr. "Golden Spike: National Historic Site." *National Park Service, Historical Handbook Series,* No. 40, 1969. Available online at http://www.cr.nps.gov/history/online_books/hh/40/index.htm.

PHOTO AND ILLUSTRATION CREDITS

Cover and Title Page: George Grantham Bain Collection, Prints & Photographs Division, Library of Congress, LC-DIG-ggbain-14052.

Chapter One: Popular Graphic Arts Collection, Prints & Photographs Division, Library of Congress, LC-DIG-ppmsca-03213 (p. 10); PH Filing Series Photographs, Prints & Photographs Division, Library of Congress, LC-DIG-ppmsca-19191 (p. 12); The Granger Collection, New York (p. 14); Prints & Photographs Division, Library of Congress, LC-USZ62- 44075 (p. 17); Prints & Photographs Division, Library of Congress, LC-DIG-ppmsca-08372 (p. 19).

Chapter Two: Printed Ephemera Collection, Rare Books and Special Collections Division, Library of Congress, Portfolio 134, Folder 13, Digital ID: rbpe-13401300 (p. 25); Prints & Photographs Division, Library of Congress, LC-USZC2-2531 (p. 29); George Grantham Bain Collection, Prints & Photographs Division, Library of Congress, LC-USZ62-104428 (p. 31); Brady-Handy Collection, Prints & Photographs Division, Library of Congress, LC-DIG-cwpbh-00631 (p. 34); Prints & Photographs Division, Library of Congress, LC-USZ62-37423 (p. 36).

Chapter Three: J.S Pughe, Illus. in: Puck, v. 49, no. 1251 (1901 February 27), Prints & Photographs Division, Library of Congress, LC-DIG-ppmsca-25503 (p. 41); The Granger Collection, New York (p. 44); Prints & Photographs Division, Library of Congress, LC-USZ62-120393 (p. 47); Detroit Publishing Company Collection, Prints & Photographs Division, Library of Congress, det.4a10152 (p. 49); Detroit Publishing Company Collection, Prints & Photographs Division, Library of Congress, det.4a13508 (p. 51).

Chapter Four: Prints & Photographs Division, Library of Congress, LC-USZ62-13018 (p. 57); Popular Graphic Arts Collection, Prints & Photographs Division, Library of Congress, LC-DIG-pga-04171 (p. 60); James Albert Wales, Illus. in: Puck, v. 9 (1881 April 13), Prints & Photographs Division, Library of Congress, LC-USZC4-6400 (p. 64); Prints & Photographs Division, Library of Congress, LC-USZ62-7618 (p. 66); Prints & Photographs Division, Library of Congress, LC-USZ62-43587 (p. 68).

Chapter Five: George Grantham Bain Collection, Prints & Photographs Division, Library of Congress, LC-DIG-ggbain-16308 (p. 73); Photography Collection, Miriam and Ira D. Wallach Division of Art, Prints and Photographs, The New York Public Library,

INDEX